SHROPSHIRE, HEREFORDSHIRE
AND MONMOUTH

Hereford

IN THE MARCH AND BORDERLAND OF WALES

By A. G. BRADLEY

Author of "Highways and Byways in North and South Wales"
"Owen Glyndwr" etc.

SHROPSHIRE HEREFORDSHIRE AND MONMOUTH

WITH ILLUSTRATIONS BY W. M. MEREDITH
AND A MAP

LONDON

CONSTABLE & COMPANY LTD.

1911

Originally published in 1911 by
Constable & Company Limited, London

This edition © 1994 Lapridge Publications

0 9518589 4 7

Printed and bound for

LAPRIDGE PUBLICATIONS
25 CHURCH STREET
HEREFORD HR1 2LR

by
Redwood Books, Trowbridge, Wiltshire

TO

MY WIFE,

MY FREQUENT COMPANION

IN THIS AND ALL FORMER RECORDED

WANDERINGS

Preface

WHEN the question arose of issuing a second edition of *In the March and Borderland of Wales*, it was decided to divide the book, which consisted of two somewhat distinct districts. Its lesser and latter part dealing with Glamorgan is therefore published separately and concurrently with this volume.

From the literary and historical point of view and that of the armchair reader, the break in topographical continuity mattered nothing. But having in mind with a fresh edition, the potential traveller in this Border Country, one feels that he is not often likely to include Glamorgan in the same pilgrimage or visit. Furthermore, that as a local book it would be handier, more compact, and to the point if the Glamorgan chapters were published separately; while precisely the same reasons apply in this case for similar treatment. This is not a guide book, but the record only of leisurely wanderings made during the course of three summer months spent in this Border Country.

A. G. BRADLEY.

RYE.

vii

ROCKFIELD, NEAR SKENFRITH.

Contents

CONTENTS

List of Illustrations

xi

LIST OF ILLUSTRATIONS

LIST OF ILLUSTRATIONS

CHAPTER I

HEREFORD

TO those who know it not—the vast majority, that is to say, of the people of England—the name of Hereford is vaguely suggestive, I imagine, of a haven of ecclesiastical peace in a mild unexciting atmosphere pleasantly pervaded with the odour of cider. Through travellers from the north-west to the south-west pass by it nowadays, however, in hundreds of thousands, and if their vision penetrates beyond the untoward surroundings inevitable to most railway stations, they will catch sight of the square tower of the cathedral and the lofty spires of two or three churches springing high into an unpolluted sky above a slumberous-looking city lying in a plain. A moment later they are rumbling over a broad river whose dimensions and situation will reveal itself to the meanest geographical intelligence as the Wye, queen of all English and Welsh streams.

Hereford may be in these days but a humdrum cathedral town deeply concerned with cider and red and white bullocks, but it has claims in the past that lift it wholly above the ordinary English city or borough of its class; since for long ages it was a frontier town, with all the rich and moving story that significant fact implies. It shares the historical characteristics of Carlisle, Chester, and Shrewsbury, and for centuries led a life of tension amid a clash of arms which circumstances made impossible in Devonshire, Kent, or Norfolk. What Chester and Shrewsbury were to the northern and middle Marches of Wales, Hereford was to the wider and in many respects more turbulent Marches of the south.

From the earliest times of the fierce Silurian resistance under Caractacus, to Roman arms, all through the hurly-burly of the fringe of Saxon conquest and the long protracted struggles of the Welsh and Normans, the men of Hereford and district were always of necessity in the very thick of the fray. They may almost be said to have slept by their arms till the accession of the Tudors put an end to civil, racial and private strife and to the feudal period. It might therefore well be that Hereford with its tributary district had played a sufficiently strenuous part for its reputation, and had fairly earned the life of leisured ease and the quiet enjoyment of one of the most favoured districts in Great Britain. English school children can, or could, prattle readily about Percy and Douglas and moss-troopers and the much miscalled " Merry Carlisle." But I do not suppose that one in a thousand of their seniors has the dimmest notion of this other border strife, quite as fierce and picturesque, which raged so continuously on the banks of the Wye, the Severn, the Usk, and the Dee. And this strikes one perhaps as the more singular since the balance of power and the fate of English kings and factions rested more often on the men who ruled and fought beyond the Wye and Severn than on any other single part of the realm.

The outward expression of Hereford to-day, unlike that of Shrewsbury, Chester and Carlisle, who still wear the relics of their ancient armour, is so eminently peaceful as to induce forgetfulness of her ancient character not merely in the minds of her visitors but even among her own people. She lacks too those wonderful vistas of timbered houses, that in those ancient bulwarks against Gwynedd and Powys carry the thoughts back something more than halfway towards the days of their warlike pre-eminence. And this is the more curious, though not for the moment relevant, as her tributary districts are much richer in this respect than those of either Shrewsbury or Chester. More too even than Shrewsbury is Hereford enveloped in natural scenery of a high order. For Shropshire only rises above the ordinary level of pleasant midland landscape on its Welsh side and in its southern districts, while Hereford looks eastward over a region which is a good deal more than this, and is still further fortunate in that most imposing background furnished by the Malvern Hills.

But it is only with the western half of either of these counties that we are here concerned, and when I pitched on Hereford as a main base for operations along the south Welsh border, I already knew enough of both to feel some confidence in the selection. I am free to confess, however, that I regarded it in the beginning mainly from the strategic point of view : but this comparative indifference changed into warmer feelings as time went by and the placid charms of the old Wye-side cathedral town, which are not inconsiderable, seemed

2

to make a grateful interlude to full and sometimes arduous days spent far afield.

It is not easy to separate a country town from its environs, and those of Hereford are wholly pleasing. But without any display of Norman towers and battlements, or very much of Tudor gables, there are certain charms here that even Shrewsbury, and still more Chester, lack. For with a sufficient atmosphere of antiquity there is also a comforting sense of elbow-room and dignified repose ; a typical county and cathedral town, in short, extended over a generous space, and resting on the banks of a classic stream that with all its breadth still holds the sparkle and buoyancy of its mountain birth. No factory smoke pollutes the air of Hereford, while hogsheads of beer or cider groaning countrywards on brewers' drays represent in quite harmonious fashion a leading industry. The streets are mostly of a generous width, and at times, as in the " High Town," where the pulse of commerce beats fastest, expand into areas almost suggestive of a continental " Place." But as a saving clause perhaps in the interests of antiquity there still lingers in the heart of Hereford, even as the neck of an hourglass, a narrow artery to which all these generous streets and open spaces inevitably lead. Here, in this narrow entry to the High Town, opposing streams of wheeled traffic present at most times, particularly on market days, a spectacle of congested animation : a cheerful confusion of footmen and horsemen, of farmers' gigs and parsons' pony traps, of milk carts, smart country turn-outs, hackney carriages, brewers' drays, and cyclists in various stages of suppressed impatience. Even the motor here assumes a chastened spirit, and with protesting snorts drops into line behind the grocer's cart.

Hereford complains with much justice that it is overlooked both by tourists and what the Americans call " home-seekers." With good schools and an excellent train service, cheap markets, good boating, fine roads, and a lovely neighbourhood, and lastly a cathedral of more than average musical activity, there would seem to be a good deal in it for the great class of the widowed and the retired with incomes of three figures and a mislike for Continental banishment. Nor should it be overlooked that there is a most admirable public library for the general reader, and a really fine reference library for persons of more serious literary habit. The air is of course mild and lays no claim to stimulating properties, but this

3

quality after all applies to almost all of the more notable haunts affected by the class in question.

But I did not come to Hereford to exploit its residential advantages, and what concerns me chiefly in the first instance is the doings of the ancients, who cared neither for schools nor libraries nor boating, and not a fig for climate, and I tell its story from the beginning, not without some qualms as to the readers' forbearance, and tell it as briefly as reasonable lucidity permits of.

A recent historian of a neighbouring county commences the story of its chief town with a sigh of pious relief that there at any rate no Romans had broken ground and shrouded the beginning of his tale in obscurity.

Hereford, like Brecon, owes nothing directly to the Roman, but curiously enough cherishes a similar tradition regarding its origin. For as the Welsh town is said to have been built out of materials brought from the great Roman station of the Gaer, so with as much probability is the creation of Hereford attributed to the abandonment of the Roman-British city of Kentchester about the same distance away. The popular derivation of the name is Hen-fford, or the old road, and there is a tradition moreover of a Roman bridge here over the Wye. Roman memories, however, are thick enough in this part of the country, for no portion of what we call the ancient Britons were so fiercely obstinate in their defence as the Silurian tribes who held the country now covered, speaking broadly, by Hereford, Monmouth, and Glamorgan. Tacitus has left familiar evidence of the prowess of this martial stock who stood around Caractacus, and a thousand years later gave its irresistible long-bow to England. The special qualities of the Silurian are attributed by some to the fact that the Celtic conquerors of Britain, the big round-headed fair-haired men with bronze weapons, failed to conquer and assimilate them with such completeness as elsewhere. The swarthy-featured high-cheekboned, long-headed Iberian of an earlier Britain, whose stone weapons went down before the bronze, is supposed to have retained more distinct personality in south-east Wales and made a blend with his conqueror of a robuster type than common. Enthusiasts who are also authorities without claiming any survival of exceptionally robust qualities, profess to see the Iberian in some purity of mental and physical characteristics even now on the limestone highway and the red fallows of Gwent and Morganwg. It is interesting to learn from Mr. O. M. Edwards that we have

4

had Gwentian poets of merit in the seventeenth and eighteenth centuries who were in all essentials true representatives of the prehistoric race. The Saxons, as we all know, were brought to a standstill on the Welsh border, and in the protracted struggles between the Welsh and Offa, King of Mercia, the country round Hereford took a leading part. The germ of the city lay about six miles to the east of the Mercian king's famous dyke, which was not in the best opinion a rampart but merely a delimitation. But Hereford seems to have been of slight military importance, though the centre of a diocese since 690, but it was fortified as a protection against the Danes, who were particularly active in this corner of Britain during the tenth century. Indeed, the Danes, harassing both races, but mainly the Mercians for obvious reasons, and pushing in between them up the Wye, effectually discouraged any further encroachments upon Celtic Wales. The Norman advent rather accentuated the old racial boundaries, as it was merely a case of one aristocracy displacing another ; in England promptly and almost completely, in Wales partially and gradually.

It was at Sutton Walls, four miles from Hereford, the traces of which are still conspicuous, that Offa treacherously murdered Æthelbert, King of the East Anglians, while his guest and the accepted suitor of his daughter. This crime contributed to the rise of Hereford Cathedral, which the repentant or frightened Offa richly endowed in expiation of it, besides founding St. Albans. A small church no doubt already stood here, as the diocese had existed since the seventh century, and now at the end of the eighth a greater fabric arose over the body of the royal and canonized victim, St. Æthelbert, whose name is still identified with the stately pile we see before us to-day. Sutton Walls remained the Mercian palace till the union of the Saxon kingdoms in 827.

With that first insidious influx of Normans encouraged by the monkish, half-French, and wholly weak monarch, Edward the Confessor, Hereford was more closely identified than almost any part of rural England. The great Saxon earl, Godwin, who swayed both England and Edward for much of the reign, had carved Herefordshire out of Mercia as a special earldom for his son Sweyn, a younger brother of the famous Harold. Sweyn however did not prove equal to his dignities, but outraged public feeling so violently by a liaison with the Abbess of Leominster, that he was banished from the country. And now, some twenty years before the conquest, Edward seized

5

the opportunity of bestowing the earldom on his chief Norman favourite and nephew Ralph, who immediately introduced Norman subfeudatories and a swarm of Norman followers. Castles of unfamiliar Norman fashion, hateful alike to English tenants and Welsh neighbours, arose at Ewyas and elsewhere, and the tyrannical conduct of these intruders justified the hatred. Sweyn's four years' term of banishment over, he returned to Herefordshire, and his natural resentment at the state of matters found ample sympathy in the men of his country. He at once claimed and as quickly received his father's sympathy, but before any effect could be given to it, Godwin was driven across the Channel by the jealousy his dominating influence had aroused among his fellow earls. Sweyn had to go with him, and Ralph, who seems to have retired, was once again in power. But in the meantime the border Welsh had taken matters into their own hands and defeated these premature Normans and their lukewarm Saxon tenantry with considerable slaughter at Leominster. This event and other signs encouraged Earl Godwin to return to England, which he succeeded in doing to such effect that the Norman favourites fled in panic across the Channel. The Normans of Hereford fled with the rest, but Ralph, as the king's nephew, was made an exception to the rule and retained in his earldom. He was a poor creature, however, as his English subjects were to learn to their cost. For in 1055 Algar, earl of the East Angles, being under a cloud, collected a force in Ireland and then proceeded to kindle the warlike zeal of Griffith, Prince of North Wales, and so effectually that a joint and ferocious attack was made on Herefordshire, absolutely devastating its western districts. Ralph, himself in Hereford, prepared his men to meet the onslaught, but with a stupid comtempt for the customs and aptitudes of his adopted countrymen mounted his English footmen on untrained horses, and with this efficient squadron set out to meet the nimble Welsh. The latter made short work of the unhandy troopers, and then proceeded to burn and sack the city and slay every one they could catch within it. They likewise destroyed the cathedral and its entire clerical staff huddled, as it is said, under the west end. The aged Bishop Athelston alone escaped, but only to die of a broken heart. This catastrophe brought Harold, the great son of Godwin, to the western earldom. How he punished the Welsh and conducted the most successful campaign ever yet made into that country is a matter of history. This finished, he set to work to rebuild Hereford and secure its safety by ample fortifications; this being the last event of note in the Saxon period.

William of Normandy paid Hereford something of a left-handed compliment by despatching thither his trusted friend Fitz Osborn, whose advice had led to the invasion of England, to confront the unconquered Welsh and the half-conquered West Mercians. Fitz Osborn not only introduced Norman soldiers and burghers in abundance, but also the laws of his own lordship of Breteuil in Normandy, which had great permanent influence on those complicated usages which became in time stereotyped as the " Custom of the Marches " for centuries to come. The dismantled castles of the earlier Normans were rebuilt and many new ones erected to be held by Norman knights tributary to Fitz Osborn, while Norman burghers were attached by valuable privileges to small chartered towns

CONNINGSBY HOSPITAL, HEREFORD.

which grew up round them. But the story of the Norman Conquest of Wales, quite a distinct one from that of England, partly effected by kings but mainly by adventurous barons on their own account, is a long one, and on the top of so much earlier history might be an unreasonable tax on the reader's forbearance, and must be left to develop itself as opportunity occurs. It will be enough for the present to have shown how Hereford became a royal English city, and remained for centuries the outpost of royal authority, not only against the native Welsh but against the haughty turbulent Marcher barons, whose principalities stretched almost to its

7

gates, and who were often more formidable and more trouble-some than the Welsh themselves. For it was not as a rule the men of Devon or of Lincoln or of Northampton and their over-lords that banished sleep from royal pillows in the long period between the Norman conquest and the battle of Bosworth, but the great barons beyond the Wye with their war-hardened battalions of Welsh and English, their close touch with the Welsh chieftains behind and their consummate arrogance, born of independent conquest and a quasi-independent tenure. The Royal pro-consuls that filled the post at Hereford would fill a page with names famous in their day or always. To give the doings of kings who have hurried there with defensive or punitive intentions, or occasionally for refuge, would be to write pages of English history in the wrong place. But while a score of grim fortresses yet defy time within easy range, that of Hereford has absolutely vanished. The castle green, a delightful pleasaunce of levelled turf and gravelled walks lifted high above the river that any town might well be proud of, is all that keeps alive the memories of its long and perilous watch. Some encircling slopes of turf crowned with foliage of recent growth faintly suggest the lines of defence first drawn, as is thought, by Harold himself, while stretches of ornamental water on the inner side define in part no doubt the ancient moat. Yet in Leland's time there were ample remains of the " fayrest largest and strongest castle in all England."

Looking westward from the terrace above the broad rapid river, over green meadows and a stretch of country whose broken nature is invisible from so low a level, the long, dark ridge of the Black Mountains fills the western skyline and catches the setting sun. To the north of the Gadir, which is nearer three than two thousand feet in altitude, you can see where the extremity of the range at Hay Bluff drops sharply to let out the Wye, that, only just released from the rocky gorges of Erwood and Aberedw, comes rushing swiftly past Hay and Glasbury. Above the broad expanse of the castle green, which was laid out by Bishop Beauclerk, a grandson of Charles II, and Nell Gwyn (who was born in Hereford), rises the massive tower of the cathedral, that is so curiously linked with the tragic fate of an East Anglian king. It was more than twenty years after the destruction of the older building by the Welsh that the first efforts were made to replace it and the present fabric commenced by Bishop Loring. Probably the first great function held within its walls was the crowning of Stephen there after a three years' siege of the castle. It possesses some exceptional interest from the variety of styles it exhibits, though the deplorable work of Wyatt after the west tower fell in 1786, carrying with it the west front and part of the nave, is an ineffaceable blemish, and the shade of the luckless architect is invoked with imprecations many times a day by every self-respecting verger. " Injured by Wyatt, saved by Cottingham, restored by Gilbert Scott" is the triad chaunted with somewhat wearisome iteration in the handbooks. Wyatt's west front, which to judge from pictures must have resembled the back view of a block of London flats, has been recently replaced in exquisite taste and at great cost by a structure worthy of so famous a site. In the north and south transepts, notably the former, and in the arches under the great central tower, a mass of fine Norman and Early English work compels the admiration. The north transept, the particular glory of the cathedral, was built to receive the shrine of Bishop Cantelupe, the curiously carved pedestal of which alone survives as a reminder of the fact and of his services. Another famous bishop, Acquablanca, sleeps in the same building, of which indeed he was the creator and has been more fortunate, his tomb and effigy remaining the most perfect in the cathedral. This prelate is said to have been " held up " and despoiled by Robin Hood, whose traditional respect for the dignitaries of the Church was doubtless modified in the case of so obvious a foreigner. The south transept is mainly of massive Norman work and much dignity. The choir is also rich in the same features though almost unduly sombre in atmosphere. There is a fine Early English chapel much restored in the last century, with a spacious crypt beneath it, the latest creation in the country of its kind, though the twelfth century, the date of this one, seems remote enough !

There is also a beautiful little chantry highly decorated and with vaulted roof in the Late Perpendicular style, named after its builder, Bishop Stanbury, and another of about the same date associated for like reasons with another famous prelate, Audley. The quaintly carved shrine of St. Æthelbert is still preserved in the cathedral, and chief among the curiosities of the building is a map illustrating the conception of the earth's surface entertained by one monk at any rate in the year 1305. The learned Hakluyt, too, was a Herefordshire man, and it is instructive to note the enormous mental gulf

9

between the broad-visioned Elizabethan geographer and the appalling darkness of Richard de Haldingham whose ideas are those of Romans and Greeks grotesquely mingled with conventional tributes to Jerusalem, the Garden of Eden, and the cathedrals of England and Wales. A chained library is among the other relics, while the organ has some historic interest as having been in its original state a present from Charles II. The cathedral is rich in effigies, some notable for their execution and others for the names or times they remind us of.

But of what avail and what a weak concession to literary convention are these brief notes on the interior of a cathedral! Perhaps so much may be venial, nay almost inevitable, but anything further would doubtless be skipped by any reader whose good opinion I should value. Nothing is more tiresome to the layman in such matters, at any rate, and above all in his distant arm chair, than an overdose of architectural description. The lucid interpretation of a cathedral is a serious matter and will fill a pamphlet at the least, and may easily be elaborated into a volume. But failing the companionship of some discriminating local expert, most of us take the pamphlet itself on a leisurely progress through such a building as this, when its pages reflect at once the glories of the reality and illuminate them. There are appreciations of Hereford cathedral by persons who spend much of their time within it, notably a little book by the present Dean, and I will leave the visitor meditating a visit to the shrine of St. Æthelbert to their more elaborate guidance.

On the south side towards the river lie the cloisters and also a quadrangular cloistered building known as the Vicars' college of the Perpendicular period that should not be missed. On the far side of the lawn the cathedral school, an ancient and still vigorous foundation with some recent additions and richly endowed, imparts a higher education to about a hundred boys, some half of whom are boarders. With a fine boating course and the best cricket ground in the county, a strong teaching staff and scholarships to the Universities, the Hereford lads have not much to complain of. The school, moreover, imparts that academic touch which is needed to make the complete cathedral town of the most approved traditional pattern. Indeed, as a specimen of the ideal type I am inclined to think Hereford is without an equal in England.

Some of the others are too commercial, some too big, some too small, some too ugly, others again too canny for quite the real article. Hereford has every qualification that Trollope himself would have demanded. It has a soothing air free from disturbing fumes, expansive and delectable cathedral precincts, and is laved by a beautiful and famous river. It has the quiet old-fashioned but not uncheerful streets proper to a cathedral town, and tortuous byways where well mellowed red brick or sandstone houses proclaim the names of doctors and lawyers upon brass plates that have probably been con-

OLD GUILD HOUSE.

nected with law and physic in Hereford since time was. There is a county neighbourhood of the appropriate description for a complete cathedral town. Nor is there any overshadowing commercial centre within reach, nor disturbing exotic elements of any kind to make a jarring note in an artistic whole that the creator of Mrs. Proudie and Archdeacon Grantley, would have revelled in if accident had not given him Salisbury, which is also admirable. I would recommend the cultured American who is peculiarly susceptible to the atmosphere of English cathedral towns, and thinks of them more tenderly perhaps than the average up-to-date Britisher, to seek the realization of his dreams in Hereford and avoid thereby all risk of disillusion.

There are two ancient churches worth notice in Hereford whose spires, next to the cathedral tower, are the dominating note in those distant views of the city which can be enjoyed from so many points. All Saints is noted for its fine carving, its chained books, and the baptismal certificate of David Garrick. Restoration, though, has been busy here as with its still older neighbour, St. Peter's. The latter was founded by Walter de Lacy, whose name is as familiar in the Marches as that of the Conqueror himself. De Lacy met his death by falling from the walls of his own church during a visit of inspection. The pride of Hereford in the matter of domestic architecture is the beautiful timbered house which in the Tudor period formed a part of "*Butcher Row*," a street similar to the still extant and well-known one in Shrewsbury. This superb specimen of "black and white" was the actual Guild house of the trade, and is profuse both within and without in grotesque carving. It stands now in dignified isolation at the end of the High Town, parting two streets, and does duty as Lloyd's bank.

The latest conspicuous addition to Hereford is a most imposing Townhall, whose interior is, I am quite sure, everything that the municipal authorities and their successors yet unborn could desire, but whose outside is regarded with feelings much more mixed. It must be admitted that a palace of terra-cotta plumped down in a region of red sandstone and black and white architecture, and under the shadow of a cathedral, is somewhat of a shock. Hereford is rich too in old almshouses, where in romantic, low-browed lattice-windowed courtyards, querulous and contented age mingle their reminiscences of sufficiently commonplace and narrow lives, no doubt. Almost might one be tempted to join them at times, even to donning the garb of a popinjay, so captivating are these haunts of ancient peace, founded by pious noblemen and charitable traders.

By far the most interesting of these is the hoary, collegiate-looking building outside the city in Widemarsh known as the Conningsby Hospital, and founded by Sir Thomas of that name in the days of Elizabeth. Here with a demesne behind it of several acres, one side of a charming little stone quadrangle flanks the street with the air of an Oxford college in miniature. Entering the gateway beneath the arms of the founder, you are taken charge of immediately by an old gentleman who proclaims himself the corporal, or appointed captain of the eleven veterans whose presence in these hospitable shades proclaims the fact that in their other life they were " soldiers, sailors, or gentlemen's servants " of meritorious record. The low-pitched eaves bowery with creepers, the rugged time-worn stone roof, the dormer windows and lattice panes surrounding the little quadrangle with its central well makes a picture well worth the slight physical effort necessary to enjoy it. The ancient motto of the hospital is a Spanish one : " Be soldiers, doers not talkers," which let us hope has retrospective application only and is not intended for the current guidance of these leisurely old persons !

Outside in the grounds and beyond the little gardens, to whose cultivation the old gentlemen's sphere of activity is limited, stands upon well-kept turf the ruins of the monastery of the Black Friars, founded in 1276, and among them is a fine specimen of a hexagonal preaching cross surmounting a flight of steps. It may be mentioned also that the hospital stands on the site of an old commandery of the knights of St. John of Jerusalem and that Edward III and the Black Prince once stood together within these precincts at the dedication of the knights' church, this long time vanished. The successors of the Conningsby family are now patrons of the hospital, and their head holds the old title of "Commander." There is, moreover, a quaint little chapel in which the state family pew remains as an interesting relic.

The livery of the pensioners, on Sundays and highdays, consists of a coat with breeches and garters, all of bright scarlet. A casual visitor of imperfect vision to the cathedral service might well mistake a group of these gorgeous old gentlemen for a bevy of doctors of divinity in full war paint, being held in reserve among the congregation for some tremendous concluding ceremony. This Widemarsh suburb, too, is notable as the scene of the escape of Edward I when the young prince was brought here as a prisoner after the battle of Lewes, and as a hostage for the demands made on his father. The story runs how, being in the possession of a fast horse he rode races with his attendances till he had sufficiently exhausted all their animals, after which he showed them a clean pair of heels and galloped away to Dinmore Hill. Here some of the Mortimers who were privy to the scheme met him and escorted him safely to their castle of Wigmore, a few miles away.

Hereford, as already shown, was familiar enough throughout the middle ages with crowned heads ! but the crown was mostly worn over the helmet and martial urgency was usually the motive of their presence. Nowhere probably was the chaos represented by the twenty years of Stephen's reign more complete than among the already half-independent Marcher barons and the Welsh princes, relieved for the time from fear of the crown. The second Henry was here in his Welsh wars. John sought refuge in Hereford when his outrageous exploits had made the home counties too hot for him, and indeed was much attached to the neighbourhood. Henry III, in his prolonged conflicts with the native Welsh and his own barons, was constantly in Hereford. All three Edwards—the first as a warrior prince not yet conqueror of Wales, the second in panic, the third alone, as we have seen, on peaceful and pious intent—made sojourn in the border city. Through the wars of Owen Glyndwr the faithful city was in a constant state of panic : the country was ravaged to its very gates, and the frantic letters from thence praying for succour are among the chief literary curiosities of the period. Again and again the tramp of hosts, gathered from the continent and from the border counties, mustered here at the personal call of Henry IV, or of his famous son, with intent to crush the "damned Glendower." In the Wars of the Roses, Mortimer's Cross, but a dozen miles away, sent its most illustrious captives, Owen Tudor, begetter of kings among them, to their doom at Hereford. It is said that this progenitor of our English monarchs, still but a private gentleman though his sons had been elevated to great earldoms, could not believe that his execution was seriously contemplated. Even when actually at the block in Hereford market place he looked for a reprieve till the last moment. It was not till his velvet collar was removed that he resigned himself with the words : " This head that shall lie on the stock was wont to lay on Queen Katherene's lap." As a matter of fact it was placed on the highest step of the market cross, and a mad woman combed the hair and washed the face and made an illumination of a hundred candles round the grizzly trophy, which so far as we know burnt themselves out. It was at Hereford, too, that the younger Despenser, the second Edward's hated favourite, was hung on a gallows fifty feet in height.

At the opening of the Civil War in 1642 Hereford was held for the Parliament by Lord Stanford, lord lieutenant of the shires of Hereford and Gloucester. Lord Hertford, who had raised an army for the king in Wales, came presently over the border, but avoiding the city, marched straight for the Severn. Stanford, who had collected all the trained bands he could muster in Hereford, hurried after him, and on the same ground as the more famous action in the Wars of the Roses fought the battle of Tewkesbury, in which he was completely victorious. The Welsh infantry under Lord Seymour were illtrained and ill-armed, and their discomfiture was completed by artillery. " The poor ill-armed Welshmen led like asses to the slaughter," says a contemporary, " and over two hundred were buried in pits." Within a fortnight, however, Hertford was in front of Hereford and was again beaten, leaving several hundred more of his raw Welshmen dead upon the field. Soon after this, however, Stanford and his forces were called away and the town was abandoned to the Royalists.

In April, 1643, the Parliamentary troops under Waller attacked the border city, which after a hot brief fight was surrendered with a great number of local celebrities inside it. Among them were Lord Scudamore, Sir William Conningsby, and many others, including ladies, all of whom, except Scudamore, who was allowed home on parole, were sent to Gloucester.

But after a time the Parliamentary forces were again called to more urgent work elsewhere, and in 1645 the city had been some time in the hands of the king's friends, Sir Barnabas Scudamore being governor. The neighbourhood, however, was growing restive under the constant call for drafts to strengthen the garrison, and the common people at length banded together and marched on the town, demanding redress. Rupert was hurriedly despatched from Chester to save the situation, which he succeeded in doing for the time.

After the disaster of Naseby and the almost more serious capture of his private correspondence, the king came in despair to Hereford with a view to thoroughly exploiting the loyalty of the Welsh. He arrived there in June and kindled only a moderate display of enthusiasm. Still the neighbouring gentry flocked in to pay their respects, and some fresh levies were gathered into the city. Prince Rupert, however, at this moment fell out with the king's other advisers and took himself off to save Bristol. Gerard, the active but not overwise Royalist leader who was so conspicuous in Wales and the border, now entered Hereford with two thousand men, and not before they were needed, for soon after the Scottish Covenanters

15

sat down to besiege the city. The latter had only succeeded in rousing the ire of the country people by their acquisitive propensities when they were compelled to raise the siege by the success of their enemy Montrose in the north. At the same time the unfortunate king once more entered the city. Lord Scudamore's brother Barnabas was now its governor. Hereford continued a great resort of the Royalist cause till December in that same year 1645, a week before Christmas. Colonel Birch, " once a carrier, now a colonel," from Bristol, and Colonel Morgan, the governor of Gloucester, carried it by surprise and captured therein some fifty men of rank and position. The weather being very severe, Governor Scudamore and fifty others escaped across the Wye on the ice. This put an end to Hereford as a factor in the struggle, and it is perhaps hardly necessary to add was the last warlike drama it was ever to take part in. Like all western cities, however, Hereford seems not to have been beyond a suspicion of Jacobitism, if we may judge by an entertaining address delivered to its citizens, after or during the rising of the first Pretender by that stout old Whig, Sir John Conningsby, at that time lord lieutenant. It] is worth quoting, howsoever unparliamentary in language, and is certainly more creditable to the worthy baronet's loyalty than to his manners.

"Gentlemen, d—n ye all. I'll have ye to know, that I am your Lord Lieutenant and Lord High Steward of this city, and, d—n ye, I'll do what I please with your city. I hear there are some of you for the Pretender, a — fellow whom his own mother disowned. I am informed that when a lady of strictest virtue and best reputation would depose on oath that an impudent rascal said this fellow was rightful heir you refuse to take her depositions. I speak to you, Mr. Mayor and Mr. Tailor, that art a low Jacobite, a fellow without a soul. I hear that a pack of worthless wretches met in the market house, and drank the Pretender's health and proclaimed him king. There are but three honest men in your town, Tom Bailey, Dr. Lewis and Sam Birch. I've opposed this fellow's father, I've opposed the son, and though King George be the best king on earth, d—n ye, I'll oppose him too if he should pretend to alter our laws and constitution. Look ye, gentlemen, I designed to have sent ye no more soldiers, do you hear ? Prosecute this rascal of a butcher. If ye do, I'll take care of a jury. If not, I'll send ye soldiers that shall use you as you ought to be used. I'll fetch 'em from hell, but I will d—n ye. So I bid ye heartily farewell."

At the time of the first Edward's final suppression of Welsh independence, there seem to have been some wealthy Jews in Hereford who lived in great style. There is a record of one who gave a most sumptuous entertainment at the marriage of his daughter, where was a great profusion, we are told, of rich silks and cloth of gold. There were theatricals and open air sports, and displays of horsemanship. The bishop threatened any of his flock who accepted invitations with all the penalties of the church, and carried out his threats, too, for numbers were excommunicated. Doubtless these hospitable Israelites had waxed fat from the king's need of money during the Welsh wars. And when these were over, and again after the rising of Glyndwr, those statutes against Welshmen, which read so strangely now, were in full force in Hereford. No Welshman born in Wales could purchase land in the county nor be a burgher of the town, nor hold any office, nor have any privilege. Nor could any Englishman marrying a Welsh woman hold office or enjoy any civic rights. There were flourishing cloth mills, too, on the river in Henry VIII's time ; but the king who did so much for Wales in uniting it with England seems to have had a spite against Hereford, for he pulled down its mills, apparently from mere malice, and threw hundreds out of employment, " to the utter impoverishment and defacing of said city," says a petition to his daughter Queen Mary during her reign. And while on the subject of Tudor Hereford, there is a remarkable old tract extant, of date 1609, describing in quaint language a Morris dance, performed in that year by a dozen old men averaging a hundred years apiece. This dance of death was held in the Golden Valley some dozen miles to the westward in celebration of a visit of James I to a country house in that delightful vale. It is headed " Old Meg of Hereford shire for a Mayd Marion and Hereford toune for a Morris dancer, Western men for gambouls, Middlesex men for tricks above ground, Lancashire for horn pypes. Worcestershire for bag pipes. But Hereford for a Morris dance puts down not only Kent but very near three quarters of Christendom."

" The merriest month of the year brought forth a number of knights and squires and gallants of the best, sent from many parts of the land to meet at Bacton. The horses having run themselves well-nigh out of breath and wagers at great sums beeing won and lost ; it was now ploted to lay a scene in which age should play a part. There were four musicians whose age made 423 years. Then came the Morris dancers, twelve in number, headed by James Jankin of Langenen a gentleman by birth but not loved of fortune, not so poor as to be pitted, nor so rich as to be envied, 98 years and married a wife of 52 and had a child by her. After him blithfully dancing John Willis o' Darmington a bone setter so skilled in setting others bones that he would not let his be out of Joint and went foote by foote with the formost aged a 100 years. Next little Dick Phillips of Middleton smartly shaking his heels age 102 with a son of eighty William Warton of Marden who never swore in his life as he was an old fisher and excellent fowler and born in the first year of Henry the eight'th age 102. Here slips in William Moss who contrary to his name had no moss on his heels age 96. But how like you John Law of Madley a taylor in his youth a hozier and born before the dessension between cloath and velvet breeches, carrying four score and seventeen summers on him. Or what say you to John Careless a dweler in Holm Lacie and known to be a tall man till now, known to be a bit crooked age 96. And William Mann of Elgeton, an old soldier and a lusty labourer, forty years since being grievouslywounded, he carried his liver and his lights home half a mile, and for all these stories he arrives at four score and seventeen and dances merrilie. But look you who comes here John Hunt the hobby Horse wanting but three of a hundred. And welcome John Mands born at Cradley a very good two-handed swordsman of the age of a hundred.—And now give way for the Mayd Marion, old Meg Goodwin the famous wench of Eardisland. This old maid was at Prince Arthurs death in Ludlow and had her part in the dole. She was three score years a mayd she says, and twenty otherwise and since has been thought fit to be a Mayd Marion of age 109. And for a good wager it were easie to find in the county four hundred persons more within the years under or three years over a hundred. The musicians and daunccers had long coats of the old fashion sleeves gathered up at the elbow and hanging sleeves behind, red buffin stript with white, gardles white stockings, white and red roses on their shoes. One six a white Jew's cap and jewel, and long red feathers, the other six scarlet Jews cap with jewel and white feather. After the daunce was ended various courtiers that won wagers at the race took the colours and wore them in their hats. And do you like this Morris daunce of Herefordshire ? are not they brave old youthes ? Have they not the right footing ? the true head, the carefully lifting up of one leg and actively bestouring of the other.   Old Hall the fidler pronounced the prologue :—

"A race quoth you behold a race
No race of horses but of men—
Men born not ten miles from this place
Whose courses outrun hundreds ten,
A thousand yeares on ten men's backs
And one supplies what other lacks."

Finally comes a list of distinguished spectators :   Herberts, Somervilles, Lewes', Scudamores, Carys, Cornwalls, Basker-villes and many other names still familiar in the county.

We may well have doubts as to the accuracy with which these frisky veterans had kept the record of their years.   Still the period in which they had matured was one of liberal diet for the peasantry, compared with later ones,   Soft climates, moreover, are conducive to longevity, and the kindly soil of Hereford was prodigal to the poor as to the rich.

And before leaving Hereford and its ancient junketings an old copy of the *Rules of the Archenfield bowmen* lies before me.   This has nothing to do with Crecy or Owen Glendwr, but is the regulations of an archery club in the days of George III, and Herefordshire, it may be noted, is not only within the district that gave the longbow to England, but maintained modern archery through those periods of dark depression that saw within easy memory the ancient pastime extinguished in most parts of England by other and more active innovations. This particular society, however, seems to have placed con-viviality in the first rank, for every fortnight during the summer they opened the proceedings with a substantial repast at three o'clock ;' after the cloth was removed, the banquet was pro-longed for another hour, when the president ordered the company to the butts ; in the meantime, apparently, many wagers in both liquor and money had been made, the proceeds of which had to be turned over to the general fund.   It was also laid down that any members who turned Benedick had to pay a five pounds fine to the club.   One may perhaps be permitted to wonder what the shooting was like after such prolonged festivities, and how it would have compared with the accuracy of the modern archer primed on tea and strawberries.

CHAPTER II

TO PONTRILAS AND THE MONNOW VALLEY

HAVING said all that, with the space at my disposal, seems desirable for the moment about the ancient city of Hereford, I purpose to recall so much of my summer wanderings on the Welsh side of the county as a few chapters will admit of, and in such fashion as will trench on the province neither of the guide-book nor of the county history; on the book of pure utility, that is to say, or that of serious reference. I trust this fact will propitiate in advance any of those local enthusiasts, and more power to them, who might otherwise be looking for sins of omission in the matter of objects of interest in their own parish, and possibly find the parish omitted in its entirety. Nothing would be easier than to plod from village to village, and note down most things that are known about each in reasonable grammar; but a topographical dictionary requiring not less than three or four volumes to a county would scarcely commend itself to the taste of the most omnivorous reader outside the district.

My modest aim, so far as I have any, has hitherto been to plead in the best fashion I am able for a greater interest in British scenery, and above all in the associations therein involved, and to remind some, maybe, what a fund of pleasure lies close at hand which many take infinite trouble and go far afield to seek. It is a further privilege, of course, to pursue such aims or fancies in those parts of Britain which touch the sense of romance and history more readily than most through the medium of inspiring scenes. "There are thousands of well educated persons in this country," wrote an authority of some weight only the other day, " who have a real desire to know something of those portions of it in which they live or visit, but are not prepared to wade through the unrelieved technicalities and ponderous tomes of the antiquarian and the county historian." Perhaps it is this type of person who is much in my mind when penning the records of my various wanderings, in which, however, I venture to record many things which are by no means history ancient or modern. It is not often the literary critic, as may readily be imagined, who notes with sorrow the omission of the particular parish pump or lightly suggests the inclusion of a further tract of country covering perhaps five hundred square miles. For he knows about the number of words that go to a book, and the point of view with which a publisher would regard a volume swollen to the size of a family Bible. He also knows by experience the difficulties of combining lucidity and interest with compression, and the sort of fate a book would have which endeavoured to give satisfaction between its covers to the local patriotism of, say, two hundred and fifty village antiquaries and entertain the outside reader as well. " We liked your book very much so far as it goes, but we shall never forgive you for going up the other side of the valley and saying nothing about the Roman milestone in the coach house, the site of St. Tudno's cell in the vicarage field and the lovely view of the river from John Jones' cottage." This is the amateur and the friend, of course, and we get eventually pardoned. The village sage on the wrong side of the valley, however, takes longer to propitiate, for which I am sorry, as entertaining for him a very great respect.

It seems inevitable somehow that on leaving Hereford I should drift off at once to Pontrilas, ten miles away on the south-west point of the county—and also on the Monnow, one of the best trouting rivers on the border or beyond it. For in these early June days, the Mayfly was struggling, though with faint success, against that fortnight of north-east wind which played havoc with the pear crop and even modified the prodigious prospect of apples that had loaded the orchards in their bloom. But these wails of perry manufacturers and tremors of apple growers and growlings of anglers, the first and the last being almost the only west country mortals who had a grievance last season, did not sensibly diminish the glory of the June landscape on that pleasant uplifted highway which runs to Pontrilas on the Monmouth border and thence to Abergavenny.

As you cross the mediæval bridge which spans the Wye below the boathouses, there is a most effective glimpse of the foliage of the Palace Gardens dipping to the stream, and of the old Episcopal Mansion behind with the cathedral towering in the background. And it was while walking in these gardens, it may be remembered, that Bishop Macgee remarked to his brother of Hereford: " If you will give me your river, I will give you my See." Nor have many bridges perhaps been trodden by such a host of kings, princes and warriors bent on epoch-making service or on mere ruthless deeds than the one borne by these ancient arches—for it led into South Wales. A straggling suburb, big enough, however, to be worth burning even in quite remote times, lines the highway for some furlongs, showing most varieties of architecture from the days of the Tudors to those of the jerry builder. Hence there is a long easy drag for a couple of miles before you are fairly up on the rolling plateau which spreads away between ridges and ranges of hills to the bounds of the old Marcher country. Looking back over the Wye valley the city of Hereford is fair to see ! the stately pile of the cathedral rising amid its girdle of foliage, between the winding river and the clean old town free in these summer days of any suspicion of smoke or fog. To the north and to the south, isolated hills of no mean altitude and ridges clad to their summits with the mantle of leafy June, rise in somewhat bewildering and inconsequent fashion to an eye still unfamiliar with the local topography. Many of them carry dykes and ramparts around their crown, hidden from distant view by the foliage that riots in such profusion on this borderland. For this country would seem in ancient times to have been a very cockpit of contending races—Silures, Romans, Roman-Britons, Mercians, Danes have all in turn occupied these hill fortresses beyond a doubt. Dinedor, which lifts a less shaggy head than most of them, some six hundred feet above the Wye and not far below the city, is the most conspicuous and much the most seductive to the ordinary pilgrim. I do not know of any prehistoric fortress that combines such a range of outlook with so fair an enclosure of undulating lawn and noble forest trees as that encompassed by its boldly marked ramparts.

But in the meantime, as we follow the Abergavenny road, more notable perhaps for distant views than foreground detail, but pleasant to travel on whether by trap or cycle, it may be noted that the Wye on its journey toward Hereford is but a short distance off. Hidden in a narrow trough between the wooded steeps of Breinton and the waving park lands of Belmont, it is running briskly over gravelly shallows, or gliding

ON THE WYE ABOVE HEREFORD.

with deep current between lofty and leafy banks. It is a river more adapted perhaps to the strenuous than to the loafing oarsmen, and furnishes periodical rapids to lend excitement without serious danger to the many boating excursions that pass up it on summer days. Belmont is an old country seat converted of late years into a seminary for the Roman Catholic priesthood; and the chiming of bells, which is inseparable from these haunts of the ancient faith, and the deeper notes of striking clocks sound pleasantly from below.

A cycle is of course the ideal method by which to see a country-side for the man or woman who is on terms of intimacy with that modest and serviceable machine. The automobile has no doubt immense fascinations as well as utility, but as at present used does not suggest itself as a good vehicle for leisurely exploration or the enjoyment of scenery. A horse and trap is an obvious alternative for numbers of persons, but your slug of a horse is a trying companion on the road, and with anything better you cannot look about you as freely as when rolling slowly along on a cycle, though this is doubtless news to some who do not use one. Moreover sound and reasonably active Britons like some form of exercise when taking a holiday, which stimulates both mind and body and puts them in a good temper with themselves, and with the homely fare they sometimes have to put up with. A traveller with a taste for such leisurely appreciation of the country side as this book invites to, uses his machine as a means to a delightful end, and its handiness goes without saying; for during digressions from the highway you may leave it behind a hedge if no house be near. If a long walk in the hills is the programme for the day, you may run easily at your own time in the fresh of the morning to their base instead of taking a train with all the ties then and after involved as the " hardy pedestrian " of old was compelled to do. And again, if the weather break upon you unexpectedly and curtail your day, you can do a little pace-making and peradventure cheat the storm, or most of it, instead of suffering meekly a prolonged ducking, or kicking your heels for an hour or two in the waiting room of a wayside station. I like to praise the cycle, for I have tested to the full the abiding nature of its manifold and elastic services, and it is impossible to go much about England without a deep sense of the inestimable boon in a more general way it has been to the country. Cheap sneers at its expense not often heard nowadays seem too infantile for comment. Another point in its favour well known to all who combine it with other physical exercise, is the actual rest which the change of method and attitude involves. The sense of reasonable fatigue induced, say, by a fifteen or twenty mile walk over hills, or what is harder a long day's wading up a rocky stream, is scarcely at all aggravated by a moderate run home on a cycle of say five to ten miles, the relief to the spine being so marked that the leg work seems a mere trifle.

But with all this gossip about road travelling the distant hills above Pontrilas will be looming larger and the high wooded ridge of Orcop and Saddlebow running along the sky line to the south-east. The isolated hump of Garway rises a thousand feet into the sky immediately ahead of us, and the long bank of the Black Mountain trails away upon the west. All around us are the warm Herefordshire fields fat with the abundance of June. Clover and ryegrass are already lying in swathes upon their prickly stubble, giving way to red fields ribbed with turnip rows, where the infant plants, waging their annual struggle with the fly, trace themselves in faint green lines along the drills. The meadow grass not yet tinged with the faint purple blush of maturity is biding its time, and the wheat is slowly thrusting soft green ears out of its sheath, in doubt perhaps whether it is worth going to so much trouble for eight and twenty shillings a quarter. But more prominent on both sides of the road are the wide spreading pastures where the meek, white-faced, red-bodied bullocks in sleek summer coats, who have carried the name and fame of Hereford to the ends of the earth, are crunching the grass or ruminating in the shadow of tall straggling hedgerows or wide spreading trees. The starlings have already begun to pack with the precocity which distinguishes them, and to gather in hundreds from the chimneys, walls, and ivy-clad trees where they were hatched. Black-faced Shropshire sheep or the long-wooled Rylands of native fame, which with wool at eightpence a pound have dropped out of popularity, are much in evidence, and not a little bored by their lusty lambs whose approaching exit to the market will doubtless be small cause for maternal sorrow. There are no villages worth mentioning in evidence ; for this is a region of large farms and big stackyards, and roomy farmhouses.

About half way through our stage, however, at St. Devereux, it will be well to make a diversion, turn down a lane to the station, cross the line and continue for yet another half-mile to where the little church of Kilpeck with its scanty remnants of an ancient castle crowns a gentle slope above the rivulet of the Worm. The church, which is one of the most perfect specimens of pure Norman work in England, needs no apology for occasioning this diversion, but I shall make the castle site a pretext for saying some few things of which I must unburden myself before we get to Pontrilas. Otherwise I shall feel that my reader is not properly equipped for crossing the Monnow into Monmouthshire and the country of the March.

Now this little Worm brook from a point a mile or two short of Hereford to its junction with the Monnow at Pontrilas, formed for several centuries the western boundaries of a peculiar people, to wit " the men of Archenfield." This district, shadowy now in the modern mind and in name long disused, contains some forty and odd parishes. Roughly speaking it bears the shape of a diamond, its northern point approaching to Hereford, its southern touching the Monmouth border. Its bounds are clear, the Worm and the Monnow forming the two west sides of the diamond, the curving Wye those on the east ; furthermore the two lower sides, east and west, are bounded not merely by the Wye and Monnow, but by the counties of Gloucester and Monmouth respectively. By a further stretch of geometrical accuracy Herefordshire might be described as a circle with its capital in the centre and Archenfield, that was, a southern segment of this circle. Now I should not make the reader's brain reel with all this boundary running for the sake of telling him that the region therein enclosed was conspicuous for perry or cider, or for pretty girls. It has indeed a most curious story, and one unique even among the racial curiosities of the Welsh border, if the reader will suffer the moderate amount of ancient history necessary to its production.

Now when the Mercian Saxons drove the Welsh for good and all beyond the dyke traced by Offa, in the eighth century, the Silures or Welsh of Archenfield were permitted to remain a homogeneous community, retaining their laws, their customs and their language. They had probably encouraged this exceptional treatment in some way, and thoroughly justified it by a quite curious and continuous loyalty to their conquerors and an uninterrupted hostility towards their own people across the border. By the tenth century the Mercians had somewhat overleaped their dyke, which, though untraceable nowadays south of the Wye, ran not far to the westward of our present road, and annexed part of the Welsh district of Ewyas without any serious expulsion of its inhabitants. This too remained an outlying fragment of Mercia and later on of Herefordshire, under somewhat similar conditions to Archenfield. But we shall be there later, and Archenfield is our immediate concern. There are " Little Englands " in Pembrokeshire and also in Gower among the Welsh to this day, but here was a little Wales in England which has lost its characteristics to be sure long ago, but which retained them for about five centuries, a sufficiently long period to merit notice.

There are some curious passages in Domesday relating to the customs which governed this little state within a state. If a member of it, for instance, slew a king's vassal he paid twenty shillings to the king and a hundred as a forfeit. If the victim were a Saxon thane's vassal the penalty was ten shillings. If an Archenfield Welshman, however, slew another Welshman it was ordained that the relations of the slain " meet together and plunder the slayer and his kinsmen and burn their houses until about noon on the morrow when the dead man's body may be buried." Of this plunder the king took a third, " of all the rest they are quit." Again, six or seven of the best Archenfield Welshmen are required to answer the call of the sheriff to a shire mote, showing what thorough-going Herefordians they had become. The local laws relating to arson and theft are also mentioned, but most significant of all is this : " When the army marches against the enemy (the Welsh) they form by custom the vanguard in the advance and the rearguard in the return." Such were the Welsh of Archenfield in the time of Edward the Confessor, and they appear to have retained their homogeneity with some modifications well on into the thirteenth century, if not much later. How long it took the Welsh of the forty parishes to merge into indistinguishable Herefordians is a matter for the local antiquary and not for us here.

English blood no doubt flowed a little more freely into this district in later times. But the peasantry of purely agricultural districts were nowhere very accessible to such infusions till recently, and almost all the names on tombstones from Ross to Pontrilas and from Hereford to Skenfrith are Welsh, and scarcely less so on the present ratepayers' lists on church doors. About half the place-names too are Welsh, and many of the others are probably but old Welsh names anglicized. As for me I had read so constantly about the doings and sufferings of these "Men of Archenfield" in border and Welsh history, and indeed not seldom had to chronicle them myself with a slightly conscience-smitten sense of vagueness as to their precise significance, that a closer acquaintance proved quite comforting—more so perhaps than its relation has been to the reader. The feeling between these people and their kinsmen over the border was even more strained than that between the English and the Welsh, and when the latter crossed the border even up to Glyndwr's time they

COTTAGE AT KILPECK.

always fell on the fertile hills and valleys of Archenfield with peculiar relish and exceptional ferocity, the compliment being duly returned whenever the opportunity offered. An Archenfield rustic to-day would resent the imputation of being a Welshman with as much heat as any other border Saxon, and would probably have no remote conception that he had ever been a jealous guardian of Welsh customs. There was and is of course a great deal of Welsh blood all over Herefordshire, indeed Cromwell's officers write of the Welsh language as being very commonly spoken in Hereford itself.

Of Kilpeck castle nothing remains but a solitary ivy-laden fragment perched on the high tump which looks down on the windings of the sober Worm, whose youthful restraint is doubtless due to its English origin, for all other west Hereford streams rise in the Welsh hills.

It was more serviceable on this very account perhaps for flooding the hollow beneath the rampart during war's alarms and for forming fishponds for the Benedictine monks who remained here till they were turned out like many other foreign orders in 1422. Kilpeck was granted by William the Conqueror to William Fitzhamon and figures in Domesday as Chilpecte in Irchenfield. Both castle and church were standing in 1124, for the latter was presented by Hugh, first owner of Gloucester. The succession continued, as Hugh's son, Henry de Kilpeck, is recorded as owing King Stephen thirteen hawks and being heavily fined for trespassing in pursuit of game in the forest of Haywood, which stretched northward towards Hereford. Perhaps for somewhat the same reasons which nowadays occasionally secure a situation as keeper for an old poacher, a de Kilpeck was soon after made bailie of this very forest, and then the male line ran out.

King John appears to have been fond of staying with the family, but with characteristic ill grace he refused to allow his hostess, the ultimate widow, to marry the man of her choice, though she offered him fifty marks and a good horse for the concession. He finally coerced her into marriage with a Fitzwarrenne, of which turbulent race we shall hear a good deal if we ever get to Ludlow. Through female lines Kilpeck went to the Walronds of Wiltshire and then to Allen de Plankenet, who, though a great warrior, utilized his ex-officio wardership of Haywood to some effect as an enthusiastic farmer and reclaimer of land; the parish and manor of Allansmore, through which we passed on our way here without comment, being an eloquent and imperishable tribute to a border baron who made occasion to turn his battle-axe against the woods and his sword into a ploughshare. In Edward III's time when so many successions were snapped upon the blood-stained fields of France, Kilpeck became again vacant and went to the Earls of Ormond, and remained in their possession with slight interruptions till the feudal days were over and rich lawyers and merchants were purchasing landed properties for cash.

It was Sir Walter Pye who thus prospered in the time of

James I, and acquired Kilpeck with other estates, which, with the enormous reputed income, for the period, of £25,000 a year, he was no doubt able to keep up in good style. As a matter of fact, however, he soon left Kilpeck to the bats and owls, and very naturally so, as the Welsh had long ceased from troubling, and a Norman fortress could have had but scant attraction for a millionaire who had seen beautiful Tudor houses springing up about him all his life. His son, however, was no money grubber but quixotically the reverse, for he sacrificed most of his great fortune to the cause of the hapless Charles, even to patching up the shell of Kilpeck Castle and trying vainly to hold it. His son again was no less single-minded, for he

KILPECK CHURCH.

spent what was left in the still worse cause of James II, and died a ruined man with the sole consolation of being Baron Kilpeck ! This is perhaps a suggestive, if somewhat dry, genealogical record of a border castle. It would be better if we could get a gleam of some of the unchronicled dramatic episodes that shook the fortress in the Welsh wars. Still, even so much of its story may yield some food for thought as one stands on the castle mound and looks out towards the wooded ramparts of the Golden Valley, and the land of Ewyas and the ever dominating ramparts of the Black Mountains far beyond.

And now for Kilpeck church, which is but a stone's throw

from the castle tump. As I have said, it is regarded as the most perfect specimen of an ancient little Norman Church, in Herefordshire at any rate, and learned societies as well as zealous or curious individuals come to see it from all parts. Few of them probably give much thought to the castle, as there is nothing left of it worth mentioning. But here we have a beautiful Norman doorway elaborately carved, both on pillars and arches, with allegorical figures of Adam and the serpent and the tree of knowledge. All round the eaves of the church, which consists of a nave, chancel, and apse, there is a continuous string of the weird faces and forms which haunted the fancy of pious builders and architects in the eleventh and twelfth centuries. Within, there is a beautiful little vista of Norman arches, while the merit of the windows lies in their simple and perfect accord with the rest of the building and its period. An ancient and simple-minded sexton, whom I extracted together with the key from a picturesque cottage at the remote end of the picturesque little village, afforded me no instruction, which indeed is hardly needed at Kilpeck, but much entertainment. He was a mediæval sort of type, a Saxon one, and not altogether out of harmony with some of the gargoyles round the church eaves in which he took a quite refreshing pleasure, and was determined that I should not miss one of the seventy.

Back again in the high road there is nothing much to detain us, unless it be the two picturesque farmhouses and a church which constitute the hamlet of Wormbridge. One of the former is a good specimen of a small Queen Anne manor house with a brown stone roof. On the slope to the bridge over the Worm is the plain but ancient church in a large graveyard, where the departed men and women of Archenfield sleep beneath the murmur of a fir grove. Traffic is light, fine though the highway be, for no tourists are hereabouts in June, nor much indeed in any other month. Betimes a cloud of dust comes stealing slowly up and develops on closer acquaintance into a flock of panting sheep fresh from the dip tub or their annual sousing in the brook.

But however quiet the highway, the tramp seems always with us. No main road so sequestered that the members of the weather-beaten brigade with brick-red faces and depressing garments do not frequent it. The industrial regions of Monmouth and Glamorgan would be, I presume, the Mecca, real or theoretical, of the Herefordshire vagrant. It is interesting to fancy that one can sometimes distinguish the sheep from the goats, though I take it a workhouse official is the only person approaching an expert in this branch of social science. There must be so many, too, who are not quite one or the other. Some of the goats beyond question must have a vein of sentiment or poetry within them, and though deplorably culpable in sponging on us poor ratepayers, are, no doubt, outside the roll of common men. A grassy bank in June and the shade of a beech tree with only a crust, as an alternative to the bottom of a coal mine and a beefsteak, might well find supporters among philosophers as well as loafers. And all the world knows that Masters of Arts and retired officers, not on retired pay, march in the ranks of the Highway Brigade. Even the simple drapery of the common roadside hedge may give pleasure to some of them, for even this in June will reward inspection ; I do not mean a hedge covered all over with briar roses or honeysuckle and banked up with foxgloves which will fill the eye of any one, but an ordinary flowerless hedge of restrained impulse and conventional appearance. It is surprising how gratefully it responds to some slight passing notice, what a store of various shades and textures it presents, what a fresh and fluttering patchwork it is of elm and ash, of thorn and elder, of oak and beech, of hazel, maple and briar before the summer dust and summer suns have dimmed its lustre.

As the long slope runs down towards the land of Ewyas and Pontrilas, the gate of the Golden Valley opens wide into the west. All in full sight the romantic parish of Ewyas Harold waves up and down with its meadowy lowlands, its uplifted commons of heath and gorse, its scattered white homesteads and cottages, its ancient mound and girdle of encircling wooded hills and its dimmer background of mountains. But we shall be there later, while as to Pontrilas, perched on a high bank above the Dore, the Dulas, and the Worm, now united for their speedy confluence with the Monnow, there is in fact very little of it. It is chiefly noticeable as the point where the single-track line threading the Golden Valley to Hay-on-Wye joins the main line. This little road has had its ups and downs. Some years ago I remember, when a stranger in the land, I had taken it on a certain occasion into my scheme of travel for the ensuing day, and at the same time taken too much for granted. For it was not till I had bundled out my effects on the Hay platform that I discovered it to have been in a state of suspended animation for some twelve months. So much for putting foolish reliance on a two-year-old Bradshaw in a country inn. Its dark days, however, seem now over, and it is once again in full operation, and Pontrilas has resumed its importance as a railway junction. A cluster of houses inviting no particular comment adjoin the station and represent the village. But a beautiful old Tudor manor house of much distinction stands just below by the roadside and near the bridge and stream.

This is Pontrilas Court and in days gone by it belonged to a branch of the Baskervilles, one of the most ancient and potent families in Herefordshire. For the Baskervilles did literally come in with the Conqueror, hailing from the neighbourhood of Dieppe, took a leading part in border matters from the very first, and are still flourishing on their native soil. The Court is now embraced in the adjoining estate of Kentchurch, the home of the Scudamores, who can boast of almost as long a local record, and of at least equal prominence in the border history, and of whom a word or two later. The old house stands within walled grounds a stone's throw back from the road, and a short avenue of limes bisecting a square of mellow turf leads to the door. Its Tudor gables and lofty chimneys and mullioned windows still bearing the arms of the Baskervilles, and its red stone walls half draped in creepers, make a most effective picture. Within there is great store of oak panelling, and at the back a quaint old garden of generous area spreading to the banks of the stream. For some time Pontrilas Court was an inn, and a favourite haunt of anglers, which one can well believe, having regard to the beauty of the mansion and the further fact that the Monnow has always been held as the best trout stream in all these parts.

Before crossing the bridge it may be noted that the first skirmish of the Civil War in South Wales took place here. But the most famous spot, for many reasons, in all this district is Kentchurch Court, already alluded to, and the road thither follows the Herefordshire bank of the Monnow for some two to three miles. It is a castellated stone building, and for the most part but a century old. Some of it, however, is so ancient as to cherish a tradition of having sheltered Owen Glyndwr during the declining years of his stormy life ; Scudamores have owned Kentchurch since the fourteenth century, and its squire during the Glyndwr period married one of the Welsh chieftain's daughters. Monnington-on-Wye, whose owner married another, makes a similar claim, and the yet stronger one of being the

D

scene of Owen's death and sepulture. Kentchurch claims at least an equal right in the tradition of these closing scenes of the great Welshman's life. Outside opinion inclines to Monnington, but however that may be there is a corner of Kentchurch which has always gone by the name of Glyndwr's Tower, and it is natural enough that in the interval between the abandonment of the struggle and his death, Owen should have sought peace and shelter in one or both of his daughters' houses, seeing he had no longer any of his own.

Both Monnington and Owen will confront us again in these pages, so we will turn now to Kentchurch and note its effective though lowly situation with far extending lawns and finely timbered levels stretching to the Monnow, and above all with its ancient and famous chase climbing the steep slopes of Garway in the immediate background. This mountain park, where the deer wander through brakes of fern and beneath scattered oaks and yews of fabulous age and enormous girth, is a feature of the neighbourhood. There are probably few better examples anywhere of a wild mediæval chase lying adjacent to a private residence : for any temptation to interfere unduly with nature in recent centuries seems to have been fortunately repressed. The result is singularly effective as the park clambers with varied and broken surface nearly to the top of Garway, which, as already noted, is almost a thousand feet above the tide. Near the Pontrilas entrance to the lower park stands the ancient but restored church with its adjacent vicarage, the latter still occupied by one of the oldest and most accomplished of local antiquaries and historians. The original Scudamore, I believe, came out of Wiltshire, possibly attracted hither by the joint ownership during the early Norman period of manors in both counties by one Alured of Marlborough, a great personage hereabouts. His descendants of a younger branch also acquired Holme Lacy on the Wye below Hereford, and later on a peerage which remained for some generations in a family, that has been conspicuously seated in the county for six centuries, and taken a leading part in making local history for most of that period.

The *genius loci* in another sense of Kentchurch is a mysterious personage who flourishes now and again on a country tavern signboard as " Sion " or " John of Kent." His supposed date is the fourteenth century, his profession unknown. His name and fame, however, are undoubted, though nobody is quite agreed as to who or what he was. A monk with a passion for magic and mystery perhaps, who entertained himself by playing on the fathomless credulity of these Celtic folk in Archenfield and Ewyas ? A theory exists that this John of Kent was only a pseudonym used by Glyndwr, who in his later years had more or less reason for not proclaiming his where-abouts upon the housetop. Or perhaps in his old age and retirement he liked to retain a little of the mystery that was attributed to him throughout his period of power ? Kent-church, by the way, is a recently Saxonized version of Keyn-church, and St. Keyn was one of the score or two of Welsh

KENTCHURCH COURT.   OWEN GLYNDWR'S TOWER.

saints begotten by Brychan the old Welsh king who owned and gave his name to Brecon town and county.   Across the Monnow is the county which Henry VIII, grouping the lordships of Gwent and other fragments together, created and designated Monmouth, accounted an English shire by geography books, legal instruments and people who live remote from Wales, but an absurd anachronism and against nature.   Its green slopes rise sharply here from the river bed, laced with hedge-rows to the lofty ridge where stand, wrapped in slumber, what is left of the quaint old border town of Grosmont and its once famous castle.

35

And on the edge of the river the rank meadow grass with its bloom-powdered heads of foxtail, fescue or cocksfoot presses heavily against the alders and tangled briars that fence the stream.

The corncrake grinds out his harsh notes like the winding of some gigantic salmon reel, mysterious short-winged succulent bird who, when flushed by a dog, seems to reach the nearest fence with difficulty and laboured flight, but somehow or other achieves in spring and autumn long voyages over stormy seas. The ousel, too, is sure to be on the scene, skimming the water with swift steady flight, or perched immovable on some mossy rock in midstream, his white breast suggesting at the first glance the lodgment there of some passing foam flake, and his intermittent piping lost in the chorus that in mid-June still fills the grove. A careful look into any of the stiller pools will be sure to reveal more than one lusty trout, and possibly, by way of illustrating the oft-quoted couplet, a grayling.

But the latter is less in evidence near the surface than his bolder and, I always imagine, slightly contemptuous neighbour. Indeed there may be good cause for jealousy in the Monnow, for the grayling is an importation, and perhaps not a wholly wise one. A much worse and self-invited intruder, too, will probably show himself at the surface of the larger pools in such shape and size as might make an unsophisticated trout fisher's heart stand still at the spectacle.

Now the chub is a fitting and useful denizen of the Thames or Ouse, but he is an outrage in a Welsh stream, and has proved an unmitigated nuisance in all the tributaries of the Wye. He has taken unto himself more and more of late the airs, without possessing a single saving grace, of a mountain fish. He will breast any rapid and disport himself in some rockbound romantic pool amid the Black Mountains, as if he belonged there and owned it like a kilted grocer on a Highland grouse moor. But brass and push and energy will achieve anything, and the chub has all that. Born, or rather spawned, with a fancy for a fly which is creditable to him, in his proper sphere he will take yours sometimes under the very nose, for all you know, of some well-intentioned mountain trout and fill twenty yards of precious water with panic by his lubberly antics.

But the loiterer by the Monnow in early or mid-June may well be privileged to get a glimpse of that beautiful process of nature familiar enough to the angler but scarcely at all, I fancy, to those outside the craft, to wit, a rise of Mayfly. As a mere spectacle—a big rise of Marchbrowns or duns, though stimulating and significant to the fisherman, would possibly appeal but slightly to the layman other than the entomologist. But no man with a soul within him could be indifferent to an orgy of Mayflies regarded merely as a spectacle. Purely as an exhibition of insect frolic and trout-madness the open banks and smooth flowing waters of the Kennet or Itchen would perhaps be the best stage of observation. But for a thoroughly artistic setting I would take my novice to some leafy vista of a rapid stream like the Monnow, where you may have an upward stretch of fifty yards perhaps of glancing water tumbling through chequered shadow and sunshine into a long deep pool at your feet. Here you may watch these graceful wantons of a summer's day (or, to be literal, two summer days) come sailing down ; first as solitary skirmishers, next in small clusters, and then perhaps in strong battalions visible at the furthest point of sight, and gradually developing the full glory of their long delicate braided bodies of saffron and olive, their forked tails and beautifully pencilled wings.

There is no sort of method in the Mayfly's brief rush through life. Some are floating helpless and bewildered on the water with vainly fluttering wings, others are pursuing a straight and steady course as if bound for Monmouth. Many are rising with the mere joyous ecstasy of a new existence to the height of the tree tops to flutter slowly down again to the sphere they were born to, ever varying in hue as they pass from sunshine to shadow and from shadow to sunshine, above the changing surface of the stream. It is an odd thought that the Mayfly will have been holding its annual carnival here between shaggier banks and marshier meadows in the days of Alured of Marlborough. That patriarch's views on the widely diverse nature of his Kennet and his Ewyas trout would be curious hearing. Nor was the fancy that took me so far fetched, since by a really singular coincidence I found myself one day last summer throwing the identical fly over Alured's Monnow trout that I had presented to the notice only two days before of the remote descendants of those that had owned him as lord in far away Wiltshire. The possibility of such a thing would probably surprise the shade of Alured much more than the coincidence. He may even himself have been a fisherman, for he figures only in the peaceful domain of legal parchments and not so far as I know as a blood-letter.

You may climb if you will up the steep slope to Grosmont

by either lane or field path, but if tied by wheels of any kind it will be necessary to return to Pontrilas, cross the village bridge over the Dore, and a mile further the old buttressed arches festooned with ivy that span the Monnow. Just here we leave the Abergavenny road to pursue its course up the river valley, and in the angle formed by the parting ways stands what was once a famous old coaching inn, known as the *Monmouth Cap*, and recalling a once popular form of headgear that Shakespeare, if not history, has made by name at least familiar to most of us. The house is now converted to private uses, and our steep road, leaving it in the valley, climbs circuitously along the shoulder of the upstanding ridge from which

GROSMONT.

Grosmont looks out both into England and into Wales. A drowsy-looking village enough nowadays, Grosmont even yet retains some vestiges of a more stirring past. It was once a chartered town, and the castle which helped its importance and guaranteed its security, or tried to, still rears its ivy-laden walls amid embowering trees in an adjoining meadow, with the pride of pose characteristic of a true fortress. Far below, the Monnow can be seen glittering and twisting out of the green levels of Kentchurch, to be forced by opposing hills into sinuous loops that suggest the strange contortions of its great confluent the Wye, before escaping eastward towards Skenfrith between the big mass of Garway on the one hand, and the yet loftier ridge of the Graig upon the other. Grosmont was the most westerly of the group of the " three castles " which lay here in a line right on the March of Gwent, Skenfrith and White-castle making up the trio.

But what gives Grosmont some further distinction beyond that of its situation is the fact of its having been the scene of a critical encounter between the forces of Glyndwr and those of Henry V when still but a boy prince. For the latter was scarcely eighteen when, with the co-operation of the wise heads and strong arms of Gilbert Talbot, Sir Edward Newport, Sir John Greindor and other veterans of this struggle, he occupied the castle at a moment when the Welsh, flushed with success, had once more flung themselves upon the English border.

It was early in March in the year 1405, and the sixth of the war, that Glyndwr's doughtiest lieutenant, Rhys Gethin or Rhys the Terrible, had appeared above the Monnow with 8,000 irregulars from Gwent and Glamorgan. This Rhys was the leader who, five years previously, had won the bloody battle of Pilleth in Radnorshire, immortalized in Shakespeare's *Henry IV*. He now devastated Grosmont to such effect that it never recovered for all time ; the traces of its ruined streets being still visible in the surrounding fields when Camden paid it a visit. Prince Henry and his friends, who occupied the castle with a small disciplined force, and some further help from Hereford fell swiftly on the Welsh while demoralized by the sack of Grosmont, and utterly routed them, a thousand being slain with slight loss to the victors. Following up this success with prompt vigour, Henry of Monmouth encountered the enemy again a few days later in Breconshire in a yet bloodier fight, killing Glyndwr's brother, who was so like him that there was a brief outburst of illusive joy among the English, and capturing his son. There is a letter extant written by Prince Henry to his father after the battle of Grosmont, and I have printed it elsewhere, in which, after describing the fight, he tells his father that he has captured one great chieftain of the Welsh, whom he would have already forwarded on to him but for the fact that " he cannot yet ride at ease," which shows some consideration towards a Welsh rebel for a fifteenth century soldier. Any-thing more different from the Prince Hal of Falstaff and company, and it is to be feared of the popular fancy than this hardworked energetic youth absorbed from the sixteenth year onward in the arduous strain and sobering trials of the struggle with Glyndwr, could not readily be imagined.

These two victories so cheered up the king, whose whole

reign had been embittered by Glyndwr, that he came down himself to Hereford with one more of his many attempts to crush the accursed magician. But if the latter had failed for the time in arms his political acumen had saved the situation. For his friends in the north had created such a diversion that Henry had not crossed the Monnow before he was hurrying off again to Yorkshire. When he had crushed the Percies, scandalized many even of his friends by executing Archbishop Scrope, besides one or two of Glyndwr's Welsh emissaries, he turned southward only to hear that Owen had been reinforced by 10,000 Frenchmen just landed at Tenby, had marched across Wales and was approaching Worcester.

I was almost forgetting another dramatic scene of which Grosmont was the stage. For that injudicious and much buffeted monarch, Henry III, in his callow days was not content with being beaten by Llewelyn the Great and driven to an ignominious peace with that stalwart prince, but he must needs fall out with all the Marcher barons in the same year, 1233. Having confiscated their estates—or rather declared them to be confiscated, which was not quite the same—he still further aggravated the situation by granting them to his Poitevin and Flemish favourites, themselves the chief cause of Henry's troubles. The Marchers and Llewelyn, who came nearer to heading a united Wales than any prince before or after him, then made common cause. Against them marched the king, with a large army, mainly foreigners, and occupied Hereford. But all the stock having been driven into the castle wards or out of reach Henry moved on to Grosmont, hoping that a better living for his army might be made out of the March of Ewyas and Overwent. His army camped around the town and castle while the king lay inside, all of them, however, confident in their numbers. But at daybreak on the feast of St. Martin's the Marchers and the Welsh fell upon the royal troops and hapless foreigners, who abandoned everything with such precipitation that there seems to have been hardly any bloodshed. The wealth of the spoil probably checked pursuit, for the entire baggage of the army, with all the king's money and provisions, everything in fact but the royal person, which was safe in the castle keep, as well as five hundred horses, was annexed by the victor. Many even of the king's friends fled down the hill to the Monnow in their night-shirts. What a sight that great stampede would have been from the top of Garway on that November morning ! After this the king recrossed the Severn.

Modern Grosmont is represented by a single straggling street, serene and restfully astride of its lofty ridge. There is an old market hall in the centre, and a few quaint gabled houses dip down a byway, as if to give the distant mountains in the west a chance of rising high above them and making an effective picture. An ancient church just off the street, with a central tower and spire, both sexagonal, and a great display of roof both east and west of it, is not only suggestive of Grosmont's former importance, but well worth seeing for itself alone. The short transepts under the tower serve all present needs of worship, while a large nave, disused and bordered with fine columns and pointed arches springing from uneven timeworn flags, is more simply eloquent perhaps of the rude past than any wealth of ornament. In the chancel there are seven lancet windows with wide splays on either side, and in the ample churchyard sloping to the south there is a forest of tombstones marking the dust of departed Morgans, Powells, Prossers, Pritchards, Watkins',

GROSMONT FROM THE SKENFRITH ROAD.

Gwatkins', Gwillims', and such like Silurian clan names, with a good solid groundwork of the still more familiar patronymics common to all Wales. There is also an inspiring outlook thence to the south-west, over coiling valleys and between enfolding hills, to the Brecon Mountains, with the Skerrid, finest of all isolated border hills, lifting its rugged peak above the glens of Pandy and marking the gateway of the Vale of Ewyas. But we shall explore those pleasant regions before the summer is much older, and it is five miles from here to Skenfrith, where we should have been ere now.

It is somewhat of a byroad that runs thither, but quite a reasonably good one for either man or beast. A wayside rustic described it to me as a " dead road with two pitches," meaning in border phraseology a road without any misleading branches, and two sharp, short hills. But in any case it is a pleasant and not arduous route, lifted for the most part a good height above the Monnow valley, which for some distance it follows. Nor are you likely to meet upon it either a motor or a tramp. It hugs the richly grassed and wooded foothills of the great hump of Graig, whose summit rises some 1,300 feet upon the right bank of the river. And for much of the time you are confronting the broad, southern slopes of Garway, laced for a space upward with the varied patchwork of a secluded pastoral and woodland county and rising above into vast sweeps of fern. In the trough below the Monnow plays hide and seek among the foliage, fringed by green ribbons of meadow whose perennial freshness defies the longest drought that we in the blest country shall ever see.

Like much of the Welsh border this is a region not only of big hills but of big trees. Oak and beech and even elm of such size as console the dwellers in midland and southern counties for some physical deficiencies of landscape flourish here midway between the sparkle of mountain streams, and the summits of almost mountainous heights. The warm, red glow of a fallow or turnip-field, plashed here and there on hillside and valley, is a further asset to the wealth of this steep Gwentian landscape. Homesteads and cottages are seldom garish. Whether of stone or timber and wattle, whether tiled, slated, or thatched they are almost always in some sort attuned to the landscape, and in a country rich in orchards as well as in woods, they have a knack of only suggesting their presence by a glimpse of wall or roof or gable in such fashion as the artist loves. So riding the boundary, as it were, with the old England of kings' writs and sheriffs, members of parliament and Crown laws on the one hand, and the March lands where none of these things obtained and a great baron was a little king on the other, we strike downwards into the Abergavenny and Monmouth road, which carries us quickly to Skenfrith and the Monnow's bank once more. Here again on an even smaller scale than Grosmont, and lying low in a narrow valley, is an ancient hamlet, pressed on one side of its short street so close against the ivied walls of its sheltering castle as actually to lean on them. There is little within but an isolated keep, which standing on a mound shows its head above the outer defences. But what with the mass of foliage that clothes both walls and tower, and the village orchards which seem to fill up the vacant spaces, and the genially intimate terms which it appears to be on with the every-day life of the hamlet, Skenfrith castle is more picturesque perhaps than suggestive of its former glories. Indeed, the whole place is very much so. The church at the far end of the castle keeps up in its precincts the serene umbrageous atmosphere of the place in general, and furthermore is not only a good and unspoiled specimen of Early English work in arch and window, but has a quite wonderful bell tower in three stories, supported by timbered shafts with a narrow stone pent roof over each ; unique in appearance so far as my experience goes, but not, I believe, uncommon in this region in pre-Restoration days.

SKENFRITH.

The castle site is, I fancy, pre-Norman, and was seized by Hamelin, the Norman conqueror of Over Gwent. Later on it shared the fortunes more or less of Whitecastle and Grosmont, the other members of the *Trilateral*, and served the same end.

Which Anglo-Norman owner built this one matters little here, though Brian de Wallingford was a famous person, as there is no space for such story as it may have. These castles, though technically just outside royal jurisdiction, seem to have been used rather in the interest of the Crown than of the Marches. Feudal boundaries in those days were not too literally interpreted, and in such attempts as I may incidently make here to lift the veil behind which the story of this part of England lies for all but a handful of students or local enthusiasts, generalizing is inevitable. The intricate conditions which

43

governed the Marches virtually forbid anything else, and parenthetical detail would be superfluous indeed.

The village bridge linking England and Wales, if we regard Monmouth as Wales, at Skenfrith is an old stone structure of three arches, beneath which the Monnow glides darkly and soberly to spread out below into wide sunny ripples washing the edge of pendent woods. It is a bridge for the angler to smoke his evening pipe upon, warmed with a good dinner and the memories of a good day. And the thought is doubtless prompted by a snug-looking old inn which stands at the end of it, and was in former days, its landlord informed me, a favourite haunt of the disciples of Izaak.

Among the Lansdown MSS. in the British Museum there is a curious paper relating to Skenfrith Castle, which throws some light upon the treasure legends of Wales and the Marches. It is dated April 28, 1589, and is addressed to the lord treasurer, Burleigh, by a Welshman incarcerated in the Tower of London for some offence. The latter begs permission in quaint English to delve for treasure beneath the castle, on behalf of the Crown, success in his endeavours being the price of his liberty. "The voyce of the country," writes this sanguine person, "goeth there is a dyvill and his dame, one sets upon a hogshead of gold, the other upon a hogshead of silver." The Welshman undertakes however to eject both the he and she-devil from their respective situations : "by the grace of God and without any charge to the Quene or your lordships. If the treasure be there I will look for something at your hands, for the countrey saith there is great treasure. No man in remembrance was ever seen to open it, and great warrs hath been at it and there was a place not far from it whose name is Gamdon, which is as much to say the *game is doun*."

CHAPTER III

EWYAS HAROLD, AND THE GOLDEN VALLEY

JUST westward of Kentchurch and Pontrilas, sweeping over low wooded ridges to the Golden Valley, or climbing southward over the ever-ascending ramparts of the Black Mountains, lies the land of Ewyas—region of euphonious name and ancient landmarks, and beyond measure beautiful. Opening wide in the foreground between the encircling ridges rising near at hand above the swift rivulets of the Dulas and the Dore, with the lofty mound of its long vanished castle overlooking the valley, spreads the parish of Ewyas Harold. That a region so fair in the things that are and so rich in the things that were, should have failed to inspire some fortunate wight whose lot is cast among them, would be strange indeed.

It is quite providential that the normal course of ecclesiastical preferment should have fortuitously placed the present vicar of Ewyas Harold within these irresistible influences. For I am betraying no confidence and at the same time perhaps justifying my estimate of the stimulating properties of the local atmosphere in attributing in part to these the zeal which produced the best history of a parish I have ever read. Moreover it is so unusual as to be almost a coincidence that Kentchurch and Ewyas Harold, two adjoining parishes, should each be thus fortunate. It would be an ungracious act to criticize the efforts of any, whether parish clerk or finished scholar, who puts on record as a labour of love—for this is what it usually amounts to—the annals of his own countryside. But it is not often that a district finds a chronicler who can satisfy at once the archæologist, the literary critic, and the merest layman in such matters, and Mr. Bannister has surely done all this.

Mr. Bannister thinks there were kings in Ewias (the old spelling),—the district that is not the parish,—between the departure of the Romans and the descent of the Saxons on this border land, and before, I presume, the tripartite division of Wales by Rodri Mawr. One of them, indeed, King Clidach,

45

was too saintly to live, his virtues, by contrast no doubt, proving such an abiding irritant to his neighbours, that they put him out of sight. He was a sportsman nevertheless, for it was while waiting for a hunting party by the banks of the Monnow, and filling in the time by meditation on sacred subjects, that they fell upon him and slew him. And when his sorrowing subjects tried to drag the body away on a wagon, the yokes of the draught oxen and their gear snapped at every effort to move the load. So recognizing in this the divine intent rather than any shortcomings in their own traces or the tenacity of the mud, they buried him where he fell, and built a shrine over him and devoted the surrounding acres to heaven for ever as a place of sanctuary and refuge.

He was classified as a martyr and the shrine was known as Merthyr Clydach. It worked miracles on pilgrims for generations and survives to·this day in the name of Clodoch, a place just below Longtown, across the big hills yonder.

The Dulas brook prattles gently with the piping voice of a dry June through the pleasant village scattered along its narrow levels, and among paddocks and orchards ; while on the northern slope the church of St. Michael with massive and squat old tower lies back a space ; the vicarage standing on a terraced hill above. The castle mound and moat coated with rank grasses and crowned with a pair of self-sown oak trees, dips its feet in two meeting streams a few furlongs away, as complete an example of extinguished glory as you could wish to contemplate. This is Ewyas Harold ; all the greater Ewyas lay behind it on the Welsh side of the here untraceable Offa's Dyke, and it seems that part, at any rate, of the district had come to much such terms with the Mercians as had the men of Archenfield so amply treated of. Like them its Welshmen had given over, though a little later, their whole-hearted allegiance to their late foes, reserving only their laws, language and customs. Like the others they sent their representatives to the shire mote or cheerfully paid a fine in honey, if they were too busy to waste their time in county legislation, which probably appeared a superfluous Saxon fad. But when it came to serious business and a Welsh war was on hand, they were ready enough, and, like their compatriots of Archenfield, claimed the privilege of advancing in the front and retreating in the rear. I have already told how the Normans pushed in here during Edward the Confessor's time and erected one of their earliest castles on this great mound which had previously carried a Saxon burh. Ralph the Timid, made, unmade and recreated Earl of Hereford within a brief space, had allotted Ewyas to a Norman follower, one Osborn, surnamed Pentecost. In the French panic created by Godwin, Osborn fled north to the King of Scotland and not across Channel like most of his kind, and the castle and lands were given a little later to his nephew, Alured of Marlborough, whose tenure was confirmed at the Conquest. In the meantime the stone castle, that hated badge of Norman pretension, had been demolished. Soon after the Battle of Hastings, Fitz Osborn, already alluded to as William's greatest viceroy and Earl of Hereford, rebuilt not only Ewyas but planted several other castles for the better aweing of the Welsh and but half-conquered border Mercians. This stirred up their leader, " Edric the Savage " to a final effort, which with the help of the Welsh of Gwent and Brycheiniog, otherwise Monmouth and Brecon, kept the hands of the Norman garrison sufficiently full for the next three years, only those of Hereford, Ewyas and the sister fortress of Richard's castle near Ludlow holding out. The tide of devastation swept once more over the unfortunate county, but ill recovered from the wasting of Griffith and Algar's Welshmen in 1057, and the sack of Hereford which had brought down the Great Harold to its succour and to his conquering progress through Wales. William Fitz Osborn, with his feudatory Alured of Marlborough, had built a stronger castle on the foundations of the other. And in time reinforcements came and the Welsh were driven back to their mountains and order restored. The arm-chair reader, at any rate, will not care to have the castle of Ewyas Harold rebuilt for him from its grass-grown foundations, nor probably will he feel an interest in the number of acres Alured kept in his own hands, and what tracts he set to knights on military tenures, or how many villeins or borderers owed him

FARMHOUSE AT RICHARD'S CASTLE.

service on the lordship, and the names of all occupants including nine Welshmen in the village who farmed 720 acres for a quit rent in honey. But all these interesting details have been rescued from oblivion by Mr. Bannister, and will be acceptable enough to any one looking upon the site of their habitations or walking among the graves of their descendants. One cannot help being struck, too, in all like transactions of this period, at the enormous quantity of honey in demand throughout West Britain, at any rate, and by inference at the amount of mead and metheglin which must have found its way into the iron interiors of our ancestors.

It was near the close of the eleventh century when young Harold, son of Ralph the Timid, succeeded Alured of Marlborough in the lordship of Ewyas, and though rich in lands elsewhere, both in France and England, he made his chief abode in the castle by the Dulas and gave his name to the church and parish for ever. Had he been more than a child in that fateful year 1066, he might, according to Freeman, have been a claimant for the throne, being great-nephew and nearest of kin to the Confessor, and his mother an English relative of the great Earl of Godwin. He may have been thirty when he came to Ewyas, and died there at seventy, a good old age for the Marches. He founded the priory of Ewyas Harold as a cell and offering to the church of St. Peter at Gloucester, and his son Robert was the doughtiest foe of Welshmen on the whole border. There was yet another Robert of Ewyas, and his daughter Sibilla took for her third husband the famous Roger Clifford of that Ilk on the Wye, brother of fair Rosamund, but best remembered as founder with Sibilla above mentioned of that great Cumbrian house, the Cliffords of the North. By 1300 the line had broken, and John Tregoz, greatest of all lords of Ewyas, was seated there and summoned to Parliament as one of the higher barons of the kingdom. He left ten daughters and a great division of property, covering in its disposition no less than 124 folio pages of closely written Norman-French. After a short interval of De la Warres, the lordship was absorbed in that of Abergavenny, which fell to the Nevilles, who still retain its honours. It was after the Wars of the Roses, doubtless, that the castle like most others was abandoned. There were still a few remains of it in Leland's time, but by the Civil War the last stones had been carried away or rooted up by the villagers. As a final word it is interesting to learn that in the year 1300, the parish contained thirty-seven free tenants and seventy-five villeins, which making the usual allowances to a household would give the Ewyas Harold of that day about the same population it now boasts of.

The church has been so much restored, it scarcely calls for notice, with the exception of the tower, which is square and massive and contains some Early English windows. Within is a recumbent effigy of the Tregoz heiress, as is supposed, who took the lordship to the De la Warre family. Forty years ago it was opened, and a small cavity, a few inches wide, containing the fragments of a metal vessel, in which it is supposed the lady's heart was deposited. The priory was dispersed in 1358 and everything removed to the mother foundation at Gloucester, on which occasion unusual precautions seem to have been taken by the Bishop of St. David's that the vicar should not be left to starve together with his church. His lordship forced the abbot in this case to endow the church before he abandoned it, and a long agreement defining precisely what the parson was to retain is preserved and reproduced in the present vicar's chronicle already spoken of. It is curious reading and is said to be almost, if not quite, the only document of the kind extant. This flitting of small priories, to the detriment of the church they left behind, seems to have been a common grievance in the century before the Reformation. In the fat graveyard of Ewyas Harold we have again the Watkins', Gwatkins', Gwillims, Prossers and the whole list of South Walian patronymics enjoying, if the term be permissible, a virtual monopoly of the headstones and monuments. From beneath the tower the shades of a once too convivial parishioner administers a snub to the passer-by, as if fearful that even in the grave he would not be sure of escaping the eye of the temperance reformer :—

> Reader, pass on, nor waste your time
> On bad biography and much worse rhyme,
> For what I am this cumbrous clay immures,
> And what I was is no concern of yours.

There is a delightful walk hence over the humpy ridge which parts the waters of the Dulas and the Dore and the village of Ewyas from the fine old monastery church of Abbeydore at the mouth of the Golden Valley. For all the higher land is an undulating common of heather gorse and fern, through which broad green ways of crisp sward spring under the feet; a place not wild enough for curlew, but on that June afternoon when I crossed it with the vicar the skylarks were mounting in full chorus and peewits were circling with insistent cries, and a noble outlook over the hills and vales of Ewyas was here. A sharp pitch downward into the vale below, a short stretch of leafy lane in the flat, a glimpse of a pleasant vicarage set back amid lawns and foliage, and the noble abbey church of Dore broke upon us of a sudden by the roadside.

It would be evident that something much more than a parish

ABBEYDORE CHURCH

church was here, though its use as such is plain from the large crowded graveyard around it. It is a cruciform building in Early English style of high pitched roof and great elevation. A square embattled tower is set curiously in the south-east angle of choir and transept, and rises high above the lofty gables of the roof.

But what we see now is after all but a portion of the building raised here by Robert, the son of Harold of Ewyas in 1120 for a colony of the new order of Cistercian monks. The traces of an immense nave can be easily marked, extending westward half across the heaving grassy surface of the churchyard. All remnants, too, of the monastic buildings but a long ruinous wall have vanished.

Giraldus Cambrensis has invested the old abbey with exceptional interest by singling it out as a mark for his especial invective, and raking up all the scandalous stories that were current about its abbots and monks in his day, which was practically theirs. It was Cistercian, moreover, which in itself was enough for Gerald, and it had an abbot or two, contemporaries of his own, who seem to have been as voracious landgrabbers as they were gluttons and roysterers. Our famous Archdeacon of Brecon, with his racy pen and biting satire, none the less convincing for his intimate knowledge of Wales and the border, is quite merciless in his strictures on Abbeydore. A brother cleric, the celebrated Walter Mapes, Archdeacon of Oxford, himself a Herefordshire man, battered this monastery and monasteries in general with broadsides of metrical denunciations, many of which Gerald, putting into his own easy and mordant prose, discharged with unconcealed delight at Abbot Adam and his monks. The worm seems at last to have turned in the said Adam's successor and namesake, who replied with somewhat tardy volleys in verse, though with what effect we know not. Unlike those of his opponents their merits, even though they had the solitary one of truth, do not seem to have been worth preserving.

Giraldus declares that while he was on a visit to the Bishop of Hereford and eating his Christmas dinner with him, a brace of these Abbeydore monks turned up at the episcopal quarters. The hospitable bishop inquired of his servants whether there was plenty of fish and other edibles such as were required by the rigid regulations of their order. But Gerald, in characteristic and caustic fashion, remarked to his host that it was not fish but a dispensation to gorge themselves on meat that these two precious Cistercians of Abbeydore were after. Whereupon the bishop put Gerald's assumption to the test, and doubtless much to the latter's satisfaction found it correct; and the archdeacon had the further pleasure, if he is to be believed, of seeing them make complete beasts of themselves under the episcopal roof. Another story of Gerald's concerns an honest vicar of an adjoining parish, who having frequently been of service to the Abbey of Dore found himself one night a guest there. Having been himself entertained on somewhat meagre fare, he embarked on a tour of observation through the establishment, not perhaps without his suspicions. These proved too well founded, for he ran his hosts to ground in the very act of feasting themselves in right loyal fashion in an inner chamber on all the luxuries of the season, and quaffing mead and wine out of silver cups.

One, Adam, who presided here at the end of the twelfth century, was the most conspicuous of all the abbots, and mainly, according to Gerald, through his iniquities. If land was to be annexed even forgery was no obstacle. For having cast covetous eyes on some property at Bacton near by, the cunning abbot invited the knightly owner to dinner, and having made him hopelessly drunk, produced a previously prepared deed of gift of the coveted farm and then proceeded to forge the owner's name at the foot of it. When morning and sobriety came to the knight and he was shown the document, he indignantly repudiated all knowledge of it, whereupon Abbot Adam sued him at law and bribed the judge, so says Gerald, and won both the suit and the farm. No owners of land in the neighbourhood, private or corporate, were safe from this acquisitive cleric, nor did he always take the trouble to make them drunk or forge their names, but according to these hostile chroniclers filched churches and benefices from weaker brethren without so much as a by-your-leave. Gerald accuses him of bribing patrons and even bishops, and of seizing the abbey of Teschort and turning it into a barn. More daring enterprises even than these did our abbot carry through. In 1198 a bloody battle against the Welsh in Radnor had just been fought, with the rout of the latter and the loss of three thousand men. A baron of Herefordshire, who had made one of the victorious party, knowing Adam's wiles, suggested to him that he should go to King Richard, then in Aquitaine, and give him to understand, without actually mentioning names, that he, the baron, was the hero of the victory, Adam being doubtless able to improve the occasion to his own advantage. Thus armed with an introduction to the very much absent king, Coeur de Lion, which was all that he wanted, he urged the fact on his Majesty that there was a barren tract of three hundred acres of Crown land near Abbeydore which served no better purpose than as a harbour of refuge to bandits and Welshmen, and was in short a curse to the country. He concluded by offering the king, to whom money for his remote enterprises was always scarce and welcome, 300 marks for the grant of it. Deplorably ignorant of these home concerns as the lionhearted king doubtless was, he was not quite such a fool as Adam thought, but at least demanded some sort of independent opinion as a preliminary to the transaction. This the abbot, when he got home, proceeded to purchase of one Ralph of Arden in Herefordshire, who, for a moderate consideration, was prepared to swear anything. So the bargain was carried through, and Adam acquired for his monastery a fine level fertile property, the timber alone off which he sold for three times the sum he gave for the property, almost reminding one of the possibilities set forth in the prospectus of a modern colonial land company.

It might be supposed that this land-hungry divine was satisfied. Not he ! for having now established easy relations with the king he paid him another visit on the continent and got two hundred acres more and a mill from the royal forest at a nominal sum. But when John came to the throne his suspicions were aroused, for he knew this district well, as we have seen, and he promptly stripped the abbot of this last acquisition. But later on, when the king got into such trouble with the church, he was compelled by Archbishop Langton to give it up again, which he only did with much justifiable protest, and even then the monks of Abbeydore did not feel secure in their tenure. So when John, late in his reign, weak and dispirited, was seeking consolation in his favourite haunts of Archenfield and Ewyas, the second Adam, the poet, already referred to, pounced upon him and successfully importuned him to confirm the grant. Thus the story ends badly, save that neither parties to it were virtuous, so it does not much matter.

We also know how the monks of Dore went to the widow of Robert of Ewyas the founder, and made her a monk on her deathbed for reasons too obvious to enlarge upon. But the reader must not take Walter Mapes or Giraldus too literally in these matters, and the Cistercians were economically the most valuable of all orders to the nation. They were the most enterprising of agriculturists, and were notable for making waste places bloom in a manner quite marvellous to the slipshod native. That they succeeded in getting grants of land from royal forests may be looked at from another point of view than that of Giraldus, for these same forests were apt to be inferior or barren tracts, and their partial reclamation was all to the people's good and the monks' credit when gaunt famine, the handmaid of rapine, stalked about the land. For men could starve then in Herefordshire while Cheshire or Wiltshire had abundance, and not only from the effects of war.

I don't know whether a ripening wheat crop of four quarters to the acre looks the same to an unsophisticated eye as one of two, or not. But I am quite certain that a mediæval cornfield with its microscopic yield of three to six bushels would excite some comment from the veriest cockney to-day. I have been much in countries where such depressing spectacles are quite common, and sometimes try to fancy the old English cornfields when this was their average yield. The Cistercians, too, were great breeders of horses, both saddle and draught, and they were of course pre-eminent as sheep and wool growers. They were a reforming order of the Benedictines, and were founded oddly enough by an Englishman, one Hardy, at Citeaux in Burgundy, from which place they acquired their name. They came to England early in the twelfth century. Tintern was one of their first foundations and Dore was even earlier. Much was done to the church before us from time to time in the way of embellishment, even in the middle ages, and the functions which each little addition entailed seem to have been the cause of strife between the Welsh partisans of the diocese of St. David's and those of the Bishop of Hereford, for each considered the abbey of Dore to be within their diocese.

But all the later work that matters now is the restoration, in 1635, by John Lord Scudamore, a personal friend of Laud. By this nobleman the church was re-roofed and the tower built, besides necessary internal repairs and the erection of a carved wooden screen. Indeed the interior is as striking as the outside, being in the best style of Early English. Where the now vanished nave joined the transept are four lofty and wide arches. The choir has three bays with a large lancet window in each, while to the east of the choir is a double transverse aisle and an ambulatory running all round the transepts. There are five chapels with vaulted roofs, resting on graceful clustered pillars, some of the capitals for their beauty of carved foliage being regarded by experts as almost unmatched. There is a remarkable stone slab, too, 12 feet long, with a strange story of adventure attached to it, for a communion table, and in the windows above some fine old glass.

In the chapels are effigies of knights in chain armour, among them the founder of the abbey. In the Hoskyns chapel is an altar tomb of 1665 commemorating a famous lawyer of that noted Herefordshire breed, who about the restoration removed from their estates here to Harewood near Ross, which has only recently lost them. Indeed I have heard somewhere that a Hoskyns could ride in those days on his own land from one seat to the other. Then there is the carved wooden screen already mentioned, as erected by the seventeenth century Restorer, which shuts off the choir, now alone used for service, from the rest of the church. And above its centre are carved the Royal arms with those of Lord Scudamore, and the diocese of Hereford on either side. There is much more detail in this noble church than it is fitting to take note of here, at the same time there is a little too much of the whitewash period still in evidence.

It was a few days after the visit above alluded to that I paid another to the abbey of Dore, betimes in the morning, and on this occasion, taking a cycle with me, set my face up the Golden Valley, with a view to crossing its eastern wall near the head and returning down the left bank of the Wye to Hereford. Now the Golden Valley was not so named from any fatness of its soil, though this would not have been inappropriate, nor yet from any treasure buried in its hills, but merely from the inability of the French monks to pronounce Welsh. The little river Dore which waters the valley and the abbey precincts was originally of course "dwr," a familiar Welsh word for water that stands for the modern name of a score of Welsh streams. This was clipped into Dore, or Dor, by the unaccustomed tongue of the strangers, and then in later generations was curiously enough treated by the Anglo-Herefordians as Norman-French and translated into English with an undeniably pleasing effect. To the stranger adventuring it, the Golden Valley has nothing wild nor grand to show, but only a level floor of meadow and pasture half a mile or so in width, and gently sloping banks of more grass, or grain, or orchards. It is hemmed in on either hand with high walls of woodland, which for its whole length cut it off on the east from the lower country of Herefordshire, and on the west from the more broken and Welsh-like valleys that abut upon the Black Mountains. It is a smooth, a fertile and a gracious region, yet always narrow enough to retain its character as an isolated and not unromantic vale.

As you pass on to Bacton, but a mile or two above Abbeydore, its ivied church tower on the hill has something in the way of a Tudor monument within it that is almost worth an inspection, even if time were pressing, not on account of its artistic merit, but from the humour both of the illustration and the accompanying letterpress.

How different are these Elizabethans in their mode of exit from those grim Borderers or Crusaders in chain mail, wholly disdainful, it would seem, of the curiosity of after-generations, over whom you may dream dreams but of a surety never smile. Blanche Parry of Newcourt in Bacton parish, however, kneels at full length in her official costume in Bacton church beneath a canopy and before a marvellous effigy of her haughty mistress, Queen Elizabeth, in hoops and crown. And on a tablet above she tells us in some thirty lines of delightfully quaint verse how she devoted all her days to her as " maid of honour to the maiden Queen." " Traenyd in princys courts with gorgeous wyghts " was she, and what a splendid mouthful is that same phrase, " gorgeous wyghts."

Whose fleeting honour sounds with blast of horne
Not dovtynge wante, whyllst that my mystres lyvde,
In womans state whose craddle sawe I rockte,
Her servaunte then, as when shee her croune attcheeved
And so remaend tyll deathe my doore had knockte
Preferrynge styll the causye of eache wyghte
As farre as I doorste move her Grace hys eare
For too rewarde decerts by course of ryghte
As needs resulte of sarvys do, ne each weare
So thar my tyme I thus dyd passe awaye,
A maede in courte and never no mans wyffe
Sworne of Quene Ellsbeths bedd chamber, allwayes,
Wyith maeden Quene, a maed dyd ende my lyffe.

It was in this parish too that the famous Morris dance, described in the last chapter, took place during a visit of James I to the Squire Hoskyns of that day at Moorhampton Court, now a farmhouse. As the road leaves the western side of the vale and darts across the level meads through which the Dore wanders, and the little somewhat grass-grown railway track cuts a straighter course, there is a charming backward peep of the old abbey church rising two miles away out of the green levels ; while as we turn northwards along the further bank a breezy stretch of low ground spreads away between its wooded slopes towards the distant gap, beyond which the town of Hay lies upon the banks of Wye. Farming is on a generous scale in the Golden Valley. Hay harvest was in progress on the late June day I have in mind, and the machines were running long courses over broad level meads bounded by the alder thickets which marked the windings of the Dore. The long straight swathes were whitening almost as soon as cut in the bright sunshine, and in the soft dry summer breeze which rippled over the still uncut grass and rustled among the fresh green heads of wheat and barley on the slopes above.

But there would seem to have been an interval in the prosperity of this remote Arcady after the Cistercian monks and their high standard of farming for those days had gone. For Roland Vaughan, a younger son of Bredwardine, just over the hill in the Wye Valley, and a contemporary and relative of Mistress Blanche Parry of Bacton, was the owner of New Court in that parish, and was filled with the enthusiasm of his

VOWCHURCH.

day for all adventure and experiment. As author of a rare tract, entitled, *Most approved and long experienced water works*, he gives a dismal economic picture of the valley: " The richest yet for want of employment the plentifullest place of poore in the kingdom, there be within a mile and a half of my house every way five hundred poore habitations whose greatest means consist in spinning flax hemps."

This philanthropist was very much before his time and was not unlike his namesake and kinsman, who a few years later, with a handful of Welshmen, tried to make the desert bloom on the savage peninsula of Avalon in Newfoundland and failed, as his successor Lord Baltimore failed. But the Bredwardine Vaughan had no Newfoundland to deal with, but rather in his own idealistic phraseology, "The golden vale, the Lombardy of Herefordshire, the garden of the old Gallants, the paradise of all parts beyond the Severne." And he proposed to "raise a golden wilde in the Golden Valley being the pride of all that countree bordering on Wales." The practical side of this scheme was irrigation, the other a sort of socialistic community, and I believe traces of his dykes still exist. He seems to have succeeded in planting his settlers, but like almost all philanthropic colonizers of independent

PETERCHURCH.

Britons only to discover that he had raised a nest of hornets about his ears. Even the young parson did not suit, for they told him he had "planted a Machiavel among them a cunning usurer." But greater and as worthy men as Vaughan have failed in this business.

The villages of Vowchurch and Turnaston lie right in our path, and concerning them there is a somewhat improbable legend of two pious ladies who combined to build a church, but falling out on the question of a site, decided on building one apiece. In the heat of argument one remarked to the other, "I vow I will build my church before you turn a stone of yours." A couple of miles beyond the spire of Peterchurch shooting high into the air above the low-lying roof trees and orchards of the adjacent village, makes a pleasant picture in the gradually narrowing vista of the vale.

Here again is a church of some repute and considerable size with a good deal of Norman work visible, a choir chancel apse, to say nothing of a mysterious monolith in the churchyard. But what would distract the attention for the moment of the keenest archæologist from all these things is the model of a huge fish placed high in the south wall which confronts you on entering the building. It is let into a stone tablet and has a gold collar round its neck with a ring. I have seen some strange things in remote churches, but the record trout of a river is generally to be found mounted in the village inn or the squire's house, not hanging on the church wall amid the tablets of the departed great. The help of an eyeglass did not wholly remove this irreverent impression, and as I discovered from an informing circle of villagers in the inn later on that my doubts were justified. For this mammoth fish is said to be a trout taken by the monks of old in the Dore hard by, with the collar and ring as depicted attached to its neck.

The better way for getting back to the Wye and the Hereford district over the eastern wall of the valley is to pursue the latter some three miles further up to Dorstone ; not because the lane that from thence climbs over the woody barrier is better than the one which mounts Stockley Hill from Peterchurch, though it is a little shorter ; but from the fact that by following a more devious route to the west of the Dore, both Old Castle, a moated farmhouse perched on the hill, and the ruins of Snodhill castle could be inspected. And again within a long mile of Dorstone is a well known cromlech known as Arthur's stone. The ridge to be surmounted in either case is just under a thousand feet in altitude, but the stony lanes which wriggle over it squeeze through a friendly notch in the summit at somewhat less than this. Not for wheels, however, are these flowery and precipitous ways, the local farmer's cart and pony of course excepted, but to be adventured only by the pedestrian or the cyclist who can of course lead his machine over without any difficulty. On this particular afternoon, almost the longest and one of the loveliest of a gorgeous year, I breasted Stockley Hill by preference, clambered up tortuous lanes between tangled hedges thick with briar rose, and with honeysuckle clustering rankly above banks knee deep in fox-gloves, ferns and gorse. This upland country is one of small farmers and small steep enclosures, whence loaded hay-carts come lurching between crazy gateposts down perilous steeps into the narrow way with a great clattering and a wealth of Herefordian Saxon.

But these uplifted lanes are lonely enough for the most part ; deep and red as those of Devon ; thickly fenced with hazel, elder and ash sapling and fortuitous patches of yew and holly, where the smaller songbirds, the finches, linnets, and yellow hammers, chirrup and pipe. Here and there some gathering of forest trees, beech or oak, break the hedgerows with their big heavy mossy bolls, clutching at the rude roadway with their long roots and for short periods shutting out the sun. And the cushats, which abound in this border-land, keep break-

THE HEAD OF THE GOLDEN VALLEY.

ing with great uproar and needless alarm from unsuspected perches in the leaves above, and offer such a series of pot-shots as they only give to an unarmed wight. And the common or even the green woodpecker will be apt to show himself in this kind of country and go jerking across the foreground with raucous note, for you will see more of him on the Welsh border than in any region known to me. Looking back betimes, which one is often glad to do for a two-fold reason, the Golden Valley seems a mere depression, its western ramparts but a ripple as the eye rises over the waving ridges behind it and rests at length on the broken skyline of the Hatteras and the Mynydd dhu. But the narrow crown of Stockley Hill surmounted the descent on the further side is not easily forgotten : first on account of the uncompromising directness with which it plunges down at an angle of forty-five to the vale below, and secondly for the fine scenic effects with which this heroic method of descent provides the hardy traveller.

For the banks here rise thirty or forty feet above the deep sunk lane, and when I went down between them were a perfect blaze of foxgloves and ragwort, of briar-rose, honeysuckle and flowering elder, springing from deep carpets of ferns. And far beneath lay outspread the many-tinted lowlands of Herefordshire, with the Wye curving through their centre. Bright patches of red fallows lay splashed about amid the tender green of fresh-cut meadows, the darker tones of the pastures, the varied shades of the unripe grain fields, the hop gardens, the frequent woodlands and well timbered parks. Homesteads and country houses, villages and church spires all played

VILLAGE CROSS AT MADLEY.

their part upon the canvas if in somewhat shy and not too obvious fashion. Blue in the background, some linked together, some isolated, rose the heights of Mansell and Foxley, of Burton and Wormsley, of Nupton and Brinsop, all wrapped in foliage to their summits. It was such a treat as you may enjoy, to be sure, any clear summer day, and from any sufficient eminence in west Hereford. But this deep trench of flowers and leaves gave a brilliancy of setting and foreground to the more distant scene which lay within its frame.

But enough of this; the descent accomplished, our adventurous lane filters tamely out into a firm high road, which will eventually land you in Hereford or Hay if you follow it either nine miles to the east or rather more to the west as whim or necessity dictate. By the first route you would pass through nothing of special note but the village of Madley, whose old church is one of the finest in the county. But my own inclinations turn to Moccas and then over the Wye to Monnington, and thence home on the far side of the river. There is no occasion to linger on the pleasant shady road which, hugging the foot of the woody heights of Stockley ridge that we have just crossed, on the one side, and with the Wye unseen but not far off on the other, leads to the Moccas turning. As I passed down there I noticed in the well-kept garden of a picturesque black and white cottage some fine cherry trees loaded with ripening fruit and all alive with little wooden windmills fastened to the boughs and spinning noisily at a prodigious rate. I ventured a remark on the subject to the good wife who was standing in the porch with communicativeness written all over her ruddy face. " Indeed, sir, if it was not for those things we should not gather a cherry, and even now I don't know as the birds will leave us many."

Before turning down the lane towards Moccas and the river, I would suggest to any reader who should find himself here, not to do so without a look at Bredwardine. For this enterprise merely means a mile or so along the Hay road, which is bordered with dainty timbered cottages in the black and white style, and for most of the distance skirts the romantic glades of what is known as Moccas deer park. Like that of Kentchurch the term chase more aptly describes these stretches of wild fern-covered glade, that sprinkled with magnificent forest trees hug the foot of Stockley ridge. Bredwardine is a small village which boasts a delightful situation at the foot of, and conveniently accessible to, those fir-tufted heights known as the Knapp and moreover of reasonable propinquity to *Arthur's stone,* a large cromlech on the heights above. It is also adjacent to a once famous castle and a later Tudor mansion, and to an ancient little church containing the effigies of one or two potent mail-clad lords of the said castle, and lastly to a quaint stone bridge over the Wye at an exceptionally picturesque elbow of the river.

Remote though Bredwardine is from the haunts of men, there is some evidence in the wayside inn between the village and the bridge, that its charms are not unknown. For there is not only a comfortable parlour where the more exclusive rambler may refresh himself beyond the gaze of the sun-burned haymakers in the tap room, but there is even a visitors' book. What strange reading these chronicles of provincial wit and humour make, and what a tale they tell of the ruling passion of the British holiday maker! Steak and porter, ham and eggs, tea and buns, smoke and steam again in columns of infamous but enthusiastic verse, as one turns over the blotted pages. The prowess of Smith as a trencherman as celebrated by his waggish friend Brown is a common note, while Jones declares in the metre of Longfellow's " Excelsior " that it is only the imperishable memory of Mrs. Quegly's hams that keep him so unswervingly faithful to " this charming spot." The ladies come in anon and tell you in much underlined prose that the toast and raspberry jam of the *King's Head* are things to " dream " of, or " fit for gods," or such like stuff. What did these fair creatures do, dear middle-aged reader, when you and I were boys, and there were only three square meals in the twenty-four hours ? Was the aching void endured in those days without a pang that is in these a matter of life and death, and cuts into the business and pleasures of men and women as relentlessly as " calling over " at a public school ? Perhaps the craving that now consumes so many people two and a half hours after a heavy lunch had not then developed, like an appendicitis. But amid all the praise of bottled stout, ham and eggs in bold clerkly characters, you will find perchance the brief autograph of some noted antiquary or some colonial bishop, or of Hiram E. Wilkins from Chicago, in that conventional caligraphy of the Western American which never yet revealed a hint of character, even to the wizard in such matters.

On the castle mound which rises high above the river, amid an abundance of foliage, not a stone is left either of the ancient fortress nor yet of the Jacobean house which followed it, though of the latter I have seen somewhere a quaint sketch. The scene from the sharp curving and much-buttressed bridge is one of the most captivating in all this portion of the Wye.

A Tudor farmhouse half smothered in ivy and flanked by great stone-roofed rambling barns of a scarcely later period overlooks the bridge, while downward the stream ripples merrily over gravelly shallows and between fringes of willow, to where deep waters lie in the shadow of a lofty wooded steep. And away beyond the old castle mound, the church peeps out through the foliage of a nearer ridge, while amid all this pleasant blend of wood and water a gap remains just large enough to show a glimpse in the far background of the sharp fir-crowned summit of the Knapp.

I must not try the reader's patience, just yet at any rate, with the story of another border castle. It is enough to say that this one here takes its name from a Norman baron on whom William the Conqueror bestowed the land; that for many subsequent generations it was in the hands of the

THE KNAPP NEAR BREDWARDINE.

Baskervilles and then fell to the Vaughans. Now within the church are two effigies, one of sandstone somewhat mutilated, but with sufficient remaining detail to identify the mail-clad knight with Walter of Bredwardine, whose chief claim to our notice is the fact of his being the grandfather of the second effigy, and this is of alabaster, a perfect and beautiful representation of a knight clad in rich plate armour, his head resting on a helmet and his arms crossed on his breast. The Lancastrian collar and certain other details indicate with tolerable certainty that this is the famous Sir Roger Vaughan who fell in the act, as is said, of saving the king's life at Agincourt. It was he and his relative, Sir David Gam, according to the popular story, who shared the glory and were knighted as they lay in mortal anguish on that immortal field. Gam is generally credited with having suggested Shakespeare's " Fluellen." He was a Breconshire man, and a member if not progenitor of the illustrious race of Gams, who are said to have owned at one time or another every estate in the county, but have been extinct, in name at any rate, this many a day. Davy Gam was a retainer of Henry IV. and first achieved notoriety by going to Glyndwr's first Parliament with a view of killing him, but was detected, seized and held in durance vile for twelve years by the Welsh chieftain, to be ultimately ransomed by the king himself.

But returning once more to Moccas, there is here a large mansion with lawns and park lands sloping to the Wye, which glides between them for some distance in deep and placid current. There are traces are of an ancient castle in the grounds, but the Cornewall family have been seated here since the seventeenth century in the present house and its predecessor. A legend runs that an enterprising youth of that stock, then landowners elsewhere, was caught poaching deer and seized by the keepers of the then owner of Moccas. This was a Vaughan widow and daughter of that Sir Walter Pye of Killpeck, who, it may be remembered, accumulated such vast wealth only for his descendants to squander in the Stuart cause. At any rate, thus runs the tale, she was so captivated by the good looks of the young transgressor that instead of locking him up she married him, and Cornewalls took the place of Vaughans at Moccas. A private bridge here spans the Wye, which for a trifling toll you may cross into the parish of Monnington, whither I would fain be without further dallying, though the little Norman church at Moccas is, I believe, well worth a visit. But in Monnington churchyard lies the dust, so at least we all like to think, of the great warrior and patriot, Owen Glyndwr.

After crossing the Wye, an unfenced road carries one over a wide expanse of parklike pasture sprinkled thickly as becomes its obvious quality with the stocky frames of the loud-patterned Hereford cattle. A moment later one may see a long and double line of ancient and lofty fir trees, stretching apparently for a mile or more towards the west. Within the row you find a noble avenue of these red-stemmed veterans, almost exotic in this land of luxuriant hardwood timber, and by so much the more distinguished. This is known as " Monnington Walk," and a local superstition relates that along it

Glyndwr used to escape into Wales, when hunted from his daughter's house at Monnington. Thirty or forty yards of turf spread between their columns, and a short journey beneath them of half a mile or so brings you to the old brick farmhouse known as Monnington Court, with the church abutting on its garden. At the end of the lawn a wicket leads into the secluded churchyard. The little church has been mainly rebuilt within the past two hundred years, though its sturdy tower has been battered by time into sufficient harmony with the air expected of it. For even a first claim to the dust

MONNINGTON CHURCH AND COURT.

of Glyndwr is no light standard to live up to in Wales and the Marches.

The reputed grave of the hero is within a few feet of the porch. There is nothing to mark it but a rude crumbling slab of slate-stone lying flat upon the encroaching turf, without mark or superscription. Early in the last century, following up the tradition of Owen's interment here, the grave was opened and the bones of a man of large stature were unearthed. Nothing definite, however, could be gathered from this, and the scant remains were put back, the grave filled in again and this rude slab placed or replaced upon it.

Glyndwr was a man well over forty when he left his estates near Oswestry and Corwen, burnt his boats behind him and in the year 1400 raised his standard on Plinlimon. He was a gentleman of fortune and education and had seen much of courts and camps. His wife was of an English border family, the Hanmers of Hanmer, still planted on their ancient seats in Flint. Three of his daughters were already married to Herefordshire squires, Croft of Croft Scudamore of Kentchurch and Monnington of this manor. Another was espoused during the war to his captive, Sir Edmund Mortimer, as every reader of Shakespeare well knows. Margaret of Monnington seems to have been the younger. But we know little of the doings either of her or her husband, or how he conducted himself in the critical position in which his marriage must have placed him.

The year 1410, just a decade after Owen's first rising, roughly marks the period at which he ceased to be a power to be reckoned with, yet though most of his people and such of his lieutenants and councillors as had survived the war had fallen away from him, as well they may have, the tough old hero himself refused to surrender, and with a hardy band of desperate followers still remained in the mountains, making intermittent but savage raids, of which we hear but faint echoes. He lived for yet another five or six years, a period of life replete with legends and conflicting tales regarding his movements. But we know that in 1412 he was still " out," as the king himself made overtures for the release of David Gam. In the next year, when Prince Henry succeeded to the throne, he issued a pardon to all Welsh rebels, not excepting the chief. But Glyndwr, though in miserable plight, was still intractable. In 1415 the young king, who had learnt so much of war from his life-long enemy, must have been influenced by some touch of generous feeling towards him, for he sent special envoys to hunt him up and give him his free pardon. From some cause or another, though Glyndwr was by now quite powerless, the mission came to nothing. But on returning from the Agincourt campaign Henry tried again, sending this time as envoy Glyndwr's own son, together with Sir Gilbert Talbot, who had acted on the previous occasion. But the elusive mystery of the magician stuck to the great Welshman till his death, for whether they could not find him or whether he were actually dead never transpired. Every tale and legend represents him for the closing years as a mysterious solitary wanderer, and no doubt the enemies he had made and the havoc he had wrought rendered some kind of concealment desirable if not necessary. Some say he assumed the guise of a reaper bearing a sickle, others that he died in a wood in Glamorgan. But the common people for generations were quite sure that, like Arthur, he was sleeping with his warriors, their arms beside them, in some impenetrable cavern waiting for the trumpet to sound which should call them to the delivery of their nation from the Saxon yoke. The most natural and sensible version of Owen's retirement is that which places it in one or other of his daughters' houses, and the burial tradition of Monnington is pretty strong—not strong enough to justify a memorial stone, and not sufficiently known apparently to make the picturesque and sequestered churchyard in the faintest degree a place of pilgrimage. Moreover when Glyndwr gets the monument he deserves at the hands of Welshmen, for he was statesman as well as warrior, and was fighting a man who half of Britain after all regarded as a usurper and murderer of the wretched Richard, it should be on some conspicuous Welsh hilltop, not a quiet Hereford churchyard. The ridge above Corwen would perhaps be the most fitting site, for Corwen was virtually in his own domain, and puts in a third claim by the way to his dust.

No figure in British history has been so overlooked as that of Glyndwr by English historians, save in the case of one or two specialists of his period, who then meet him face to face and cannot help themselves. Wales and the Marches were relatively a far more important part of the kingdom in those days than in these, and Owen for long periods made himself virtually master of that whole region. Here and there a Marcher baron held out within his castle walls, but Owen at one time or another captured most of these and destroyed great numbers. "Deflored by Glindore," is the brief significant note with which old Leland only a hundred years afterwards dismisses his report of fortress after fortress.

Owen had been squire of the body to Henry of Bolingbroke, (not, I think, as was formerly stated, to King Richard), and it was Henry's treatment of him, when he came to the throne, that stirred the fiery scion of the line of Powys to turn a few partial and hopeless movements, in which he had no part, into a formidable and lengthy war. He effected treaties with foreign powers, made and unmade bishops, and devised

schemes for the civil and ecclesiastical government of Wales.
When apparently crushed he would spring up again in a month
or so with a fresh force and devastate Hereford or Shropshire.
He was facing enormous odds, and his methods were deliberately ruthless, nor did Wales recover from his scourgings
for over a century. Henry IV paid a tremendous penalty for
his short-sighted treatment of his old servant, who for almost
his entire reign was the longest and sharpest of the thorns that
were planted in the side of that vigorous but much harassed
monarch. Great armies marched into Wales, but they could
do nothing whatever with Glyndwr, and as the elements seemed
so often to fight in his favour, it was no wonder that a fixed
belief that he could " call spirits from the vasty deep,
and was not in the roll of common men," obtained among his
enemies from the king himself to the meanest soldier that
shivered under the Royal banner in the Welsh mountains.
And yet this trifling shabby stone, scarcely observable in the
grass under the porch of Monnington church, is his reputed
resting-place. Nay, worse than that, for the last time I was
there an ancient person was mowing the long grass which
outside the shade of the yew trees was threatening a hay crop
in the little graveyard. I had not encountered him on any
previous visit, though he told me, with the not ignoble pride
of your genuine rustic, that he had lived in Monnington " man
and boy this seventy-five years come Michaelmas." A shock
was now impending, for on complimenting the perspiring
veteran, who was glad enough to lean awhile on his scythe, on
the possession of so famous a grave, he regarded me with dull
vacancy. |I thought he might be deaf, but was mistaken, for
he shortly brightened up, and led me to the comparatively fresh
headstone of a well known farmer who had been thrown from
his horse or cart in recent years and killed. I listened to the
particulars of the tragedy, and then referred to the more
ancient one of Glyndwr and pointed to the grave. My friend,
however, shook his head; he had never heard of the person to
whom Monnington owed such small measure of fame as it
enjoys in the outside world, which was the more curious as a
former rector had been somewhat zealous on the subject. He
had a dim notion, to be sure, that a casual stranger at long
intervals would come in and contemplate the stone below
the porch, but the name Glyndwr conveyed naught whatever
to his mind or senses. There was a famous gentleman, however, buried in the church, and some lines about him on the

wall, he informed me, and the building being open, though of no particular interest, I strolled in, and was glad I did, for the tomb or rather the bust of the sexton's hero, the only one in the little building, took my fancy. It all seemed so futile, this marble bust of a young man named Francis Perrot, with long hair and collar of the period 1667. It seems he was the third son of a country squire, living several parishes away, and why the records of his noble deeds were presented to the limited circle which the congregation of Monnington church must always have provided I know not, and it struck me that the young man had some presumption in coming from Moreton under Lugg to pose so aggressively as the hero of Monnington, when Glyndwr, even if only by repute, lies out in the cold in a nameless grave. No doubt, however, he was a fine young fellow, and here lies his farewell message, or rather that of his eulogistic mourners :—

> Stay, passenger, and if thou hast one tear,
> Bestow it on the noble dust lay'd here ;
> Here Perrot lies whose great capacious mind
> In 's native limits scorned to be confined.
> To the unknown dangers of enraged seas
> And foreign enemies more fierce than these
> His valour him exposed. Venice may boast
> The aid he lent her to defend her coast
> 'Gainst unbelieving Turks. Then wisely he
> Commits his credit to posterity.
> Those who by virtuous acts enshrine their name
> Live in the records of eternal fame.

As I left the church to which Master Francis Perrot had entrusted the preservation of his eternal fame, the scythe of the same old sexton was again swishing leisurely through the graveyard grass, regardless of the slayer of Turks within or the hero of Wales without. The bees were humming, and the little stream that edged the enclosure was piping gently in its deep ruddy bed beneath a tangled maze of leaves. The milk cows were champing lazily in the home pasture before the Court, and over the mossy lawn young ducks and chickens were wandering now as they wandered once, perhaps, beneath the fostering care of Glyndwr's youngest daughter.

You may look hence over the Wye Valley and across the groves of Moccas to the blue hills of Wales. If Owen of Glyndyfrdwy had chosen the spot in which to close his eyes on a world he had so greatly agitated, he could of a truth not readily have found one more fair. At his birth we all know that the front

BYFORD ON THE WYE.

of heaven was filled with fiery shapes, and the flocks stampeded in terror from the hills, and stabled horses were found standing up to their fetlocks in blood. But surely no great leader of men in times so recent ever slipped out of this world so quietly and so mysteriously.

The old house wherein the hero is supposed to have died contains much evidence of its former dignity—a fine timber roof, a huge fireplace, and some curiously carved arms of the Tomkyns, who were lords here in the seventeenth century. On each side of the coat is this inscription :—

VIVE DEO GRATUS—CRIMINI MUNDATUS—TOTO MUNDI TUMULATUS SEMPER TRASIRE—PERATUS.

A mile of lane from Monnington brings you into the main

STAUNTON-ON-WYE.

high road from Hay to Hereford, hard by Staunton and Garnons castle, the seat of the Cotterels, which stand finely up under the woods of Mansell Hill and the pretty hamlet of Byford. Seven miles of broad firm undulating road leads hence to the cathedral city, passing on its way, at Bridge Sollers, the most southerly traces of Offa's dyke. A pleasant Herefordshire landscape laden with fine timber and rich in verdant meads lies all about it, with a peep of the Wye betimes sparkling in the sunshine, as it hurries from deep to deep and the mountains always on the sky-line, lest you forget you are not in Warwickshire, but in a land where men lived always amidst war's alarms.

CHAPTER IV

THE VALE OF EWYAS

THERE is something of melancholy even in the twenty-first of June, for the passing of the longest day rings the knell of the summer's youth and heralds the fading of June's freshness into the sober luxuriance of middle age. But though the early garden flowers may pass away and their successors wilt and the lawns burn brown, things are never so bad in the open country, even in the hottest of Julys. Above all is this true of regions where hills soar high and streams run fast. There are compensations here even for the passing of June, with its first pride of leaf and full chorus of bird song. If the woods of July are darker the shadows also are deeper, and present a yet more effective contrast to the glare without. The hedgerow banks at any rate show no loss of colouring. And if the wild roses are fading, the traveller's joy has laid its festoons where they lately bloomed, and the fern brakes mantling on the hillsides grow deeper and richer with each day. Nor does the gorse care anything for July suns, but blazes away as brightly as ever, while the heather begins to touch the southern slopes of the hills, and the sunnier glens with the promise of its coming splendour. Hay harvest too in higher latitudes is still going merrily forward, and helps to keep the summer fresh and cheat the calendar. Far be it from me to scorn a hammock swung in the shade of Elizabeth's or anybody else's, or for that matter my own garden, with a good book or good company. But if you could wish to encourage the delusion that 75° in the shade is a temperature too high for the enjoyment of greater enterprise or a more strenuous form of recreation, commend me to a garden lounge. If you have never spent summers in almost any other country, and are therefore tempted to unconsciously metaphorical language respecting our English temperature, it will probably be on

73

your own lawn or on somebody else's. The Briton is unduly thankless for his climatic blessings, and after grumbling at everything else that is sent him, is quite ready to abuse when it comes the most tempered sunshine that is shed anywhere in the civilized world, and dodge it round a tree in a costume suggestive of the West Indies. But out in the open country there are few days of a hot July that do not improve on more intimate acquaintance, and bring more bodily comfort at any rate to the traveller on hill or highway than to the loiterer in the shade; the alternatives are of course a mere matter

THE HOLY MOUNTAIN.

of taste, but the current phraseology shows both lack of proportion and of gratitude to Providence.

The days had just begun to shorten, though if anything to gain in splendour, when I set out for a fortnight's exploration of a region even more delectable than those we have already traversed, and as rich in interests of another kind. I use the term explore, for the valleys of the upper Monnow, the Honddu, the Grwyny, and the corresponding reaches of the Usk were hitherto only in part known to me. As seen on the map they may be likened to the fingers of a hand laid flat on the compact block of the Black Mountains pointing north-west-ward, the palm resting on the railway immediately north of Abergavenny. For purposes of description I might resort at once to the old priory of Llanthony in the Vale of Honddu, otherwise of Ewyas, which sheltered me for a week of this period, and the conventional method of accomplishing the journey would be by train on the main line from Hereford to Pandy, three stations short of Abergavenny, and thence by trap up the Honddu valley for some seven miles. But we are not burdened with luggage or concerned with transport questions in these pages, so I shall once more take the road at Pontrilas, though both road and railroad follow up the Monnow for the brief stretch of six miles to where the afore-mentioned Pandy, which means in Welsh a fulling mill, stands near the entrance of the Vale of Ewyas. Not much need be said about the narrow but admirable road which ascends the Monnow valley towards Pandy—except that it would be a waste of six miles of scenery much above the average to take the train.

As one approaches Pandy the outlook gathers dignity. The culminating spurs of the Hatterall Hills, the most easterly ridge of the Black Mountains, crowned with the grass-grown ramparts of Trewyn Camp, loom high upon the right, and the Monnow disappears up its hither side towards its own fountain springs amid the bosky uplands which surround the scanty remnant of Craswell Priory. It would be pleasant if space permitted to follow the river up the deep Vale of Longtown, with its ancient hamlet and church and old castle mound. Nor could a summer's day be more delightfully spent than in mounting to these same springs of the Monnow, which do not rise in a peat bog like every other Welsh river, but, as noted above, in that half wild tract of upland which was once the chase of Craswell monks. I was fortunate myself in visiting it under the auspices of a Herefordshire association of archæologists, naturalists and ramblers known as the Woolhope Club, called after the village of that name, which gave birth to the society quite early in the last century. We trained to Hay, and walked thence up the sequestered dingle of the Dulas brook and over its watershed, dropping down through the yard of the solitary homestead of all this pictur-esque wild to the woody dingle which holds the ruins of the priory church. We were fifty in number, and I could see caused some perceptible flutter among the occupants of that isolated grange, while we on our side had the satisfaction of noting a tall dead sapling ironed to the barn-wall, a familiar precaution in old Wales against witches. The priory was a foreign brotherhood of Benedictines, whose rents and dues all went abroad, and on that account, with many others of the kind, were not improperly if a trifle harshly ejected by Edward IV. Little more than the moss-grown foundations of their small church remain, sunk in a thicket and shaded by a big oak or two. But the enterprise of a neighbouring landowner had done some excavations preparatory to our visit, unearthing a bit of the chancel floor and step and increasing the obligation by entertaining us in sumptuous fashion on a remote hillside where one might well have been thankful for a packet of sandwiches and a flask.[1]

The north-eastern point of the Black Mountains rises high and sharply above the spot, while covering all this watershed is a broad rolling carpet of rough pasture and fern sprinkled thickly with birch and thorn, firs or scrub oaks, looking to-day very much as it must have looked when it was the fenced-in park of the old Benedictine monks. Later on we descended the valley to the edge of civilization, where the ancient little church of Craswell perched in a grove on the hillside stands possessed of a good preaching cross, and what is much more rare stone benches let into the outside wall of the building, overlooking the well-marked traces of a cockpit or ballcourt. It is a common fact, of course, that games of ball as well as dancing and cockfighting were not merely practised in the churchyard but were zealously encouraged by the Crown and church party long after the Reformation, the *Book of Sports* of James I to witness. But this is all parenthetical, for down at Pandy the rugged pile of the Great Skirrid awaits our admiration, two or three miles ahead and to the southward. Though of only some 1,600 feet elevation it is quite isolated from the Black Mountain range, and is the finest solitary height below the scale of a mountain known to me in Britain. At some dim period, the night of the Crucifixion, say the locals, and call it in consequence the " Holy Mountain," a great landslip clave its summit in half, leaving one side precipitous, so that approaching it from two directions at any rate it shows the outline of a complete though ragged peak, rising high above the wooded foreground and slightly

[1] Further excavations have since been made here, with most satisfactory results.

changing its rugged profile at every fresh bend of the road. Just beyond is the loftier hump of the Sugar Loaf above Abergavenny, and the mountains which form the gateway to the vale of the upper Usk, but these are not quite yet within our sphere of action.

In the meantime, just across the narrow valley, set at the very confluence of the Honddu and the Monnow, and tucked under the foot of the Hatteras spur, is the little homestead of Allt-yr-ynys. It is not as a small Tudor manor house, for these are common enough down here, that it claims attention, but as the nest of the great house of Cecil, whence sprang

ALLT-YR-YNYS.

the lines of Exeter and Salisbury, though now for generations but a sequestered farmhouse. An eighteenth century owner of this and other manors, a Delahay, successor to the Cecils, was so enraged with the county at his defeat in an election, that to revenge himself upon so unappreciative a generation he sold all his property in these parts to the Drapers' Company, who own it still. Allt-yr-ynys (the height of the island) is a plain little house with not much left but its age and associations to recommend it. Fifty years ago it contained a store of good tapestry, which was burnt as rubbish. There were some stained glass windows too, bearing the Cecil arms, now

77

preserved in Llanfihangel church, and a fine old Tudor ceiling may still be seen in the parlour. The Cecils were a Welsh stock, the now famous and familiar patronymic being an anglicised form of the Celtic name of Sitsyllt, which the family still bore in the time of the renowned Lord Burleigh, in whose day Queen Elizabeth once slept here. The situation has some further charm as the clear waters of the Monnow and the Honddu run together into a shallow pool below the lawn. The present occupant has held the land for half a century, and while our artist was busily occupied on one side of the stream our host of the moment, who had been in youth and

LLANFIHANGEL COURT.

prime a keen fisherman, entertained me with some marvellous stories of what the Monnow could do in the Mayfly season when he was young.

As you return across the valley to the main road there is a glimpse of the somewhat notable avenue which climbs to Trewyn House, an old gray mansion standing high up on the slopes of Hatteras Hill. Much might be told of its long story, but the more engaging Tudor pile of Llanfihangel Court is close at hand. Here, too, a noble though shorter avenue leads from the highway between gate pillars surmounted by stone eagles to the terrace, up which successive flights of time-worn steps climb to the gabled front of the beautiful old house. It was once the dower house of the Harleys, a name to conjure with for generations in this border country. Later on it was the home of the Rodney family, and is now owned by Mrs. Attwood-Mathews. As you stand on the terrace and look down over the vista of wood-fringed park land, a few gigantic and venerable fir trees remain as the survivors of an avenue that is said at one time to have extended the whole way to Allt-yr-ynys. Within doors there is a noble entrance hall rich in oak and numbers of finely panelled rooms and passages. Charles I, during one of his unhappy progresses backward and forward through the southern marches, slept here, and the highly wrought bedstead which carried him is still treasured in the room he occupied.

Talking of royal beds, I remember many years ago going over a historic house in North Wales with an eccentric old gentleman from the manufacturing districts who had recently purchased it, together with much territory, for a large sum. A bedstead once occupied by some visiting monarch had been among the household treasures, and carefully cherished in the very room he had slept in. It was apparently priced in the schedule of furniture taken over by the new owner at £5. As we stood in the empty chamber where it had rested for some centuries, the old gentleman pointed to the vacant spot and waxed eloquent on the effrontery with which the vendor's agent had tried to extort £5 out of him for a crazy rattle-trap of a bedstead that was barely fit to carry a mattress, and how he had told them to go to the devil with their rotten furniture, which doubtless brought to some one a handsome price. The strange thing was that this curious old person was quite reasonably alive to the historic value of the room, but seemed to think that £5 was an outrageous figure for the article which gave it its chief interest. Not the least interesting part, however, of the mansion we are now concerned with is the stables. There may or may not be plenty of seventeenth century stables still in use in country houses, but I do not imagine there are many where the original fittings still remain. Here, however, are the same stalls and the identical wooden pillars, circular, massive and moulded, to which the bridles of Charles's cavaliers were actually hitched.

Leaving the hamlet of Llanfihangel with its square church

tower and its queer old hostelry, and an interior more suggestive of a Dutch canvas than a British tavern, the narrow road to Llanthony pitches headlong down the steep to a stone bridge over the Honddu, and then swerving sharply to the left joins company with that delightful stream and follows it up at once into the Vale of Ewyas.

What a pleasant thing is a mill leet of mountain water in a dry July, though you are conscious that the stream below has been reduced almost to silence in the process of filling it, and the memory of the one just here gurgling in full volume by the dusty road is the excuse for this irrelevant note of appreciation. How gratefully its crystal waters lave the thirsty rushes and

LLANFIHANGEL COURT (*back view*).

grasses by the road edge on one side, or flick the pendent fern leaves and the trailing greenery of the fence bank on the other ! How the ducks rejoice in it, and what a pace they come sailing down, and even the water-flies seem conscious of their immunity from their quick-eyed foe, as they skim the surface for their short and merry day. If I were a trout I should retire for the summer solstice to these cool and bubbling depths, and indeed an odd one or two will generally be found possessed of such measure of sagacity. Still these pleasant excursions are not without their risk, for we all know what tricks Mr. Miller can play when, with the turn of a hatch, he converts his mimic river into an empty ditch, and no doubt all these things are well understood down in the main stream.

Perhaps that snug little wayside fishing inn, the *Queen's*

CWMYOY.

Head, perched on a knoll above the Honddu, may serve to mark the point where you really enter the vale. From here to the head of it is ten miles, the ruins of Llanthony standing

about midway. The first time I found my way up here I
sought this modest hostelry for a night's shelter, and my
heart sank within me as I counted eighteen pairs of waders
depending from the verandah and gently swaying in the breeze.
For at the first glance they suggested a mathematical problem
that the appearance of the house made insoluble. My
situation for the moment was evidently a hopeless one, and
the more disappointing as I, too, had waders ; but it proved
one of the most striking illustrations within my experience
of how deceptive appearances may sometimes be, for I had
the house and the sporting landlord absolutely to myself,
and we talked flies and farming deep into the night, and I
spent the next day in the Honddu in almost complete solitude.
It may not interest the reader who cares for none of these
things to know that the various owners of this phenomenal
display of indiarubber overalls were at the moment pursuing
their legitimate occupations in different parts of modern
Siluria, though the hearts of many of them were doubtless
here at Cwmyoy with their waders and rods. In brief the
Queen's Head is the centre for more than one fishing club who
rent water on the Honddu, as well as for the upper Monnow
away at Longtown beyond the Hatteras ridge.

The Vale of Ewyas, more commonly known perhaps as the
Llanthony Valley, is among the gems of Wales, a statement
I hazard with a full consciousness of the more striking claims
of a dozen or twenty valleys that leap at once to the mind
without effort. There is no sublimity of ruggedness here, no
great wealth of cataract, no wilderness of woodland, nor yet
any broad surging river. But then one does not approach the
Vale of Ewyas by way of Snowdonia, or the Cader range, or
the Berwyns, or the Cardigan Mountains. Nearly every one
who penetrates to Llanthony is fresh from the more placid
environments of the western shires, and is indeed more
often a resident therein. And this is the best way to reap
the full measure of its delight. You pass at once from what
is characteristic west Saxon scenery, though of a high order,
into a valley that might be in the heart of Wales, though not
quite of the wildest Wales—For the term " wild " is not strictly
applicable to the Vale of Ewyas, though used most freely in all
descriptions of it from time immemorial. Indeed it is this long
belt of pastoral country, of woodland, meadow and homestead,
that winds along the skirts of its enfolding mountains, craning up
betimes to their steep red sandstone breastworks or their hanging

curtains of fern and heather, that constitute its peculiar fascination. Somewhat more, too, is imparted by the fact of its being a vale that leads nowhither, unless a rude lane squeezing over the watershed near its head into the Wye Valley counts for anything. It is virtually a cul-de-sac, and once in it you can escape neither to the right not to the left except by climbing on foot over one or other of its mountain walls. And even then you would but drop into a wilderness on the one side or to the scarcely more populous uplands of the upper Monnow on the other, while if a finishing touch were needed it is the spectacle of those noble grey ruins standing in the hollow of mighty hills.

HONDDU VALLEY LOOKING UP TOWARDS LLANTHONY.

As you follow the narrow lane, which is the sole artery of the vale, the evidence of another landslip like that which split the crown of Skirrid shows on the summit of the eastern ridge, above Cwmyoy, for this too is broken short off, the course of the débris after these thousand or two years being still plain to the eye, beneath the red cliff it must have left with such convulsion. The little church at Cwmyoy is the ecclesiastical mother of the whole vale, which constitutes a single parish. I have said it is a Welsh country. The small grey roofed homesteads, their whitewashed walls glinting amid orchards and sycamore groves, nestle with their backs to the

83

overhanging moors, where the sheep graze in summer, and their face to the steep slanting meadows through which the Honddu burrows its way amid a continuous track of foliage. These are the old Welsh folk of Ewyas, but they can have had but slight intercourse with the Welsh of Ewyas Harold, still less with those of Archenfield, though they were in ancient time tributary to the lords of Ewyas Harold castle, but there were probably then but few people in the valley, and those few under the influence of the Augustinian monastery. They are of course Welsh in name, as in blood, habit and character, and some of the old folk still speak the ancient tongue. They ride on pony back, are properly clannish and nonconformist, are simple of habit and industrious, without enterprise and peaceable, but prone to much innocent hilarity if some festive gathering seems to justify an extra pint or so of cwrw, as I can personally testify, while not a few of the elder matrons can wear an old straw hat, a frilled cap, and adjust a woollen shawl and carry a basket with a pose only possible to a Welshwoman. But perhaps I am too discursive on these racial subtleties and strange cleavages that lie along the border. For most people it will be enough that Llanthony is in Monmouthshire and Monmouthshire is an English county, if nobody quite knows why. But in any case it is hopeless to think in counties in a part of the world where they are of such recent and arbitrary construction. As to the makers of so-called county atlases I should like to write a chapter on their iniquities, and if there is half a page to spare in this book I shall have my futile say.

Where the overlapping shoulders of the mountains fall back a space from the vale and form something approaching to an amphitheatre, the grand old ruined priory, set amid sloping pasture lands and ancient trees, breaks finely into view. Its situation thus moved Giraldus seven centuries ago: " In this deep vale of Ewyas about an arrow shot broad and encircled on all sides by lofty mountains, is a situation truly calculated for religion and more adapted to canonical discipline than all the monasteries of the British Isles. Here the monks, sitting in their cloisters, enjoy the fresh air, and when they happen to look upwards towards the horizon behold the tops of the mountains as it were touching the heavens and herds of wild deer feeding on their summits. A place truly fitted for contemplation, a happy and delightful spot, fully competent from its first establishment to supply all its own wants, had not the extravagance of English luxury, the pride of a sumptuous table, the increasing growth of intemperance and ingratitude added to the negligence of its patrons and prelates reduced it from freedom to servility, and if the step daughter (Gloucester), no less enviously than odiously, had not supplanted her mother." The point of Gerald's strictures, which when monks and abbots were in question the satirical archdeacon ever loved to fling, will appear presently. In the meantime let us leave the road, at the hamlet of Llanthony, where a group of picturesque cottages are set amid embowering orchards and near or about the banks of the rocky stream, and, beneath the shade of mighty trees, turn up the short farm road to the abbey.

A large stone farmhouse of later date but in sufficient harmony with the rest of the buildings adjoins the precincts,

LLANTHONY PRIORY.

while the little Norman church of the priory, still used by a scant, and rustic congregation, stands in the large outer court. Here lowing cows fresh from the pasture and lynx-eyed sheep dogs resenting one's approach wake the old walls with not wholly inappropriate echoes. Of the inner quadrangle, brightly carpeted with turf, the beautiful pointed arches of the roofless nave form one entire side. Fragments of the south transept with the sacristy and chapter house make another, while a third is occupied by the old lodgings of the monks. These last, together with one of the west towers, have been always kept habitable, and are utilized to-day as quarters for such pilgrims as have a mind to sojourn here, whether for grouse shooting, fishing, or hill walking, or the mere quiet enjoyment of a most entrancing spot. In no rural hostelry, surely, are you on quite such intimate terms with the monks of old. You squeeze upwards by the narrow spiral staircase to some large sombre chamber in gable or tower eloquent of the monastic period, and if wakeful you may listen to the owl hooting at night in the ivied ruins without, while within, according to a friend who was with me there, and who is psychologically susceptible, have much more weird and interesting experiences. Gigantic loaves are still baked in the ovens of the monastery, and excellent ale still brewed in the monastic brewhouse. Living-rooms and kitchens are all of the same period ; and none the less harmonious, perhaps, from the spirit of let-well-alone utility which pervades them, in spite of some whitewash and papering. The hostelry as such is quite unpretentious, and on the lines of a plain comfortable old-fashioned fishing inn. We had it almost to ourselves for the hottest week in July, and in the hours not devoted to more strenuous exertion, the wide window of the long parlour looked right out on to the beautiful arches of the abbey, which rise not a stone's throw away ? and to the lonely mountain ridge towering high above them, where the monks, according to Giraldus, used to see the wild deer grazing.

As the ruin contains various styles of architecture, Norman, Early English and Transition, it was probably not all built at the same time, though one or two authorities think differently and give their reasons. The sacristry is still fairly perfect and serves as a washhouse, while adjoining it are the partial remains of a beautiful chapter house.

The story of Llanthony is quite a stirring one if you are in the mood and on the spot to enjoy it, and I must find room for so much of it as is expedient here. The plain little Norman church in the outer court, flanked by a crowded and dilapidated grave-yard is the germ of the foundation. For it covers the site where St. David himself had erected a rude cell to which he could retire from the world for purposes of pious meditation. It was known to the ancients long before the founding of the monastery as Llanddewi Nanthodeni or Nant Honddu, " The church of Saint David on the river Honddy," and is still called so by the Welsh. Now in the year 1103 it so fell out that a martial cadet of the great house of Lacy, which after the Norman Conquest had wrung the district of Ewyas from these partially Saxonized Welsh, was hunting one day in this fringe of his great relative's territory. The secluded charm of the spot not only wrought on his imagination but filled him on a sudden with holy thoughts and a desire for an anchorite's life. Acting on this impulse he furbished up the ruinous cell of the great Welsh saint, which after five centuries must have needed repair, and settled down then and there to a life of religious retirement. In due course the fame of this warrior's extraordinary piety reached the court itself, and one Ernicius, Queen Matilda's chaplain, visited the recluse, and falling himself under the mystic influences of the spot and its hermit, William de Lacy, he begged to be taken at once into partnership, to which the other consented. De Lacys personal discipline was severe, for he wore his armour over his hair shirt, we are told, till it was worn out with rust. He had, moreover, taught himself letters and qualified for ordination, which he received from the bishop. The partnership was successful, and Ernicius being a person of much influence the two distinguished hermits became objects of much interest in fashionable and courtly quarters. Queen Matilda herself came all the way down to Llanthony to see them. This stimulated Hugh, the then head of the Lacys, to recognize his relative's surpassing devotion by some memorial worthy of him and his family. The beautiful fabric before us according to some was the result, Ernicius becoming its first prior. It is not at all certain that the Anchorites approved of this ambitious departure. It is quite certain that they protested, though vainly, against the rich endowments which were poured into their lap for the support of the establishment. One may remember that it required no great self-denial for a Lord Marcher to glorify his family and purchase atonement for his sins by land grants, as these were usually contrived at the expense of enemies in the shape of recent conquests or partial conquests, and the rents not always realizable assets. Let us, however, give Hugh de Lacy all credit for the enterprise, if only for the delight its remains afford to us of the present day.

The new building was appropriately dedicated to Saint John the Baptist, and was honoured with a staff of forty canons. The Pope had interested himself in the matter, and according to a prevalent fashion of the period it was connected with the new order of Black Augustinians. But the Welsh liked neither them nor their monastery, and were only less hostile to the Norman church, with its assumption of superiority, than they were to the Norman sword. So in the warlike chaos of Stephen's reign which followed some twenty

years after the building of the monastery, they made things
so hot for the Llanthony monks that the latter fled in a body
to the protection of the pious Robert de Betun, Bishop of
Hereford, who had formerly been the most devoted of their
priors. The bishop, though himself greatly harassed at the time,
harboured them to the best of his power for a couple of years.
After this a courageous few returned, but the majority had
received such a fright that they absolutely refused to move
from Hereford, and spoke of the horrors experienced in the
savage valley in almost mirth-moving terms. So the hospitable
bishop had them on his hands, and Hugh de Lacy being either
dead or indifferent, he turned in despair to Milo, Earl of Hereford, whose father had himself laid aside the sword for the
cowl and had died a monk at Llanthony, where he was buried.
Milo proved amenable, and gave them land in Gloucester where
another Llanthony arose, which was to prove a most unfilial
offspring, robbing the mother foundation not only of most
of her monks, but of her furniture, her money and even of her
bells.

For nearly half a century this older monastery in the Vale of
Ewyas languished sadly, and the occupants of her upstart and
now luxurious offspring grew to regard her with contempt
as a mere place of penance. When they heard of a fresh
addition to its scanty inmates they were accustomed to scoff,
saying, " What has he done ? What crime has he committed ? "
So stripped for a time was the old Llanthony that the brethren
had not sufficient bread, nor any cassocks to wear, nor even
breeches to go decently to church in ! But towards the close
of the twelfth century came a great reaction. Another Hugh
de Lacy, who had shared to his great profit in the Irish wars
of the Norman Welsh, looked favourably upon the old
Llanthony and lavished upon her endowments of both English
and Irish lands, and some think that a large part of the fabric
was due to him and others to his son and grandson. For
three reigns the mother monastery flourished again with more
than its former splendour, and the Gloucester Llanthony was
compelled to surrender the lands and rents it had filched from
her. The period of its final decline our best authority, Mr. St.
Clair Baddely, places at about the middle of the fourteenth century. In 1376 the prior had both his eyes torn out by three of the
canons, who were only excommunicated, the chief sinner being
soon reinstated. This little unpleasantness seems to have
been the beginning of the end. Glyndwr's hand fell heavily

on the monks of Ewyas, and in the reign of Edward IV the fortunes and *personelle* of the priory had fallen so low and the conduct of the prior was so bad, that it suffered the ignominy of being handed over piecemeal to its daughter at Gloucester. At the dissolution, the latter was valued at eight times the value of the former. The mother foundation, however, may be said to have had her revenge. For a gateway alone remains. Canals and docks have wiped it out of existence, together with the tombs and bones of generations of great earls and barons who lay therein.

But the older Llanthony remains, beautiful and famous in her slow decay : possibly matchless in her site. For if I have given the impression that only an occasional wanderer in these hills or a few antiquaries enjoy the spectacle, I must hasten to say that it is a favourite object of pilgrimage throughout the summer months amongst the quieter and more intelligent type of excursionist, who are allowed to picnic in the precincts under certain conditions. A pleasanter memory to carry back to Newport or Gloucester of a summer day thus spent it would be hard to fancy. But the old monks who made what was then the quite perilous journey to Llanthony did not come up the vale, which was probably tangled thicket overhung with shaggy woods. The route in those days climbed the lofty ridge of Hatterall from Longtown, and dropped down the steep slope to the east of the abbey. William of Wycombe, an early prior, who wrote its chronicles, has left some thrilling accounts of the fearsome hardships of the journey thither.

I am quite sorry I ever read an account of Llanthony just a hundred years old by one Malcolm, F.S.A., for if an educated nineteenth century writer can perpetuate such stuff, what might not an old monk who heard the devil in every gust of wind and saw a fiend in every bush ? One can only account for some of the Georgian descriptive writers by supposing they had never before been outside a city, and were the victims of nervous delusions. " Infinitely grand, awful, and horrific, are the convulsions in the vale of Ewyas," writes another gentleman in 1813. Mr. Malcolm's eye ten years earlier had been " bewildered and his imagination confused " when he saw the sheep " dance upon the crags of these tremendous precipices, while at the sight of the mother butted by her young not two spans from the yawning gulf he wept with suspense." This also is good : " The ancient Briton ploughs till his horses are almost perpendicularly elevated above his head, nor do his fields terminate till the spot is reached where gravity eternally prevailing would hurl the adventurer down the sides to his native dust." I don't quite know what this means, but it was seriously printed and circulated in 1803 by an F.S.A. Our narrator was caught in a heavy shower crossing the ridge of Hatteras from Longtown on his way to Llanthony, a plain climb on short fern-clad turf over a broad brow clad with heather and bilberry plants. This is how it struck the bold adventurer : " The storm approaches ! The frowning gloom suspended in collected majesty above the wailing water, arranging its volumes into dense masses till attraction or the impelling urged its departure. Then advancing the deep shades stalked along the mountains and howled hoarse music to the appalling march." I am not surprised after this that the next step of our author and his friend was to fly for shelter (though where ?), and " in gloomy questions and answers debate the propriety of further progress." In the midst of their irresolution, however, a gleam of light gave them fresh courage, " and the sun invited us to the labours of the day. What was to be done ! impossible to ascend into the vortex of the cave of Aeolus."

" Many rash actions, however," reflects the writer of this thrilling adventure, " are undertaken through the dread of ridicule, and though their reason contemned the temerity of the exploit," they set their teeth and cheered by the sunshine faced the down. Once started, " nothing remained but to preserve our footing or fall many hundreds of feet down a precipice." Oh, Mr. Malcolm ! Mr. Malcolm ! it is a pity no Prior Betun or William of Wycombe was at the abbey to shrive you when you got there ! " Our path was beset by gullies, and when necessity perched me on these pinnacles of danger reflection stung me to the quick, and I thought myself little better than the wretch who commits suicide, and, when the agitated air raged around me in hollow blasts it compelled me to seize upon a tuft of grass, and when holding on to this I ventured to turn my eyes to the eastward view where the wind groaned in continuous sound loud as the billows in the most furious tempest amidst the wilds of Ocean." We will leave Mr. Malcolm hanging on to his tuft of grass with one more quotation descriptive of the first meeting of the anchorite William de Lacy with his future partner Ernisi : " Particles of Holiness floated from William, and meeting a proper reception in the pericranium of Ernisi the same effects ensued."

This delightful book gave me so much entertainment, I do hope these fragments of it are not wholly cast upon the waters, for my conscience smites me that I wasted space on them that might have been more profitably devoted to some of the real hardships of the Llanthony monks, of which much store of detail remains to us. Indeed it must have required no common courage for a Norman Order to stand here as an unprotected outpost face to face with the sorely harassed and hostile Welsh.

But I, too, spent a long day on Hatteras ridge, and it was the hottest of the year. " The caves of Aeolus " were as silent as the grave, not a breath was stirring. The priory being 800 feet above the sea, it is only another thousand or so to the summit, where our imaginative author indulged in all these astonishing nightmares. The ancient track by which he ventured is graded gently over, but with other motives than lunching on bread and cheese at Longtown I faced the steep, and admit that I too seized a friendly tuft or rather bunch of bracken more than once, for the close grazed turf after much sunshine was prodigiously slippery. In my approach to the actual ascent I wandered from the home pastures of the abbey through a large field of upland mowing grass alive with butterflies, for which I hoped my landlord would forgive me, and there at the foot of the climb and at the head of a densely wooded dingle I came upon the roofless ruin of a considerable dwelling-house choked with grass and nettles and wild parsley that greatly puzzled me; for no fire, apparently, had ever seared it, nor was its decay that of age, nor were there any signs of garden, grounds or enclosures. The situation was picturesque but unpractical, and it suggested nothing but the possible whim of some modern William de Lacy without the hair shirt, the rusty armour, and the rope girdle, but with a less enduring passion for solitude.

Now at that moment I did not know, or to be precise had forgotten, that the poet Walter Savage Landor, from an impulse something akin to this, had acquired the Llanthony property more than a century ago. It is usually supposed that he merely purchased the priory ruins. On the contrary he took over the whole estate of valley and mountain, and his family are the absentee owners of it to this day. The venture as regards Landor's own enjoyment and peace of mind was an utter failure. He was only twenty-four, a genius, scholar, and poet, of wayward, scornful temperament and impulsive nature ; just the man to buy a landscape and repent at leisure. Moreover he sold one of his maternal estates, Tachbrooke, for the purpose ; inditing a farewell ode to the Yorkshire estate, of much beauty, but from the somewhat illogical standpoint of an unwilling and compulsory fugitive. I have seen the printed bills advertising Llanthony for sale of date 1799, when Landor bought it. All the farms being then on leases for lives, the reputed ages of each tenant and others of his family were printed on the handbills, and have an odd look nowadays. Landor, however, though his brilliancy had been fully recognized at Rugby and Oxford, had despised competition in those very pursuits which were his passion, and, though a bookish and reserved man, was at the same time so intolerant of ordinary discipline, that both his school and college declined to bear with it. " He lived," says the late Lord Houghton, " in a past world of heroic thought unaltered by the events of common life from his school and college days, and enduring for some ninety eventful years. He passed nearly the most eventful century of the world without learning from experience and almost without adding to his ideas."

One can understand that this unpractical and unsympathetic genius did not play the alien landlord in a strange and clannish valley with much success, but came to loggerheads with his conservative dependants in Ewyas within a brief period. He threw up his rôle as feudal chieftain of a mountain valley with relief and not without some embittering disputes. The ruin of this incompleted house which he commenced to build for himself amid the thickets at the mountain foot is a pathetic witness to his mistaken venture. Scarcely more fortunate in his marriage the poet sought the more congenial atmosphere of southern Europe, returning to England at seventy and dying in Bath at an extreme old age. There is a partial analogy between the impulse of young Landor to identify himself with the Welsh mountains and the efforts of his equally youthful contemporary and acquaintance Shelley a few years later. The inspiring influence was the same and the social failure somewhat similar. For if financial reasons alone drove Shelley from Radnorshire he ran considerably amuck of the squires and farmers in Carnarvonshire, though not in connection with the land reclaiming enthusiasm which bound him to Mr. Maddox at Port Madoc, for that was wholly practical. Landor had few intimates in life, though

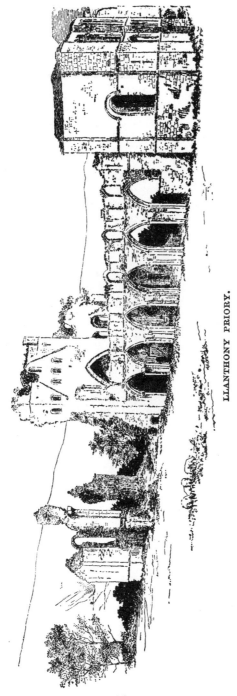

LLANTHONY PRIORY.

his enduring friendship with Southey was a marked exception. His unshakeable egotism is well illustrated in the couplet :

> Southey and I have run in the same traces,
> When we break down, what pair shall fill our places ?

The high back of Hatterall ridge is broad and soft : for many miles a rank growth of whinberry bushes densely matted with heather and bog grasses holds you knee high and sometimes much more. There was not air enough even at this altitude to stir even the wild cotton bloom of the bogs. The mountain sheep were reduced to unwonted silence, and a stray one sprang like a roe deer now and again from the scant shade of a whinberry bush, as one almost trod on its tail. A few carrion crows floated lazily about, and here and there the well picked bones of a dead sheep gave evidence of their industry. The little meadow pipit, so inappropriately named, that unfailing and cheerful companion of every mountain walk, piped and flitted in sociable propinquity. A restless curlew or two, with no longer any use for the varied notes of the hatching season, broke the silence with their normal and melancholy cry. Once or twice, too, I stumbled on a clutch of young grouse, diminutive cheepers who fluttered gallantly up from the deep heather after their affrighted parents.

The prospect from here under favoured circumstances is sublime ; even in the simmering heat of this July day it was no mean outlook. Down in the vale a thousand feet below the great grey pile of the abbey with its two west towers and its long vista of Gothic arches, lying conspicuous and solitary amid its tributary park lands, struck a wonderful note. Shooting straight up beyond it the Fwddog ridge soared higher and bolder altogether than the one I stood on. Along its feet the little white homesteads with their network of riotous untrimmed hedgerows and bright patchwork of tillage and pasture glowed in the sunshine ; the far-spreading carpets of bracken climbing from their topmost limits up the lower spurs and hollows of the mountains, and giving out even at this distance the sheeny glitter of high summer, scarcely less beautiful to my mind than the gold of autumn. Above the fern limit again the mountain turf climbed upward, broken here and there by breasts of rock, to the deep mantle of heather which clothes the long summits and the lonely plateau of the Fwddog and hangs over its edges. Just above Llanthony the ridge is broken by a rocky gorge, and the mountain stream which comes leaping down it from the bogs on the sky line to join the Honddu at the village, even in dry weather, shows a glimpse here and there of a shrunken cataract. The Fwddog is the first rampart of the Black Mountains proper. For a dozen or fifteen miles beyond all is solitude and silence ; heathery uplands and falling waters, grouse and curlews, buzzards and plovers, mountain hares, mountain sheep and mountain foxes. Looking south I could see every detail of the Vale of Ewyas, with the Skirrid rising finely at its lower extremity, and the Sugar Loaf looming more hazily on the right. Turning northwards again up the valley one could mark it growing narrower and less habitable, till the heights this side of Hay and the Wye appear to block its further course some half-dozen miles away.

It is at the far head of the valley, some half-mile above Capel-y-ffin, the rude old daughter church of Cwmyoy, with its yew-shaded graveyard, that Mr. Lyne, commonly known as Father Ignatius, has erected his buildings and founded his order of Welsh Benedictine monks. I know nothing of the establishment beyond its exterior except from hearsay. I should not venture to say anything about it one way or the other but for one reason, and my prejudices, if I had any, would not be of the least consequence. Nor am I concerned with new enterprises of creed and dogma, and have not much faith in the monastic system taking hold of twentieth century Britain, which seems to be the dream of the small handful who resort to New Llanthony for the encouragement of such futile hopes. If I were to say anything of the function which I believe takes place annually in celebration of the appearance of the virgin in the Vale of Ewyas, I should probably put my foot in it, not with the Nonconformists, who chiefly fill the valley, nor yet with the Churchmen there, but with a few excellent people, who are perhaps differently constituted from most of us. Nor do recent erections in the innermost sanctuaries of nature appeal to me, however faithfully they may attempt to adhere to the models of ancient times. Not however that the Priory of Llanthony has any approach to a duplicate in the modest establishment of the new "Llanthony" above Capel-y-ffin, so far as one may see. One bone, however, I feel free to pick with the zealous founder of the new Welsh Augustinians. For beyond all doubt he has created the most hopeless confusion in the minds of the British public in the matter of Llanthony by appropriating its name for his modern establishment some miles away.   One of the most beautiful of monastic ruins, having due regard to its unique situation, in the whole island has been quite obscured in the public mind by a modern society whose eccentricities, as plain people mostly think them, have been more widely bruited about than their more solid characteristics.   Be that as it may, should you mention Llanthony in any company outside the district, nine people out of ten will vaguely attribute its foundation to Father Ignatius, which is hard on William de Lacy and something of a shock to any one familiar with the facts and the Vale of Ewyas.[1]

Beneath us, on the English side, the Longtown valley stretched the whole length of its deep secluded trough, and the leafy course of the upper Monnow could be traced up well nigh to its source near Craswell.   Beyond again, and lower still, and less conspicuously defined, lay the Golden Valley, the outermost of all these lateral ramparts, which made the country such a cockpit for warring races in the days of old.   Down in the Vale of Ewyas the air is sweet but stimulating, as is natural to so respectable an altitude above sea level, and welcome enough to those who would lead the active life necessary to a full appreciation of this enchanting region.   For it may be noted again that some hundred and odd square miles of a mountain wilderness touches the valley here on the west, as it virtually does the Wye upon the north and the Usk to the south, rising considerably higher than Plinlimon at several points.

But for those whose strength or inclination does not run to more serious efforts, the vale itself offers innumerable rambles of an inspiring kind.   The frequent lanes which follow the bosky course of the Honddu, or clamber round the foothills above, were a blaze of briar roses, foxgloves and honeysuckle, of ragwort and blue mallow when we trod them.   Here, too, are hanging woodlands of larch and fir threaded by green ways, in which you may walk at will in the shade and look down on the sunlit vale between their dark stems, and over to the opposing hills which hide their summits in the near tree-tops.   There are no tourists about, for the picnickers

---

[1] The fact that the modern establishment is an "abbey," and the ancient one a "priory," is sometimes proffered as a feeble and hair-splitting justification of this breach of artistic and historic taste—and one altogether beside the mark.

of a day to the abbey have scant time to wander far, even should inclination prompt them. Nor is there any question of right of way or of public and private footpaths. Short of trampling down ripening oats or walking through the middle of his mowing grass without some sort of an introduction to the owner the stranger may wander anywhere in the Vale of Ewyas. Most of these devious and flowery ways lead through farmyards, where you will find everything friendly but the inevitable pack of collies, for all these people have sheep upon the hills. You will not be hunted by black bulls, an experience to which the promiscuous wanderer in North Welsh pastures is always liable, for the more amiable Hereford is nearly always yarded. The sides of the vale too are riven at intervals by delightful dingles, formed by short-lived lusty brooks that come leaping from the hills above; and your path will drop down betimes from the wood or meadow or pasture's edge, into a fairyland of gorse and bracken and dancing waters, where scattered birch and mountain ash trees stand waist deep in the rank growth, and rabbits scuttle before your feet in needless fear. Opening up to what seems, at any rate, like the brow of the mountain these bosky gullies offer frequent temptations to edge up their slippery sides by some faint deceptive sheep path, till you find yourself wading aimlessly and waist deep in the bracken or clambering round fragments of rock; starting the wheatears and stonechats, and if fortunate a rock ousel, with its strident alarm note, from the lairs they love. And nowhere do the birds of this border country congregate in greater variety than in these sheeny dingles which cleave the hillsides from the edge of the bustling farmyard in the valley to the mountain's brow. The dipper, the sandpiper, and the grey wagtail, who, unlike his pied and yellow cousins, winters in the south of England but breeds and summers by the mountain streams, have come up here from the river. The larger song-birds, the thrush, the black-bird and the starling, are in fussy and continual evidence, springing from the fern and hurrying to some tree or bush or thicket for a leisurely survey of the intruder. Both green and spotted woodpeckers are here; while linnets, finches and tits, and the whole tribe of small hedge birds, find their taste for timber fully met in the dingle, and with the further delights of gorse and fern brake and much greater seclusion. There are always wood-pigeons, in ones and twos rather than in companies, hidden somewhere in the screen of foliage which follows the torrent up into the breast of the mountain, till nothing remains of either but a silvery thread and a stunted mountain ash or two. Here the wheatear will be flitting from rock to rock, and the ring ousel be quite sure to have raised a brood in the neighbourhood, and to have marked the rowan trees at the head of the dingle for his own against the good time of its fruition. Such good company as foregathers in here has infinite attractions for the sparrow-hawk and the kestrel, who will most assuredly swing into view if you have reasonable patience, now hanging motionless with quivering wings against the sky on business bent, now scudding over the fern with the aimless innocence of a cuckoo or a dove. And upon the brow at the far head of the dingle plovers will be calling, and a drumming snipe or two may have been tempted to forego the long north sea journeyings, and raise its tardy brood which in these July days are but just hatched out. The buzzards, too, are by no means extinct in Wales, and there are always some in the Black Mountains, though kites would seem to be extremely rare, while every pair of ravens is known and cherished, as they should be by dwellers in the locality who care for these things. The valley folk are kindly, well mannered, and communicative. I ran across the rosy-faced owner of a freshly cut hay-field that I was walking over one day and spoke half-seriously of not having asked his permission, whereat he laughed for about five minutes at the bare idea of such a formula. They have a stronger Welsh inflexion in their English than their neighbours of West Herefordshire, as is natural, and an acquaintance who has lived among them all his life, and can yet speak with the detachment of another blood, tells me that they regard themselves as of different clay from their neighbours in the parallel valley of Longtown, of whom they have no opinion whatever, and with whom they never mix. Most of these families have been seated in the valley since time began, and many have held the same farms for hundreds of years. They rarely quarrel, and Churchman and Nonconformist lie down like lambs together. Much more Welsh than English in habit, and of course wholly in blood, the bitterness of Welsh sectarian feeling does not seem to agitate their quiet lot. There is irrefutable evidence, too, that the population is not nearly half what it was a century ago, when the poet Landor bought so considerable a slice of it. The sporting rights of the entire valley and the grouse moors above, which on the western ridge are extremely good and if anything almost too thickly coated with heather, are rented by a syndicate, and there is not a resident squire in the whole ten miles of the vale, nor indeed a country house. I was almost forgetting too that Southey once stayed here with Landor, who during his brief sojourn as lord of the manor inhabited that portion of the ruins now utilized as our inn. The village fathers who sleep in the weedy dilapidated little churchyard adjoining

LOOKING UP THE HONDDU FROM LLANTHONY.

the priory church, here as elsewhere Prossers, Watkins', Morgans, Prices, and Powells, seem to have had a more than common vogue for verse. English composition of any kind was never probably their strongest point, and most of the epitaphs would be worth repeating. Here is one at haphazard :—

> Thomas Price he took his nap
> In our common mother's lap,
> Waiting to hear the trumpet say,
> Awake, my dear, and come away.

99

More than one worthy, too, leaves metrical testimony that his debts are paid. But after all not the least beauty of the Vale of Ewyas is the Honddu itself. I have not often seen a more perfect sylvan stream, and to enjoy the glories of one that buries itself for miles in foliage, dear reader, you must, I fear, be an angler, and wade up the middle. It was pleasant after a long day on the mountains or below them, to drop into the cool melodious channel at the foot of the manor water below the abbey, as the sun was drawing towards the crest of the Fwddog mountain. Under such conditions of weather and water one's expectations were modest and limited, let us say, to a breakfast for two. But if the basket is light,—for the approach of night, which brings possibilities on the hottest days to those who can flog an open river down stream, puts an end to up-stream work amid a tangle of foliage,—there are other rewards. For there is some slight measure of satisfaction in beguiling and fastening an occasional fish when everything in the heavens above and in the waters beneath seems to mock your endeavour. Yet more, what a world of loveliness there is in the bed of a stream like this, at any time, above all when the sunbeams are shooting low through the leaves and playing with more witchery on the pools and rapids and mossy rocks than even in the earlier hours. The artist may paint, the poet may sing of these streams, but they mostly sing and paint from samples. They do not see them as we fishermen do who feel the rush of crystal water about our feet for hours and miles, and get to know by heart the ever-changing vistas of leaf and stream, and rock, and almost the changing melodies played by the restless water in each stream and pool.

CHAPTER V

THE GRWYNY VALLEY—CRICKHOWEL—THE USK AND ABERGAVENNY

ONE need not suppose that the old monks of Llanthony went back and forth by the valley road. Much greater people than monks in those days habitually travelled by paths that are now only trodden by shepherds or sportsmen. When the saintly Archbishop Baldwin, accompanied by nobles, priests and princes, made his grand tour of Wales in 1188, the cavalcade climbed the Black Mountains near Talgarth, crossing the pass still known as Rhiw Constabl, and descended by the sources of the upper Grwyny, on which human eye, even to-day, rarely rests. People in those days sidled along hills or climbed over their crest. For one thing they liked to see who was about, and for another the valleys were often tangled swamps. The main routes to Llanthony lay over the Hatteras ridge on the east and over the Fwddog on the west. Many are the contemporary accounts of the adventures of these Augustinian brethren met with in tempest and darkness, and among the goblins and devils that much fasting, no doubt, assisted their fevered imagination to conjure up. It is some of these, peradventure, that our friend Mr. Malcolm, F.S.A., must have been pursuing when he tried to outdo them in 1803. Even when safe in their monastery the monks had bad times in this land of outlaws and hostile Welshmen. For persons flying from vengeance would seek sanctuary with them, so often, we read, as to become a peril and a nuisance. Yet even these sanguinary times have their touches of humour. For on one occasion a man with his wife and daughters, hard pressed by enemies, so importuned the holy prior to protect and lodge them that he was constrained to break every monastic rule and to do so, and he could not get rid of them. The horror of some of the brethren at the bare notion of entertaining women within their walls is quaintly expressed in letters to a former prior, then Bishop of Hereford. Indeed, the scandal of their presence seemed almost too great for words. Now the way by which the monks and their friends travelled between Llanthony and Abergavenny was not down the valley, as we should go nowadays, to Llanfihangel Crucorny, and thence by a turnpike to the banks of Usk. But they climbed straight up the Fwddog range above them, and so dropping into the parallel valley of the Grwyny followed a trail which wound somewhere through the dense woods that clothed and still partly clothe its sides.

Or they may sometimes have crossed the ridge further down where it greatly declines in height. I have tried both, and for a person to whom fifteen miles is the same as a dozen, I would say, face the Fwddog by all means, and get the beauty of its heathery solitudes and noble prospects in the fresh of the morning. For right opposite the abbey, as noticed in the last chapter, a fern-clad gorge, riven by an impetuous stream, runs straight up the mountain face to the wild plateau, lying between the cairn-crowned summit of Bal-mawr and the lower height of Bal-bach. A plain path, trodden, if but sparingly, by countless generations, skirts the edge of the dingle high above the mimic cataracts below, till the bracken-sprinkled turf gives way to the heather and the moorland grasses. A brief stage further and we are fairly out on the pass, and straggling patches of luxuriant rushy bog land among the heath dimpled with pools of brown water, marks the source of the now silent rivulet. We have had the last peep of the stern gray abbey lying beautifully framed by the drooping hill-sides amid its pastures a thousand feet below and all around the long russet undulations of a true grouse country, not yet in bloom meet the sky. The ancient path here takes some careful tracking, and if this may seem superfluous caution with a clear line ahead, I would remark that heather thigh-deep on a spongy bottom is not the sort of going to be lightly chosen at the beginning of a good day's walk. One hears a good deal, both in prose and verse, about "springing over the heather," but this must be the heath of a Surrey common, not of altitudes where grouse fly and trout streams have their source. At the far brink of the pass a noble outlook for the lover of wild landscape lies spread beneath. The dark ridges of the Black Mountains are rolling westward in solemn procession, and if the day be clear the pale peaks of the " Bannau Brycheiniog," the Beacons of Brecon, the Snowdon of South Wales, shadow dimly against the sky. And right beneath us the Grwyny in its deep trough is just leaving the virgin wild and entering the first fringe of upland civilization. Away on the right we can see its infant streams coiling like a silver thread down boggy hollows, and hugging the feet of the Gadir range, which right before us lifts its head to the respectable height of 2,600 feet above sea level.

But I must leave the wanderer to find his way down the Grwyny valley ; no difficult task where farmhouse is linked to farmhouse by tortuous lanes and untrimmed hedgerows, still laden in this higher country with the blooms of June. The Grwyny valley might almost be another Ewyas, but narrower, more tangled, and even more secluded from the great world beyond, and the Grwyny river is another Honddu in every essential detail, though it belongs to the Usk, while the other is of the Wye. Just here, too, we run for a space into one of those eccentricities of county delimitation with which England abounds. For a long thin strip of these grouse moors and of this Welsh glen for some occult reason is a detached fragment of Herefordshire ; and our path, starting in the debatable shire of Monmouth, while it waxes more Celtic, if the term be admissible, is in actual fact re-entering England to land us again within an hour in a woody dingle below Partrishow church in the unquestionably Welsh county of Brecon. I know not what these Welsh sheep farmers in the Black Mountains have to say to their fellow countymen in the hopfields bordering on Worcester and the Malvern hills. They talk English, with a Welsh inflection to be sure, though some of the old Welsh people can still prattle in the ancient tongue, but if specimens of the Iberian Celt were in demand for scientific purposes, I should imagine this isolated thread of Herefordshire would be a not unprofitable hunting-ground.

Now Partrishow (commonly now called Patricio) church nestles in some seclusion above the Brecon bank of the stream, and it must not be passed lightly by, though scarcely capable of holding fifty people, since it is as much sought after by modern antiquaries as it was by the pilgrims of old. A rude and ancient building, embosomed in trees, and perched above a rough and deep sunk lane, it might very easily escape notice. But when you have secured the key from the nearest cottage, half a mile away, and passed through its portals, the significance of the little fabric needs no profundity of antiquarian lore for a proper appreciation of its merits. A most beautifully carved rood loft of Irish oak, the work, so says tradition, of an Italian artist of the fifteenth century, divides nave from chancel and is probably the most recent addition of importance.

The companion of my pilgrimage heather, a clerical friend from a distant Herefordshire parish, had climbed up through the mural staircase leading to the loft, and was promenading the latter with much composure, when a timely notice that such a venture was perilous and forbidden caught my eye, and, indeed, the time-worn structure was already giving out some significant indications of the fact. An old font proclaims itself by inscription as ("In tempore Cynillyn, Meiler me fecit") of the time of Cenhillyn of Tretower, who was son of Red Rhys, lord of Ystradyw (this district) circa 1060, and an entry in the Book of Llandav confirms the consecration of this and three neighbouring churches by the bishop of the diocese at that period. It was then known as the "Shrine of Merthyr Issiu" or the Martyr St. Isshow, which has become by a process interesting only to Welsh etymologists Partrishow or Patricio. What manner of church stood here before, or when the eleventh century one which the font commemorates was replaced in whole or part by the present sufficiently ancient fabric, is a futile speculation. But there are two stone altars in the small nave and a fresco of Death as a skeleton capering on the wall. Perhaps the most curious feature of the church is a building at its western end, which was a priest's cell and oratory and sanctuary of pilgrims before the creation of the church, and this, too, contains a stone altar. A holy well near by still preserves the name of the patron saint in Ffynnon Isshow, and a small stream below bears the name of Nant Mair or the brook of Mary.

Strange as it may seem to any one now standing in this quiet inaccessible backwater of modern life, a main track from the centres of Glamorgan to those of Hereford and Shropshire passed through here in ancient times. Nay, more, for it would seem that not only Archbishop Baldwin, but the great Norman lords of Abergavenny crossed this track by another, when they went to look after their precarious possessions in west Wales. One knows this from a memorable murder which took place in 1135, related at full length by Giraldus, and confirmed by the Welsh chronicle. For it seems that Richard, one of the founders of the great Marcher dynasty of Clare, set out on a summer day in the aforesaid year from Abergavenny

CRICKHOWEL.

for the far coasts of Cardigan, where he had built and garrisoned two castles. For once in a way the trail thence led through a defile which had already acquired some sinister reputation, and was, in fact, the one we are now in, wooded even yet, but then no doubt a mantle of tangled foliage from the hill tops to the margin of the stream. It was known as Coed Gronwy and sometimes as the " bad pass of Gronwy."

To the edge of this, Brian de Wallingford, warder or lord of the district at the time, had accompanied De Clare with a strong guard, and there, reluctantly at his friend's request, left him to pursue his journey with his son and a mere handful of attendants. Now it so happened that Morgan ap Owen, one of the Welsh chieftains, who had been injured by this Richard de Clare and had vowed vengeance, now saw his opportunity. So, as the over-confident Norman was riding with light heart through the woods above the Gronwy or Grwyny, two musicians walking in front of him, the one singing and the other playing an accompaniment on a fiddle, Morgan ap Owen and his friends who were laying for him fell upon the careless group and slew them to a man. Henceforward the place was known as Coed dial, or " the wood of vengeance," and is so called even to this day.

> Brecknok is full of treason and there is war in Ystrad-Towy,
>   In Ewias is found hatred and starvation,
>   In Glyn bwch are mangling and sharp words,
> In Talgarth robbery and shame, bribes and lawyers.

And this old quatrain no doubt aptly represents the pleasant state of affairs on the Brecon March in the thirteenth century. Just here below us, as the valley swerves to the west, the great base of the Sugar Loaf Mountain forms its further wall. With wooded foot and broad expansive breast, showing a score or so of scattered pastoral homesteads and a crown of bracken-sprinkled turf and red sandstone rock, it looks every inch of its 2,000 feet. But I have said enough, perhaps, to justify my preference for this method of progress from the Vale of Ewyas to the banks of Usk. For its final stage of some half-dozen miles, during which it receives the waters of the Grwyny fach and passes the hamlets of Pont Newydd and Llangenny, it still retains its glen-like character and loses none of its charm. And the Grwyny plays the same melodies beside you as the Honddu, and leaps on its way, rejoicing beneath the same unbroken bowers of leaves.

BORDERLAND OF WALES

The Vale of Usk presents to the wanderer, emerging from the bosky defiles of the Grwyny, a complete change of scene, this point of outlook being nearly midway between Abergavenny and Crickhowel, and some three miles from either. The former, with its high-perched castle ruins, stands at one of the great gateways of Wales ; the mountains receding to the north and south respectively on either side and the undulations of fertile and woody Monmouth, opening widely to the south and east, and to the sun. Crickhowel, a much smaller place, but with a castle, too, of its own, stands higher up the Vale of Usk, at a point where its mountain's sides begin to press closer on the famous salmon river, and with rocky feet to lash its

ON THE CANAL NEAR GLANUSK.

waters into more frequent gusts of rage. There are those who hold the Usk as the equal of the Wye in beauty. I know them both, almost from source to mouth, and should be hard pressed indeed to give a verdict which happily is not needful. But as the Wye has a longer course, it gathers round it by so much the longer stretch of beauty, and is on this account entitled to the precedence. Moreover, its lower portions, with Simon's Yat and the Wyndcliff to their credit, are finer than anything on the Usk south of Abergavenny. The Wye salmon have the choicest flavour, but the Usk yields much heavier catches to the rod, and is, or was till quite lately, for deteriorating influences irrelevant here are at work, by far the best salmon river in England or Wales. In the late eighties, a well-known local angler killed thirty-two fish to his own rod in one day, and there have been other catches approaching that, all, I need hardly say, well authenticated; as salmon fishing is as general a topic of interest and concern on the banks of Usk as fox-hunting at Melton Mowbray or Market Harborough. The Usk, moreover, is a most prolific, and in its higher waters, free-rising trout stream, ranking, perhaps, with the Monnow and the Cardiganshire Teify as the best in Wales, and you may still see that ancient British contrivance the coracle on the bosom of the Usk, as you may see it on the Teify and the Dee.

The Vale of Usk, too, is not only a notable artery, but it divides the great red sandstone system, with its purely pastoral and agricultural interests, from the carboniferous limestone which marks the beginning of industrial South Wales. Happily for the charms of Usk, the first rampart of this country, which in an unbroken chain of heights, looks from across the narrow vale at its sandstone neighbours, is disfigured to the eye by nothing worse than an occasional quarry. That the glare of a blacker and remoter region can be detected in the southern sky at nights need hardly be counted a blemish.

Geologists hold that all these red sandstone uplands to the north, whose peace and quiet is now for ever guaranteed, were once overlaid with a crust of limestone and coal measure, which the action of countless centuries has worn away. In support of this theory, an outlying point of the Black Mountains above Crickhowel, which still wears a cap of limestone, is cited with other evidence of a more technical description. However that may be, between these opposing ramparts, each of them maintaining an elevation of two thousand feet, more or less, but of such widely different formation and significance, the efforts of generations would seem to have been expended in adding adornment to a valley already endowed by nature with lavish hand. All the way from Crickhowel to Abergavenny, wide meadowlands, through which the Usk rolls its amber streams, are the seats of families native to the soil or of others who have taken root there. Crickhowel is a considerable village of bright and clean but venerable aspect, and is given more than village importance by the extent and character of the country that regards it as a centre. It has a market house which is attended in somewhat leisurely fashion by the smaller farmers of the surrounding hills, two public halls, and an old bridge of twelve arches which spans the Usk, from whose brink the little townlet spreads gently upward. There is a fourteenth century church much restored, and close to it a fine old residence, once the property of the Herberts, which skirts the western entrance to the town with a wall of vast proportions entered through an imposing turreted portway. Outside the town, looking down towards Abergavenny, the ruinous tower of the castle keep may be seen standing on a lump amid sheltering trees. Crickhowel was once noted for flannels and shoes, industries now no more, though the fact of their past notoriety is crystallized in Smollett's novel of *Humphry Clinker*. It takes its name from a British camp, whose clearly defined escarpments stand out in bold and striking fashion on a mountain spur nearly a thousand feet above the town. This is Crûg Hoel, the Rock of Hoel ap Rhys, whose deeds are in oblivion and his name alone preserved to fame in the peaceful village below, which nowadays is irreverently alluded to by the natives as Crick—thus are the mighty fallen. We begin to know something about the dominant spirits who ruled in these parts with the coming of the Normans, that is to say in the time of Rufus. Crickhowel is some two miles within the bounds of Brecon, but that limit had of course no definite meaning till Tudor times, except that it roughly served as such to the old Welsh province of Brycheiniog which was conquered by Benard de Newmarch and held as a March. It will be remembered (by Welsh readers, at least, it is to be hoped) that the sub-kingdom of Glamorgan was successfully subdued and annexed, not to England, but to himself, by Robert Fitzhamon and his twelve knights. Spurred to emulation, Newmarch was equally successful with Brycheiniog and a little more, and cemented his rule by marriage with a granddaughter of the first Llewelyn. Like Fitzhamon, Newmarch parcelled out his conquest among those who had helped him, and the manor of Crickhowel, in the wide district of Ystradwy, a name still retained by the portion of a single parish only, to be held on the service of one knight's fee. Later on, it passed to a branch of the famous Glamorgan family of Turberville, from whom an heiress eventually carried it to a Pauncefote, a valiant knight of the first Edward's Welsh wars. These two founded the church, and their recumbent effigies, as is most right and proper, may be seen to-day in the chancel.

In spite of Henry the Fourth's instructions to their descendants to secure his castle at Crickhowel against Glyndwr, the latter knocked it almost to pieces on his way to Abergavenny, as he did most of the Marcher castles. The next Pauncefote being a staunch Lancastrian, having no heir, settled his estates on Henry VI, which by an irony of fate went of course to Edward IV. The latter granted them to the Herberts of Raglan, from whom they passed by marriage to the Somersets, who in the person of the Duke of Beaufort hold them still, together with the mansion of Llangattock Court, just across the bridge. There had been, of course, tremendous struggles with the Welsh in this valley between the Marcher conquest of Gwent and Brecon and its harrying by Glyndwr, Crickhowel being retaken more than once before that time. The Welsh chieftains were not all wiped out by the Marcher barons ; a few of them held baronies in the lower country and many held large hill districts by recognized feudal custom within the March and tributary to the greater lords, and though often connected with the powerful Norman houses by marriage ties, this was not often taken into much account when a good chance offered to strike at the hated invaders of their country. And this Crickhowel valley was after all but a day's march from the Vale of Towy, where the Welsh princes still ruled, and the old Welsh national life smouldered fiercely and without restraint till the Edwardian conquest.

And in the lordship of Brecon, all through the middle ages, there were the Welsh courts and the English courts, to which the litigants of each nation brought their suits and conducted them under codes modified from the old Welsh laws on the one hand and from the Anglo-Norman law on the other. There were manor courts at Crickhowel and courts of appeal at Brecon, and the successors of Bernard de Newmarch held the final verdict in the hollow of their hand whether it was a case of land or one of life and death. If the last issue, however, seemed a probable one, it was not difficult for the offender to get over the mountains into the March of Glamorgan or down the valley into that of Overwent.

The chances of extradition were remote and somewhat dependent on the affection or the reverse which these neighbouring mikados entertained towards one another at the moment. The king could do nothing. The Lord Marchers had usually won these territories without any king's assistance, and upon conditions then readily granted, which soon crystallized into customs that they guarded with a jealous eye. Among these was the right

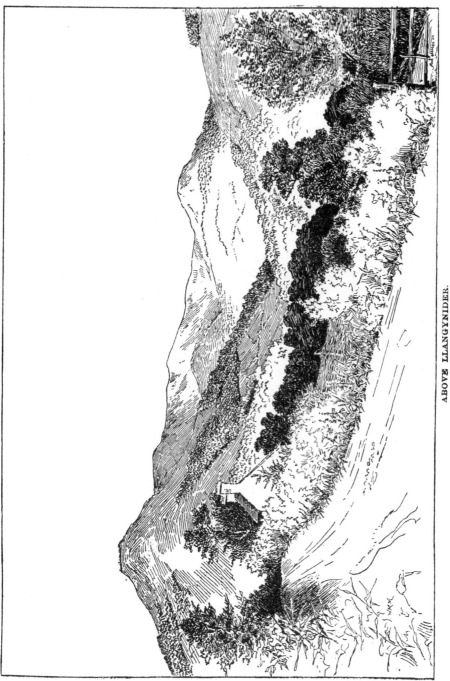

ABOVE LLANGYNIDER.

III

to make war upon each other and the Welsh. So a fugitive from the laws of a neighbouring palatinate, with bow and arrows and short sword, but no encumbrances, was often a welcome addition to the permanent staff who hung about the castle and formed the nucleus of this border baron's army. It was not till Edward IV's time that any attempt was made to alleviate this impossible state of affairs, and not till the union of the two countries in the sixteenth century, as noted in a former chapter, that it was finally abolished.

And from all this it comes that the great baronial dynasties of the March still remain identified in memory with the districts they ruled, and are as familiar by name to the native of ordinary education as the kings of England to whom they gave such trouble. No one in Devonshire or Suffolk but a stray antiquarian cares a button for the mediæval earls who built or held such few castles as have left traces. Their very names have passed away from the average mind. Their life at home, when they were there, was comparatively humdrum, their dependants docile, their equals friendly, their castles almost superfluous except in times of national upheavals, and the king's writ ran unquestioningly. The story of Wales and the borders is utterly different, and so incomparably more picturesque and dramatic that one only wishes one knew more of it.

Historical associations begin for most people rambling England, with a mind bent that way, at the Tudor period, Welsh history leaves off there. But the Marcher barons and the Welsh princes meet you at every turn in Wales, and their shadows still lie as it were over the lands they held.

The fact is that Wales, with its two warlike and warring races, was a much more important factor in the kingdom before the Tudor time, and before Scotland and Ireland came in, than afterwards. With the Union Wales lost its spirit. Its aristocracy became English in every detail. Its vast horde of small squires, their old trade gone, remained stagnant and Welsh for a time and then followed suit. Its peasantry alone remained outside. War and its minstrels, priests, monasteries and other stimulants to common life all gone, they sank into a torpor of ignorance and superstition, which, fostered by their peculiar situation, lay heavily upon them for two centuries or more.[1]

But the middle ages appeal to educated Welshmen with tremendous force. You can scarcely move a league in many districts without encountering the towers or fragments of

[1] Till the religious revival.

some ancient fortress that in its lifetime never slumbered nor slept while the spectres of Welsh princes and Norman barons still stalk about the land on terms of almost familiarity with ordinary folks, not hopelessly insensible to the past.

Wealth and taste have done much to make the Usk Valley for half a dozen miles above Crickhowel one of the gems of Wales. It is roomy enough for adornment and yet sufficiently deep and narrow to give height and distinction to the mountain walls between which it winds.

LLANGYNIDER BRIDGE.

The trough of the vale is filled by a chain of country seats of which Lord Glanusk's is the most conspicuous. Though most of them are of the last century only, the extensive planting of parks and hillsides, with woods that have now reached maturity, gives the impression from above of one continuous stretch of foliage, parted only by the glittering streams of Usk.

It is needless to say that there are many delightful gardens hidden away in the intervals of park and pleasaunce that break the woodlands of the valley as you traverse it. Some are high up on the hill ledges, others are within easy sound of the rush of the river. The cult of the garden must surely find some additional stimulus when its triumphs are the foreground to the broad breast of an overhanging mountain, and the hollow between is filled by some wide and seething salmon pool. And this is not all, for you may look up or down the valley from some of these pleasant terraces and see the river parting the woods with the glitter that only plays on streams like these, and the shapely forms of the more distant mountains, which seem here to fill both the upper and lower ends of the vale. Henry Vaughan, Silurist, the accomplished singer and Christian gentleman of the civil war period, lived and died a few miles from here up the river which he loved so passionately ; but I have written somewhat of him elsewhere,[1] and his grave lies just over the Bwlch (Pass) yonder out of our present range and in the heart region, not in the outlying flanks of Breconshire, such as we are now in.

There are few old abiding-places of note in this stretch of the Usk Valley, but abundant relics of a remote age ; Maeni heirion or " long stones," of cromlechs one or two, of inscribed sepulchral stones several, while the mention of Henry Vaughan reminds me that there is one notable stronghold of an intervening period, namely Tretower, the fortified residence of the poet's ancestors. This might have been a more fitting spot than Bredwardine to recall the fame of a family who owned both places, seeing that of the other stronghold there is nothing left but the tump on which it stood, while here there is not only an ivied tower and curtain wall, but a good deal more, within a courtyard still occupied as a farmhouse. Some years have passed since I was actually at Tretower, but an old pencil sketch of the exterior executed under some difficulties, and for that reason perhaps the more stimulating to the memory, recalls a fine gate-house and a large hall behind it, with a good roof and some other rooms of fourteenth century

---

[1] *Highways and Byways in South Wales.*

date. A Roman stone, too, was then sitting near by the gateway, bearing the brief and not inappropriate inscription, " Valent."

The poet was the ninth in succession from Sir Roger the Agincourt hero and himself the grandson of a Vychan of Tretower, an Oxonian and a cavalier, though a non-combatant, yet he rode this Vale of Usk as a simple country doctor, from his little patrimony of Scethrog, all his life. A deeply religious and reflective man, he had also an overpowering love for nature and his native valley, and used their imagery with great freedom in the mystic devotional verse which forms most of his work. A common assumption is that he modelled himself on his distant relative, George Herbert. Archbishop

CWMDU AND THE BLACK MOUNTAINS.

Trench, no ordinary judge, rates him even higher as a poet than Herbert himself, who he thinks wrote nothing equal to Vaughan's " Retreat." His affinities to Wordsworth are many. He had the same love of rural sights and sounds for their own sake. Like the other he spent his days among them, and was almost as greatly privileged in this respect as the great lake poet of a century later, for mountains as high as Skiddaw and Helvellyn rose before his windows and at their feet rolled his beloved Usk; which is invoked most frequently in his verse :

To thee the wind from far shall bring
The odours of the scattered spring,
And laden with the rich arreare
Spend it in spicie whispers here.

The " Retreat " is of course well known to critics as containing the germ of Wordsworth's famous " Intimations of Immor-
tality," etc., in a most remarkable degree.   Trench in the first
edition of his *Household Poetry*, assuming for good reasons
not relevant here that Wordsworth could not possibly have seen
what was then a very rare book, regards the coincidence in
language and sentiment as inexplicable.   Before his second
edition was published he was made aware that Wordsworth
had possessed a first edition copy of the *Silex Scintillans*, by
a person who had actually bought it at his sale.   The analogy
might be carried further to prove Vaughan a Wordsworthian
in such purely nature poetry as he has published.   Here for
instance is his morning welcome to a bird :

> Hither thou com'st, the busie wind all night
> Blew through thy lodging ; where thy own warm wing
> Thy pillow was, and many a sullen storm,
> For which coarse man seems much the fitter born,
> Rained on thy bed
> And harmless head.
> And now as fresh and cheerful as the light
> Thy little heart in early hymns doth sing.

Gwernvale, which is beautifully set on a wooded slope above
Crickhowel and the Usk, is another place of ancient note, though
the house is comparatively modern, and it was connected for
some generations with a family of spirit.   Now to the thought-
less Saxon the name of Prodgers very likely stands for the
quintessence of jocose nomenclature.   He would probably
feel that if he owned it he would not rest, though it cost him
half his fortune till he emerged a Norfolk Howard or something
like it.   It is the kind of patronymic that the fancy of the
Punch artist leaps too naturally for his greengrocer on Margate
beach.   But the Prodgers or the Ap Rogers of Gwernvale
would have been no wit ashamed of their name, nor would they
have had any desire whatever to become Norfolk Howards.
It was in high favour and deservedly so at the court of Charles I,
for Sir Henry Proger or Prodger and his three brothers not
only fought for the king to the bitter end, but returned with

his son to France for the whole of the Commonwealth period. At the Restoration one of them was knighted and made a gentleman of the Privy Chamber. Indeed the zeal of this quartet of Progers was so great that two of them were said to have personally assisted at the killing of Cromwell's envoy to Madrid. Another was the recipient of one of those royal landgrants in Virginia of which Charles II was lavish and the Virginians so deplorably regardless. However, the poor Progers ultimately experienced the proverbial fate of those who put their trust in princes. James II ignored their really remarkable services. The owner of Gwernvale, once keeper of Bushy Park and M.P. for Breconshire, came down in the world, and at his death in 1713 at the age of ninety the place passed to a daughter and out of the family, together with a great collection of autograph letters from the Stuart kings and their councillors.

SUGAR LOAF FROM ABOVE GWERNVALE.

How one does suffer, too, in the matter of Welsh derivations! In a borderland of Welsh and English, where hybrid place-names are common, Gwernvale would seem so obviously the Alder valley, as to be outside etymologist comment, though instead of Alders there are nowadays magnificent groves of rhododendrons and beautiful beech woods. Whether this is too ridiculously obvious for the Welsh etymologist who has a passion for derivations or not I cannot say. But he will tell you that the name is not what it seems, being in fact a corruption of Tir Wronow Voel, " The land of Wronow the bald," a gentleman who held it in the time of Edward II.

Now you may drop down to Abergavenny upon either bank of the river you choose, and may again admire as you approach it the situation of the border town between its lofty hills and in the very gate of the vale. Like most border towns, however, that sprung from a Norman castle, and for obvious reasons, its streets are on a slope. It is now an English and not a Welsh town both in habit and appearance, boasting a mayor and corporation, ten thousand people, golf links, cricket ground, and a famous salmon river. It is on a main line for Bristol, London or the north, has a marquis close at hand and a select and wealthy neighbourhood, so it should be happy. It manufactures nothing notable, I believe, but has a railroad which climbs the mountains across the Usk and taps the mining country which lies for the most part so mercifully hidden behind them and should bring trade and traffic. In short, Abergavenny is in itself a pleasant average country town, neither remarkable nor the reverse in its construction. It has a fine cruciform parish church of goodly dimensions, and embattled tower which in ancient days was attached to a Benedictine priory and contains a number of the tombs and effigies of those who ruled the country in the sanguinary days of old. Above all it has the scanty remnants, two towers, a gateway and a wall, of the great castle that once stood on the high mound which rises above the town on one side and the streams of the Gavenny as they hasten downwards to meet the Usk upon the other. In the time of Elizabeth the ruin was thus invoked by the indefatigable Churchyard in his rhyming prose :—

> Most goodly towers are bare and naked left
> That covered were with timber and good lead
> Would God, therefore the owner of the same
> Did stay them up for to increase his fame.

And I fancy it was the true antiquarian fervour which thus animated the good Churchyard, not anxiety for the security of the town below. The modern antiquarian, however, receives something of a shock when he finds the storied haunts of the De Braoses laid out in tennis courts and decorated with swing boats and a bandstand, and I can imagine some notables of my acquaintance demanding their entrance money back in no measured tones.

I had the castle to myself, however, one grey summer morning of late, when a wild storm seemed brewing and an ominous breeze was rustling the leaves of the tall trees which cover the mound, and of the ivy clinging to the broken walls. The evil spirit of William de Braose, the ogre of all Lord Marchers, the bloodiest of a grim breed, might almost have been abroad. And William de Braose was universally potent, for he not only held Abergavenny and a large slice of Gwent, on whose edge it lay, but had succeeded to the great lordship of Brecon. His life was long, though he ended it in poverty and exile. Amid many black deeds the shocking massacre of the Welsh chiefs of Gwent, his own vassals most of them and his bidden guests to this very castle, was his most supreme effort and has rung down the ages. For reasonable severity he had some excuse, as one of them had killed his uncle, the Bishop of Hereford. De Braose, however, gathered together a large Christmas party of these gentlemen in his castle at Abergavenny and brought the festivities to a sudden silence by

THE SUGAR LOAF FROM THE MONMOUTH ROAD.

demanding that his guests should then and there take an oath not to carry arms on their precarious walks abroad. The request was naturally resented, as the insult it was meant to be, whereupon the doors were flung open and De Braose's soldiers, kept in reserve for the purpose, rushed in and slew his guests to the last man as they sat at table.

De Braose was so powerful that even our candid friend Giraldus, when at Abergavenny a few years after the event, finds it prudent to do a little futile whitewashing. But the sons and nephews of the murdered Welshmen were not so complacent, for after waiting till they were old enough, a matter of several years, they captured the castle by assault, scuttled it and carried off the garrison, which unfortunately however contained none of the De Braose family. Being themselves assailed afterwards by a force from Hereford under the command of the sheriff, they defeated and slew that functionary

RAGLAN CASTLE.

and several conspicuous Herefordians. The redoubtable William himself had some slight unpleasantness with King John, which was aggravated by his wife, Maud St. Valerie, a notable character in border history, telling his Majesty what she thought of his conduct towards Prince Arthur, and absolutely refusing his demand for her own sons as hostages for William's good behaviour. The latter escaped and died abroad, but the hapless Maud and one son fell into John's hands, who immured them at Windsor and slowly starved them to death. A more fortunate son, however, became not only Bishop of Hereford, but owner of all his father's vast possessions. To him a brother succeeded who married a daughter of Llewelyn the Great and proved the last of the stock. Cantelupes, Hastings, Herberts, Greys, Beauchamps followed together with the stalwart Richard, Earl of Warwick, who distinguished himself against Glyndwr and elsewhere and died Regent of France. Almost ever since that time the honours of Abergavenny have been in the possession of the Nevilles. A further characteristic of William de Braose was the unblushing fashion in which he invoked the divine will as the patron of his atrocities. It was said he paid his clerk extra wages for interpolating scripture phrases into his ruthless edicts ; whether the clerk's claim was merely for extra pen work or like the late President Kruger's for moral injury we may not know. Abergavenny was the capital and seat of government of the lordships of " Overwent " or Upper Gwent, a beautiful and fertile part of Monmouth, a good corn country, but even in Leland's time " men studied more to pastures the which be well enclosed." Leland, however, found the country " sumwat mountayneous." I wonder why the modes of expression used by some writers of that day move one so ? The deliberate jocularity of the Elizabethans gains of course a further flavour from its phraseology, which was their normal English. But Leland was earlier, and had no more thoughts of joking than has the compiler of Bradshaw, yet scraps of his itinerary are surely mirth-moving in their quaint turns of constructions and delightful spelling.

Archbishop Baldwin, accompanied by his faithful henchman Giraldus, in 1188 preached the crusade at Abergavenny and many took the cross. Those who could afford it usually bought off. Having enjoyed a few days or hours of pious ecstasy and the credit of heroic intention they then quietly contributed their pound or two to the war chest and went home to fight their neighbours, which provided at least equal entertainment in a more congenial arena with a greater chance of profit. For all this country, Giraldus tells us, was splendidly stocked with horses and cattle, swine and sheep and goats. Probably it was the preliminary conflict with what our departed hero in Monnington church euphoniously styles "enraged seas," that choked off most of these well-meaning volunteers, and no wonder, considering their transport facilities. But one gathers that the wives had much to say in the matter. I

AT CLYTHA.

have quoted the story elsewhere of how the wife of a Cardigan crusader took her adventurer by his coat collar and effectually reminded him that he had a predominant partner, and the saintly archbishop may have had this and many other similar instances in his mind, when he quizzically inquired of a noble recruit at Abergavenny whether he was not going to consult his wife? The great man denied the soft impeachment, Gerald tells us, "but with downcast eyes," whereupon the archbishop, scenting mischief, swore him in without the loss of a moment. We are not told whether or no he compounded, still his money contribution was something. Those who could not pay had to go, and it is remarkable, we learn, how many

" notorious thieves, robbers and murderers " were cleared out of Abergavenny lordship and the island of Briton generally by this means and transformed into champions of Christendom. The entire Welsh tour produced 3,000 recruits, but from this number the compounders have to be deducted.

In this same itinerary the feats of the Gwent archers are duly extolled, though they had acquired nothing like the efficiency that distinguished them a century later under the first Edward. The long-bow had not yet developed, but the Welsh of Gwent at that time used short bows of elm, of whose penetration wonderful stories were told. An oaken portal four fingers thick in Abergavenny castle, for instance, had been pierced by several arrows in the last siege, their heads being preserved in the gate. The ogre of Abergavenny, William de Braose himself, told Gerald that a Welshman had shot one of his troopers through his armour-plated thigh, through his saddle and mortally wounded his horse. Still more wonderful yet, another soldier had one armour thigh pinned to the saddle, and on turning round was promptly transfixed through the other in like manner and so pinned on both sides to the saddle. The fact is that till Edward's time the English yeoman and peasant away from the Welsh border had done no great amount of steady fighting since the Saxon period. He was comparatively unwarlike, and unskilled in the use of arms, nor had he naturally any personal devotion to his Norman overlord. As a class he seems to have resented being called out to serve against the Welsh, the Scotch or the French, or anybody else whose hostilities he rarely or never felt, and he consequently deserted in most wholesale fashion. As a matter of fact he was not very heavily drawn upon till Edward III's time, when he so astonished Europe, which seems to have held him till then as a more or less negligible quantity. We are apt to imagine the Yorkshireman at least as a person always ready for a fight, but Edward seems to have held the north-man as cheaply as he did the men of the east and south when serious work had to be done in Wales or Scotland. Nothing so illuminating on the subject or more calculated to disturb a good many fondly but vaguely cherished notions has ever been published than Mr. Edward Morris' *Welsh Wars of Edward I*. It is not a picturesque or partisan history, but a complete summary by an expert, of the numbers, personnel, and efficiency of all the material the great soldier had to draw upon, collected from the records of the period, with a vast amount of information not accessible to the general reader. It was of course inevitable that the Welsh and border Englishmen, martial by habit and of necessity, should be the readiest weapon to Edward's hand. Shropshire, Cheshire, and Hereford, with parts of Lancashire and the Sherwood outlaws and foresters for other reasons, seem to have stood out till the fourteenth century and the Hundred Years' War with France, over the rest of England as regular infantry to raw militia. In the same category stood the Welsh of the southern Marches, who were by then as ready to fight the north and west Welsh spearmen as they were the Scotch, and it was in the hands of these

BELOW USK BRIDGE.

Marcher Welsh, who were the most accomplished archers of their day, that the bow was rapidly developing into the perfect long-bow of a generation or two later. One may well imagine what a contrast there must have been, discipline and martial habits apart, between these borderers and the levies of yokels from South or East Anglia who had not practised the difficult art of archery and in great part resented being dragged from home by king or overlords. It may also be noted that Edward used no troops in his long wars with Wales from east of the border counties except the foresters of Sherwood, though he was hard pressed for men. In 1297, says Mr. Morris, Edward had 8,000 infantry in Flanders, just half of whom were Welsh. In the Scotch campaign of 1298, which ended at Falkirk, the king summoned 10,500 Welsh and not a single infantry soldier from all the northern counties of England. And these troops did not go like the 5,000 Welshmen to Crecy forty years later, to act merely as light troops supporting the by that time trained English archers, with whom also both Welsh and English borderers were mixed. But they went with Edward to Scotland as the flower of his infantry, the most experienced troops; and the best archers then available. These 10,000 came mainly from the lordships of the south, and from Gwent, Glamorgan, Brecon and Pembroke. One factor, too, must not be overlooked in all these thirteenth and fourteenth century wars in Wales, in Scotland and in Eng-

THE BELL POOL NEAR USK.

land itself, namely the foreign mercenary, whom both barons and kings imported freely, particularly crossbowmen, an art requiring much drill with a weapon formidable only at short range and slow of fire with a missile which stunned and bruised but did not penetrate the joints of armour. Edward, says the same authority, saw it was useless to apply his great organizing powers to all the levies of the country, and he began with what was then the best material, the border counties and the Welsh March, and the men with or against whom he had fought so much. The two corps of longest and most distinguished service were one of 800 men from Gwent and Crickhowel and a small company a hundred strong from Macclesfield. In calling out the great levies of infantry from the rest of England,

Edward seems to have hoped that some at least would not only stay by him, but prove apt and teachable. The astonishing change that came over Englishmen and surprised Europe in his grandson's day does not concern us here, but so many historical shibboleths become articles of faith it seemed natural at Abergavenny to recall the fact that English archery, as the world understands it, did not have its birth on the village greens round London but on the banks of the Dee, the Wye, the Severn and the Usk. Finally as Edward I's reign witnessed the extinction of organized racial warfare on the Welsh border, so his death in the moment of cementing what promised to be the sane and natural union of Scotland and England, gave birth to that other border warfare which has been so much more sung and written about. In short, the northern borderer came into being almost at the moment when the Welsh borderer, as such, ceased to be.

RAGLAN CASTLE.

BORDERLAND OF WALES

CHAPTER VI

HEREFORD TO CREDENHILL, BRINSOP AND WEOBLEY

JULY had run half its course when I heard the bells of Hereford Cathedral once more chiming overhead. The turf of the precincts was just touched with brown where the far-reaching shadows neither of elm nor minster could ward off some portion of the long day's sunshine. The Wye beneath the castle green had shrunk still further down its gravelly beaches and rippled over the streaming moss-weed in feeble tones that spelled despair to the would-be slayer of salmon from Rhayader to Tintern. While, as if to emphasize the parlous state of the fishing interests, bare-legged urchins paddled in what should have been mid-stream, and angled in guileless fashion for sprats as untutored as themselves. The old town itself seemed more astir, and the stranger was already quite obvious within its gates, for the world of the great cities was beginning to stretch itself and the ripples of the movement to be felt even here. Country houses, too, lately emptied by the London season were again occupied, and the rejoicing tradesmen were skipping back and forth from shop doors to motor and chariot. Stranger motorists, too, veiled and begoggled and white with the dust of many counties, were in some evidence, pausing for a brief spell in their mad career. Local touring societies were on the war-path in breaks and wagonettes; archæologists from neighbouring counties with their disciples of both sexes, and eyes on the alert for Norman arches and Tudor chimneys; licensed victuallers of warm and jovial aspect and cheerful countenance at the near prospect of a social repast at the *Blue Lion* or the *Stag's Head*; cricketers bent on the conquest of some neighbouring village, for village cricket flourishes on the border, though only Monmouth of the four counties has, I believe, any collective significance in the committee room of Lord's. Now in Northamptonshire, which has just become a first-class county, village cricket in most parts is virtually dead. Which is the better condition?

The tourist who rambles mainly in bricks and mortar is about in Hereford, too, by the end of July. He comes by train, stops a night at an hotel, and you will see him inspecting the terracotta front of the town hall with his wife on one arm, an umbrella under the other, and open guide book in hand. After lunch he will do the cathedral; after tea call a cab and drive round the outskirts of the town, when his attention will be called to the jail, the race-course, the water works and the union; so home and to bed—that is, after dinner, of course. The next day he will proceed to Shrewsbury, Gloucester or Lich-field, and will repeat the process for which there may be much to be said. This concentrated form of touring, however, is not the sort to which England would seem most readily to lend itself, where the country is so rich, and the towns, with a few notable exceptions, so lacking in objects of interest to the intelligent stranger. It is a method, however, that might be highly commended for practical reasons to a town councillor.

But I did not come back to Hereford to discuss tourists, above all in this frivolous vein, but to do a little touring myself of another sort with the reader for my company, if he be not yet tired of me. The north-western portion of the county will now be my theme, or rather so much of it as we can cover in the course of two short chapters. In the first place, I should like to go to Weobley, some ten miles away, for reasons which will, I hope, appear sufficient when we get there, and by a slight deviation from the straight path, take in the site of Roman Kentchester, while other objects of later date will no doubt confront us. With this in view we must leave the city by the Hay Road, that ancient artery which follows the Wye out into the land of the setting sun and the March of Wales. On shaking off the last suburban villa, a stone cross standing on a sexagonal shaft, surmounting as many sided a flight of steps, marks the parting of the ways. This is White-cross, somewhat restored but originally erected by Bishop Charlton in gratitude for the departure of the Black Death in 1347. For it was here during that fateful period the town markets were held. It was at this very spot, too, that the saintly Bishop Cantelupe in 1276 heard the bells of the cathedral ring a welcome to him without human agency.

A mile beyond, we leave the Hay Road near King's Acre

Gardens, celebrated nurseries of fruit and shrubs that reflect the prolific glories of Herefordshire over many acres with infinite variety. We pass Stretton Sugwas on the right, which in former days contained a palace of the bishops, occupied by them till the end of the seventeenth century. Far away to the east beyond the woody ridges and red fields through which the Lugg is somewhere wandering, the shadowy heights of Malvern loom so large as to momentarily suggest the notion one has lost one's bearings, and is looking towards Wales. To the west, however, the old landmarks are bold and defined enough to banish at a glance any such hallucinations. For the full course of the Black Mountains, from Hay Knob to the Usk, with the Sugar Loaf and the Skirrid and all the familiar

STRETTON SUGWAS CHURCH.

landmarks so recently encompassed, now break the morning sky in broken shapes of misty blue. The wheat and oats have headed and indeed are now yellowing, and the traveller's joy has festooned the hedgerows since we followed these tortuous ways in June. The hops have made great leaps upward, and the apples in the roadside orchards are giving solid evidence that the cold east wind blight which rebuffed the Mayfly and killed the pears had small effect on their abundant promise.

Right ahead and already throwing its shadows upon us is Credenhill, the most southerly of a beautiful chain of more or less connected hills. It is a typical Herefordshire height of the normal and domestic type. Draped in rich foliage to its summit some seven hundred and odd feet up, you would never guess that the latter was encircled by deep cut defences and was the site of a British camp. On the lower slopes beneath the woodland lies a typical Herefordshire village ; irregular groups of timbered cottages, the black of the oak frames traced in squares of varying sizes over the clear whitewash covering the daub and wattle. Here is a roof of braided thatch arched over the windows, and there again one of mellow russet stone coated with wandering patches of moss. Creepers and roses twine about them, and an archway framed of yew hangs over the wicket gate. Orchards and barns fill in the vacant spaces, and where three roads meet in the middle of the hamlet, there is a fine chestnut tree on a triangle of turf which has no doubt received the confidences, the rude jests, the political opinions of Credenhill villagers for generations.

And in regard to these black and white houses it may be noted that when modern needs compel the use of the prosaic brick, the rustic borderer seems instinctively and happily to flinch from the intrusive spectacle. For he proceeds immediately to wash it over with white or pale yellow, and to trace black bands of paint or pitch tar where the beams should have been if the builder had been possessed of an artistic or conservative spirit. Perhaps, however, the builder does it of design, probably so if he is the squire. Up Mr. Eckroyd's drive a space, and standing back under the wooded hill, is the church with a Norman nave, much variety of window tracery, and some old stained glass portraying Thomas à Becket and Bishop Cantelupe. The exterior speaks for itself by the pencil of our artist. Credenhill, however, has a more famous tree than the democratic chestnut which shelters the village green in the shape of a huge elm of quite gigantic girth, which stands in the Court grounds. It is known as the Prophet Elm, and is said to foretell a death in the house by flinging off a limb.

A few hundred yards below the village, at a small station bearing its name, the highway is lifted over the Hereford and Hay railroad by an arch, and standing upon this you look immediately over two or three large fields covering in all perhaps fifty acres, and sloping gently upwards from the line. They fill the entire foreground to the near horizon, and are encompassed by the narrow road from the bridge, whose course you can mark the whole way round to the village of Kentchester, or Magna Castra, as the Romans called it. It is one of those spots like the field of Waterloo, concerning which the man in the street will tell you there is nothing to be seen, which is a solemn truth. But like the other more famous and immortal field, the site of Kentchester holds you from its

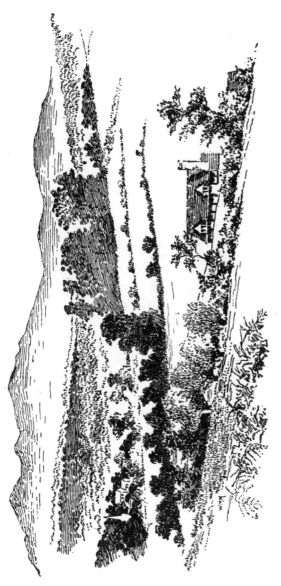

MALVERN HILLS FROM NEAR HEREFORD.

clearly marked delimitations in a single *coup d'oeil*, and if you can construct nothing on that, though half of its wavy undulations are in barley and the other half an ox pasture, or at least find no food for dreams or fancy, it is not worth while even turning aside to see it. The gates were at this lower end, but the lane fence so plainly visible follows the course of the city wall round two-thirds of the enclosure, the foundations being, I believe, traceable most of the way, while the railway virtually marks its northern boundary. When the pasture is closely grazed I am told that you can clearly mark the lines of streets and houses as I have done myself at the Gaer near Brecon, a smaller but more perfect station on the same lines.

CREDENHILL CHURCH.

It will be remembered that Hereford is said to have been partly built from material carted hence. A great quantity of relics have been unearthed here and are in the possession of various people, and some in the museum at Hereford. Villagers tell me they are still turned up freely by the plough or hoe ; coins, pottery, leaden pipes, bits of tessellated pavement, personal ornaments and such like. In Leland's time there was a block of brick work here resembling a chair, which foolish people called " the King of feyres chayre " ; this was

BRINSOP COURT.

blown up for a wager by some still more foolish person early in the last century. The camp was five-sided and lay on the Great Roman road trom Caerleon through Abergavenny to Uriconium near Shrewsbury. It inspired the muse of Wordsworth, who, as we shall shortly see, was a frequent visitor in its immediate vicinity and witnessed the unearthing of one of the Roman pavements !

> Fresh and clear
> As if its hues were of the passing year
> Dawns this time-buried pavement, from that mound
> Hoards may have come of Trajans, Maximins
> Shrunk into coins with all their warlike toil ;
> Or a fierce impress issues with its foil
> Of tenderness ; the wolf whose sucking twins
> The unlettered ploughboy pities when he wins
> The casual treasures from the unfurrowed soil.

The British camp on Credenhill probably occupied by Caractacus overlooks the site of the vanished town, and a villager loitering with me on the railway bridge one day assured me that the latter had been destroyed by fire hurled from this lofty eminence !

A couple of miles further on, beautifully embosomed among the wooded hills of the Ladylift and Foxley Range, lies the church and yet more wonderful fourteenth century moated manor house of Brinsop Court, celebrated on more than one account. Two blocks of the original house survive, in one of which is a beautiful oaken-roofed banqueting hall, now used as a granary, but like the rest of the fabric looked after with care, being in the occupation of a family who take much pride in it and farm the lands which are considerable. It is the ancient home of the Danseys, one of the oldest families on the border, but passed out of their hands some generations ago. What is not original is mostly Tudor, and the whole fabric, within and without, is difficult to write of in measured phrase, it is so wholly satisfying. Two sides only are at this time actually washed by the moat. In the front a well-kept lawn intervenes, and the entrance porch is shaded by a fine cedar, planted by Wordsworth himself. The house I shall leave to the artist ; it will be my part to relate how it was occupied in Wordsworth's lifetime by his wife's relations, the Hutchinsons, and how the poet often stayed here as well as his famous sister Dorothy. I have already mentioned the cedar, but what is perhaps as interesting is a replica of Pickersgill's

portrait of the poet, presented to the house by Lord Saye and
Sele in recognition of his connection with it. I sometimes
think there is an almost greater charm in these smaller manor
houses of high antiquity when really cared for than ones of
greater pretension. The latter inevitably suffer somewhat
from the modern requirements of a large country house, while
the others, being generally occupied as ordinary farmhouses,
are apt to look a little woe-begone. But Brinsop hits the
happy mean exactly in the upkeep and proportion of its
flower and kitchen gardens ; simple and well ordered in the
first, and teeming with old-fashioned abundance in the other,
the environs harmonize more nearly with the life which the
owners of such manors led in recent centuries, but which
would scarcely have satisfied their ambitions had they survived till this one. However that may be, Brinsop is probably
without an equal of its stamp in the county, and is moreover

THE BANQUETING HALL, BRINSOP.

set amid enfolding and leafy hills that give it an air of peculiar
seclusion from the madding crowd. The ancient but unpretentious little church contains the dust and the monuments of
many Danseys, and a stained glass window to the memory of
Wordsworth.

Back upon the main road from which this pilgrimage to
Brinsop has been effected, the wooded heights of Foxley are
soon rising upon our right. They and the mansion of Queen
Anne's time within them belonged to the Prices through the
eighteenth century, the best known of whom was Sir Uvedale
Price, who laid out Kew Gardens and was the most famous

landscape gardener of his day, as well as a prolific writer on all matters connected with his art. The Foxley woods are still rich in many of the rare trees and shrubs Sir Uvedale planted there. It is a curious coincidence that the other great planter and gardener of that period should have been a neighbouring squire, though in his case the plural number must be used, for the brothers Knight of Wormesley and afterwards of Downton were no less famous throughout England than Sir Uvedale himself.

THE MOAT AND WORDSWORTH'S CEDAR, BRINSOP COURT.

The latter, with many generations of his family, lies buried in the old church of Yazor near the new one here. Just beyond Yazor our own way shakes off the pleasant trammels of wooded heights and richly timbered meads, and swinging to the right for the last two or three miles opens out magnificent vistas to the north-westward of the hills of Radnor, rising in wild confusion beyond the Vale of Arrow. Lifted upon a gentle terrace upon the outer slopes of this Foxley and Lady lift range, as one is here, one may look uninterruptedly over ten or fifteen miles of rich undulations, where Eardisley, Lyonshall, Kington and half a score of ancient villages full of antiquarian and architectural treasures lie snugly nestling, to the lofty ramparts of mid Wales and the Radnor Marches. The familiar eye can readily mark the frontier heights of Brilly and Squilver, of Hergest and Hanter, and higher yet and dimmer in the background the dark solitudes and wild sheep walks of Radnor forest.

I have said my say of Radnorshire elsewhere, a brief and poor enough tribute to one of the fairest counties that the tempered sun of Britain shines on. Fair perhaps is an inapt word—you might truly say that of any county—Berkshire, Hampshire, or Suffolk, for instance. But I do not mean that sort of thing. Radnor belongs mainly to the type of country that men travel far to see and linger in, and to enjoy a totally new sensation, who live all the year round amid ordinary pleasant English landscape. None of them go to Radnor, it is true, unless the gouty patients who amble round the precincts of Llandrindod count ; neither do they go to Breconshire, which, though much intertwined with Radnor, and sharing with it the best of the Wye Valley for forty miles, must rank even higher as it rises occasionally to the scale of North Wales and Cumberland, while the other goes nowhere much higher than Dartmoor. But the two counties may be fairly regarded as one in a physical sense. The chances are that your neighbour at dinner could not even locate either of them, and very remote indeed that he or she have ever crossed their borders. They would be almost always incredulous at the statement that this unknown region is more uniformly beautiful than Devonshire, and sometimes rises to efforts quite unequalled in that delectable county, where, I should like to say, lest my opportunities for comparison may be suspected, I have spent not weeks nor months, but some of the pleasantest years of my life and know most and certainly the best of it. All the world has either been to Devonshire or takes it for granted. Literature has much to do with the ruts on which these things run, fiction particularly, and the western county has been fortunate in finding able interpreters among her sons. Her seacoast scenery and traditions have been a powerful asset, of course, but in the matter of comparison between counties of the same class which is really interesting, if you are in a position to make them, and not odious, I have interiors only in my mind.

Devonshire is a popular Arcady, too, with the London novelist and even with the playwright, and the Devonshire rustic on the stage would make angels weep who knew the soft rapid buzzing tones of its vernacular, and heard the strident laboured cockney Essex or heaven knows what of the virtuous Phyllis who is the leading lady of the village maidens. Britons are not enterprising when in the mood to explore the more pronounced charms of their own island, or Devonshire would not be overrun with holiday makers while the South Wales Marches were virtually untouched, nor would the coasts of Cornwall be packed every summer and those of Pembroke and South Cardigan remain practically unknown. Yet the old familiar cry is echoed from year to year that every place is crowded at that

FENHAMPTON.

season in which the majority are compelled to seek their relaxation. The natives of Herefordshire protest that their county is every whit as beautiful as Devonshire, whose seaside places they much frequent, and only a person who did not know it would venture on an offhand opinion. Their characteristics are both western and somewhat similar. High hills, tumbling waters, a red soil and that intensely vivid green which makes the centre and south of England appear almost pallid as it must always appear, thirsty and low-pitched on first entering it from the west. Herefordshire may fairly claim to have no single tract of ugly country within her borders. Now Devonshire has some large slices which no stretch of imagination could commend—that big block of the South Hams, for instance, between the Dart and Avon. Herefordians maintain that their hills are nearly always richly wooded over their summits, while the rounded hills of Devon are almost always bare on the top and chequered with rectangles of bank or wall fences. This is perfectly true, and many far-reaching outlooks in both North and South Devon that I can call to mind seem monotonous and dreary to a degree till you remind yourself of the snug wooded valleys that lie hidden amid the sometimes disheartening vista of bleak and chessboard hilltop. For its moors, Herefordshire may take unto itself the Welsh hills and mountains that half the county look at every day, and whose edges

THE LEY.

are actually within their borders, while in the matter of rural architecture the Herefordian need not worry himself, for nowhere else, may he be well assured, is there such a wealth of timbered cottages and farmhouses such as the artist loves.

Fenhampton, depicted here, is but an average specimen, and was built as a farmhouse, while The Ley, a mile nearer Weobley, though now a farmhouse, is a superb specimen of a sixteenth century timbered manor house, having been built by James Brydges in 1589.

Weobley is one of the most famous of the black and white villages of the border. To be literal it is an ancient borough which sent two members to Parliament till the Reform Act. I have heard somewhere an old saw—

> Poor Weobley,
> Proud people,
> Low church,
> High steeple ;

applicable no doubt to a former period of Weobley's life. Numbers of its beautiful old buildings have disappeared within the last century, among the rest a fine market-house built by John Abel, the greatest architect in this style of Charles I's time, and who covered the border counties with beautiful timbered buildings, including several town halls, now mostly vanished.

THE LEY FARMHOUSE.

He lived to be ninety, and shortly before his death carved his own monument, with an effigy of himself and his two wives, and composed his own epitaph which quaint production may be seen and read in the sequestered little church of Sarnesfield a few miles to the westward :

This craggy stone a covering is for an architect's bed,
That lofty buildings raised high yet now lies low his head;
His line and rule so death concludes are lockèd up in stone,
Build they who list or they who wist, for he can more build none.

WEOBLEY.

There is little suggestive of a town left about Weobley, which perhaps gives better scope for the many charming old houses and rows of houses to display themselves in sleepy and umbrageous fashion amid the rustle of orchards and pleasant strips of meadow that cover the site of its former streets. It would be good to have seen it, say, a century ago, in the full plenitude of its architectural glories, when the electors all sat free in consideration of their votes, but I do not suppose that any one gave a second thought in those days to its picturesque qualities. A legend runs that when the occupant of a house died in Weobley it was pulled down, which I can hardly believe, particularly if he had thirty-two children, as had one Weobley worthy, and the very house, one of the best specimens extant, where they were all born, is still pointed out.

A most imposing fourteenth century church looks down on Weobley, and the summit of its lofty spire must be visible from Radnorshire. It was no suggestion of insecurity in the pose of Weobley's cloud-compelling vane, that provoked to memory these artless lines as I drew the first time within its shadow, an inconsequent fragment from some forgotten eighteenth century poet that took possession of a particular brain cell at an uncritical stage of existence and has stuck there ever since :—

> Where longs to fall yon rifted spire,
> As wearied of the insulting air
> The poet's dreams, the warrior's ire,
> The lover's sighs are sleeping there.

Indeed, I have often meditated an application to that invaluable journal "Notes and Queries" for the source of this fragment, which, if not profound, is not altogether infelicitous. Most of us have some store of these old friends fortuitously gathered when the sense of cadence was overmastering, and the memory assimilated without effort what an effort more profitably directed a little later would have availed naught.

Weobley churchyard is on the wrong side of the border to be the resting-place of poets' dreams, for Phillips is the only Herefordshire bard, other than Mrs. Barret Browning, known to me, and even he is ignored by outside critics and compilers. But lovers' sighs know no geography, and of warriors I will undertake to say there are enough laid here. Best known of them, however, is that redoubtable Colonel Birch, who began life as a packhorse trader, rose to be a distinguished leader in the Roundhead army, and terminated his career as owner of the Garnstone property close by, and member for Weobley. His statue in marble beneath a handsome canopy adorns the chancel of the church, and a long inscription tells the story of his successful and vigorous life. It does not, however, include the tradition that his start was achieved by a valiant defence of his packhorse train against an attack of Royalist soldiers

WEOBLEY.

first attracting the notice of Cromwell, and securing him a captaincy of horse. Nor does it relate how well the colonel's sharp trading instincts served him later on in the administration of sequestrated Royalist estates. He seems to have acquired episcopal palaces, productive manors, and even the leaden roofs of cathedrals at scandalously inadequate prices. He was among the first, however, to welcome Charles II at the restoration, and with more consistency was a staunch supporter of William III. He made some amends in old age, however,

143

for his sacrilegious and other peculations by contributing largely to the adornment of Weobley church, and has thereby earned his right to occupying so prominent a post in it to-day.

Among other distinguished persons commemorated here, as is thought, though with no visible sign of it, is Hugh de Lacy, the founder of Llanthony Priory and probably of this church also. The inn where Charles I stopped as he passed through Weobley in 1645 is still standing, though no longer a hostelry. A pretty story, too, is told of Lord Eldon, who as a young barrister was member for Weobley. On his first visit he was the guest of the rector, Mr. Bridges, and while in the humour for giving promises, from which even the member for a pocket borough was probably not quite exempt, the rector's little girl extracted her concession like the rest. This was to the effect that if ever Mr. Scott became Lord Chancellor, and her fairy prince should happen to wear a white tie, the first vacant Crown living should be placed at her disposal. Lord Eldon himself has left the sequel in writing ; how, many years afterwards, when clothed in the majesty of office, his sacred presence was invaded one morning by a not-to-be-denied young lady, who called to his mind the promise made to a little girl at Weobley in days long gone by. His Lordship, who had naturally forgotten all about the matter, suffered his memory to be jogged so effectually as to assume that his visitor had married the potential clergyman of their ancient compact. The damsel admitted with a blush that she expected shortly to attain that honourable situation, and that it only remained for the Lord Chancellor to fulfil his part of the compact, which he did like an honest man on the first opportunity. Indeed, Lord Eldon relates that the young lady was of such business-like habit that she would not stir till he had given something more than a promise of his good intentions.

Weobley, of course, had its castle, of which no trace remains but a wooded mound outside the village, in the corner of the park, where towers the castellated mansion of Garnstone, built by Nash on the site of the timbered house occupied by Birch and his descendants. Weobley Castle was built by the De Lacys and saw much battering in the days of Stephen, who captured it once in his own royal person. In later times it came to the Devereux, and in the course of generations to the member of that family who, as Earl of Essex, led the parliamentary forces with so much deliberation and Fabian caution. By his daughter it passed to the Thynnes, who still own property here, and whose scions represented the interests of Weobley in Parliament with praiseworthy consistency till its disfranchisement. But Garnstone Manor itself was a separate property belonging to the Tomkynses till Colonel Birch bought it; that same stock whose traces, it may be remembered, we found at Monnington, where Glyndwr died. It was this once notable family, ruined by the Civil Wars, that made a fresh name for themselves as tenant farmers a century or more later in the founding of the Hereford breed of cattle as we now know it. Another celebrity of the neighbourhood was Mr. Thomas Dinely, or Dingley, who lived at Dillwyn. His history in marble would hardly call for general notice, but his *Progress of the Duke of Beaufort as Lord President through Wales in* 1687, written in manuscript and illustrated by himself, is a most delightful and unconsciously humorous picture of the time, and its scarce reproductions are among the literary treasures of the Welsh Marches. Artists of discrimination are very naturally to be often found at Weobley, and the more so as it is but one of a group of neighbouring villages where the black and white architecture of the border finds its highest expression.

In returning to Hereford the nearer way, some nine miles, the road winds pleasantly along the eastern foot of the Ladylift and Foxley hills, which on our outward journey we skirted upon the other and the Welsh side. A wooded bluff high on the right is known as Robin Hood's Butts. Now the most trustworthy accounts of the half-legendary outlaw make him, I believe, a follower of De Montfort with the rest of the Sherwood foresters. These, as we have shown, were almost the only English archers away from the borders that Edward I considered efficient and used in his wars. It is quite possible that this immortal person may have been here in the flesh, and even tested his skill against the bowmen of the Marches. It is sad to think that he could not possibly have drawn a

THE BUTTAS DOVE COT.

six foot long bow to his ear, as the bow and its science had nothing like reached that perfection in Robin's day, and though formidable enough, was by comparison to the weapon of Crecy as a smooth-bore to a rifle.

The hamlets of King's Pyon and Canon Pyon, with the fine uplifted ivy-clad church of the latter looking out towards the distant hills of Malvern, lie on the road. Rare specimens of timbered houses nestle amid the hills to the right, of which Luntley Manor is the most noted, while of the many seventeenth century dovecots of elaborate design which still survive in this part of the country, the one at the Buttas close by is perhaps the most curious. The two Pyons, however, though the relics of warlike Mortimers are to be found in one of them, suggest by way of a change the more peaceful achievements and the less sonorous name of Tomkyns. For all about here lie the homesteads in which the descendants of the former lords of Weobley and Monnington, turning their swords into ploughshares as tenant-farmers, accumulated fresh prosperity and a fresh reputation by the quality of their flocks and herds.

It would bore the reader, whose interest in these matters is probably slender, to hear all about the making of the Hereford; and, moreover, many other names notable in this connection besides that of Tomkyns would demand recognition.

Still the stocky, meek-faced, long-horned red and white ox is familiar wherever the English language prevails, and over vast areas besides where Spanish alone is understood ; indeed, South America just now is its staunchest patron. As to this south-border country, on either side of it, no other breed is noticeable till you strike the black Welshmen in the mountain valleys of the Principality. There is a legend of white beasts with red ears which King John had a fancy for commandeering when in this part of the country, but it is probable that whatever the points of the scrub stock of the border in his time may have been, the most essential attribute was a capacity to gallop on emergency. Richard Tomkyns of the New House, King's Pyon, seems to have been a successful and scientific farmer, as things then went, by the year 1720. In the next generation five of his sons were holding farms in the neighbourhood, all busy with the evolution of the modern Hereford. In the next it was an accomplished fact, and the most perfect animals hailed from King's Pyon and neighbourhood where the Tomkynses still remained as renowned breeders, sharing their fame with the Prices of Pembridge, the Hewers of Holmar, and the Galliers of Wigmore, all noted names in the eighteenth century.

The horns of the modern Hereford must be of the colour of
wax, the eye full and prominent, the nose broad and of light
colour, the main coat curly and of a rich red ; the face, top of
neck and under parts of the body white. Any more subtle
anatomy of the frame would undoubtedly be out of place here,
but it would be well to say that the Hereford is essentially
the " rustler " among English cattle. In the earlier days of
North American ranching, when no hay was saved and stock
were left to face the winter as best they might, the Hereford

KING'S PYON.

came out easily on top. Nowadays, when ranchmen give
both attention and feed to their herds, and hardiness is less
essential, the shorthorn, with his heavier weight at the shipping
age, or in north-western parlance a " long three," has forged
ahead again.[1] Every one knows, too, that Herefords rank low
as a milking stock, and the reputation is deserved when they run
with their calves ; but their friends maintain that the cows
if brought up to the pail often make most prolific and rich

[1] The Hereford came out of the recent dry seasons in Australia far
ahead of the Shorthorns in the percentage of survivals.

milkers. It is quite certain that the Herefordshire farmers seem mostly contented with them, for one does not see short-horn or Jersey or Ayrshires or other recognized milkers in the home paddocks anything like so often as might be expected. It is a comforting reflection amid the present somewhat depressing conditions of British agriculture, that the British breeder of good stock need never fear, humanly speaking, a serious rival across the seas. The American, at any rate, whether of North or South, must always " come back " for his blood. In two or three or four generations, cattle and sheep, particularly the former, fall away from the perfect standard of the show-yard or the high class breeder, and the colonist and the American will neither now or ever be satisfied with anything but the very best, being a highly practical person. The climate of this little island, which both laymen and farmers so often abuse, is at least responsible for a symmetry of form and fineness of coat, in its horned stock at any rate, that need fear no enduring rival.

CHAPTER VII

HEREFORD TO LUDLOW, BY LEOMINSTER, EARDISLAND, PEMBRIDGE AND MORTIMER'S CROSS

THE road from Hereford to Leominster running due north, a section as it were of the boundary I have set myself in these pages, is well worth pursuing, if only for the fine leap it takes about midway over the wooded range of Dinmore. Leaving Hereford, and so far as we are here concerned for the last time, you climb the long steep pitch of Aylestone Hill, on whose pleasantly wooded summit and slopes is set the chief residential suburb of the cathedral city. At the foot of the pitch on the far side is Holmer church, conspicuous for one of those detached half-timbered belfries which are not uncommon in this country, while further on Pipe-and-Lyde, with a fine outlook to the Malvern Hills, is worth a moment's halt. Indeed I could gossip at some length between this and Dinmore, but must forbear, and only stop to notice Marden lying a mile to the eastward down by the banks of Lugg, which noted trout and grayling river babbles leisurely along between high red banks through miles of gently swelling meadow-land. Marden church is famous as covering the first burial-place of the hapless King Æthelbert before the tortured conscience of Offa moved his saintly bones to Hereford, and a well exists within it even yet which broke out miraculously at the burial of the murdered East Anglian king, and is to this day, together with the church, called by his name. Sutton Walls, the site of Offa's palace where the tragedy occurred, is within a mile. It crowns a slight elevation amid the tillage and pasture lands, being encircled by a single ditch and the overgrown traces of a wall which makes its recognition easy from afar.

At Wellington, as one nears the foot of Dinmore, a capacious and woe-begone-looking edifice of red brick, with decayed coaching inn written all over its many-windowed face, stands in mournful solitude on the banks of Wormely brook. A humble tavern in a lower room keeps the spark of life still flickering within its shell. Curiosity to know more, rather than any untimely thirst, took me within one bright summer morning, for in a cider country you may at least purchase your footing in the humblest inn without risk of being poisoned. The venerable dame in possession was a new-comer and could tell me nothing of the history of the gaunt Georgian barrack, but she told me all her own from the very start. How she had been married in the year railways first reached the county, and had taken her wedding trip on almost the first train, and had enjoyed fifty years of connubial bliss with the best of husbands and best of farmers. How they ran a sixty-acre holding together all their wedded lives with a pride in land and dairy produce that had vanished in her opinion from the face of the earth; and there was much more laudation of the things that were and denunciation of the things that are, concluding with a parting shot at motors which went "howlin' by without so much as stoppin' for a glass of ale."

Dinmore Hill is thickly wooded from base to summit. It is a mile to the latter by a steady but gentle climb, with a similar drop upon the farther side; nor is it often in England that a broad high road thus runs through unbroken forests for two miles. There is no roadside fence here, but bright strips of fern-sprinkled sward edged by feathery birch trees lead at once into beautiful woods of oak and beech and ash, sloping up on the one hand and descending upon the other. Rabbits dash freely across the road from cover to cover, and squirrels leap among the overhanging boughs; and high above the world though you are when the long ascent is finished there is not much to be seen of it, when the leaves are on at any rate, for the very abundance of them.

Dinmore once had a sinister reputation. For a hundred years after the wars of Glyndwr, and even into the Tudor period, the borders were infested with outlaws, robbers, and broken gentlemen, a medley of Welsh and English from the Marches. For it was not only the ruin and havoc of war that robbed hundreds of spirited individuals of occupation, but the blood feuds that war had left in its trail, and as previously mentioned a misdemeanant had but to cross into Marcher territory, where its lord would defend him against Welsh or English or the king himself as a point of honour.

In the year 1416, as Robert Whittington and his son Guy

were riding home from Hereford with three valets and two pages; they were attacked by thirty men " armed and arrayed in manner of war;" many of whom they recognized as the servants of Mr. Richard Oldcastle, and were carried off forcibly to " a mountain named Dynemore hill." There the robbers stripped them of horses and clothes, and in the morning bore them two leagues away and imprisoned them in a chapel quite outside their local knowledge. For two or three days the captives were hurried about from one wood to another, after which they were given the alternative of finding sureties for a ransom of six hundred pounds or being taken into Wales. Choosing the former, which is rather significant, Guy Whittington, bound over by oath to return, was sent out on this business, while the others were detained in a ruinous mill. The young man succeeded in finding three gentlemen of Gloucestershire severally named who each gave a bond of £111 that Robert Whittington after his release should " give under his seal two general acquittances to Richard Oldcastle and Walter Hackluyt of all manner of personal actions from the beginning of the world to the feast of All saints following," upon which they were set at liberty. This lawless Mr. Hackluyt, it is to be feared, was of the family of the eminent prebendary and geographer of a later generation.

Dinmore even yet might offer choice facilities to the modern footpad if cycles and motors had not made his less heroic enterprises so much more risky than of old. But the traveller who would flinch from the long climb may take a wider circuit round the base of the hill, and by so doing he will see Hampton Court, one of the notable old places of the county and now owned by the Arkwright family. There was one, Sir Roland Leinthall, in the days of Henry IV, of whom Leland says : " He was yeoman of the robes to the King and being a gallant fellow, a daughter or near kinswoman of the King fell in love with him, and in continuance wedded him, whereupon after he fell into estimation he had £1,000 worth of land by the year given him of which lands he had Ludlow for part. This Leinthall was at Agincourt and took many prisoners there by which prey he began the new buildings at Hampton Court and brought from the hill a springe of water and made a little poole of it in the toppe of his home." Later on Hampton passed to the Conningsbys, of whom we said something in the first chapter. One Conningsby was with William III when he was shot at the Boyne, and was the first to apply his handkerchief to the wound. This same handkerchief was preserved at Hampton, together with an original portrait of Henry IV, given to Sir Roland Leinthall, the Agincourt hero. They are still, I believe, at Cassiobury, the Earls of Essex having

PRIORY CHURCH, LEOMINSTER.

succeeded through marriage to Hampton and sold it to the present owners.

It was one of these Conningsbys, though tradition wavers somewhat as to which, who cut a somewhat undignified figure through certain eccentric claims to various manors in the county and the methods by which he strove to enforce them. The story runs that he had a fancy for riding sword in hand to the door of peaceable squires and demanding, so to speak, their title deeds or their lives. When he turned up one day, however, on this fantastic mission at Sir John Goodyear's house of Burghope he found a man madder than himself, who did not take the visit as a joke at all but called at once for his horse, drew his sword and rode full tilt at his eccentric visitor. The latter, not accustomed to being taken quite so seriously, started for home at a gallop, and there was a great race across country for Hampton, Conningsby only just getting in and slamming the door as the choleric knight's sword clove the lintel above his head. This impulsive Goodyear, so lacking in humour as he surely must have been, paid dearly afterwards for his unreflective habits; for being inveigled on to a man of war by his naval brother who was his heir, he was murdered in the Bristol Channel. The fratricide, however, did not enjoy his ill-gotten honours, for speedy justice overtook him, and he was hung at Bristol together with his accomplices in the foul deed. Thus merrily wagged the Welsh border only two centuries ago.

Leominster is about five miles northward from the foot of Dinmore, and the whole of this district is among the most noted in Herefordshire for its apples. Yet the growers of this county and of England generally appear to let their trees for the most part grow at their own wild will, untrimmed and unpruned, and to make grass paddocks of the land they stand on. The British housekeeper knows only too well how necessary the apple is to the storeroom and how disproportionately dear. Now in Canada and the United States apples do not generally yield the grower one half the price that is paid here, low as even this seems when compared to what the consumer pays. I have seen the orchards of Nova Scotia, of Ontario, of the Pacific coast, of the northern and of the southern States, and done something more than see some of them. But in these countries, where land is of less value and labour much more valuable, and the price of fruit as I have said much lower, apple orchards are cultivated, pruned and tended with constant and assiduous care. The land is expected to give all its strength to the trees, yielding, say, ten to twenty pounds an acre, not to squander part of its sustenance on grass worth only one or two, and grass in itself is considered there as detrimental to the vigour of an

153

orchard. In a minor degree too it is not held as salutary for even well grown apple trees that their stems should be rubbing posts for stock, nor targets for the horns of playful or fly-tormented milk cows. Now even in Herefordshire, the premier apple county of England, these opinions do not seem to be generally held, the orchards being more often than not conspicuous for their picturesque disarray and the freshness of the perennial turf, which mats about the roots and catches the stray sunbeams that pierce the wilderness of boughs above. Yet cooking apples are sometimes threepence a pound even in Hereford.

Do farmers make so much money out of apples as to lack a stimulant for increasing gains ? Their private conversation, their conferences, and the local press suggest the very reverse. Yet every extra bushel in Herefordshire would mean nearly double the profit it does to the growers of Nova Scotia or British Columbia. The latter, by the way, has a seacoast climate much like Hereford or Devon, whose orchards, if memory serves me right, are equally the delight of the painter and the poet. In transatlantic orchards, those of the professed apple countries that is to say, every tree bears the mark of careful handling and constant supervision, with a view not only to its health and produce but to the ready and rapid gathering of the fruit. It would seem that no one but an acrobat could reach much of the fruit one sees swinging in English orchards. Perhaps the officials of west country horticultural societies could satisfactorily explain the reason for this immense difference of treatment, though I greatly doubt it. I have failed to gather any light on the subject from the farmers themselves, as with most of them custom is custom and there's an end of it. This past season was a very productive one, yet I feel quite sure from the appearance of the trees in August that there was nothing like the yield to the acre in the average Herefordshire orchard that is usually looked for in apple-shipping districts across the Atlantic, while as regards the soundness of the fruit it would be against every horticultural canon if the neglected tree did not suffer by comparison with the other.

I might also recall, for what it is worth, an incident somewhat to the point. During a drive one day in the south of the county we noticed a roadside orchard offering such a contrast to the average type that it might have been picked up in the Niagara district or the Anapolis valley and dropped down in Herefordshire. The trees were trim and carefully pruned, their trunks were limed and washed, and the ground beneath them worked clean by cultivator and hoe. A few days afterwards I was talking casually about the apple crop to a tradesman in a neighbouring town, who proceeded to tell me of a relative of his own from the Colonies who had bought a small orchard in the district and gone seriously to work upon it in a fashion that had caused his neighbours to prophesy speedy ruin to himself and destruction to his trees. To cut the story short he had actually quadrupled the former yield of the orchard, and the latter proved to be the identical one which had aroused our curiosity a few days previously. One can well understand how stone and perishable fruit plays all sorts of market pranks with its growers, but apples have none of these terrors, and seeing the inordinate price we often have to pay for them, and that growers thousands of miles away can afford to spend infinite time and labour on their orchards and still make money by shipping apples to us, surely there must be something amiss if British orchards are only doubtful sources of profit ?[1]

As a place of much greater importance in the past than in the present, though still the abode of over five thousand souls, a great deal might be said about Leominster if space allowed. With the exception of its noble priory church, the largest in the county and one of the oldest in England, there is not much here to arrest the attention of the passing traveller in its somewhat commonplace though narrow streets. Being at one time a great wool centre it flourished exceedingly by its cloth trade till the fifteenth century, when Worcester and Hereford, according to Leland, felt its prosperity so injurious to their interests that they schemed successfully for the alteration of its market day, which shifted the balance of trade to Leominster's detriment. Drayton waxed enthusiastic on ancient Leominster :—

> Where lives the man so dull in Britain's further shore,
> To whom did never sound the name of Leominster Ore,
> That with the silkworm's web for smallness doth compare ?

[1] The condition of the average British orchard is a matter of perennial astonishment to transatlantic visitors to this country. A week or so after the quite unauthoritative remarks perpetrated above had been put in type, a weighty article appeared in the *Field* on the British apple-grower, in which his elementary neglect of pruning and surface culture was made a leading point of, besides more venial and complicated deficiencies of treatment and marketing.

Leominster was an exceptionally "malignant" town in the Civil War, and when Waller took it he devoted some time to its reformation. The cheery little river Arrow, which rises in the Radnor moors, and another little stream join the Lugg close to the town, and mills were once plentiful for grinding the fine wheat grown in the neighbourhood.

"Lemester for bread, Weobley for ale," says Camden, is grown into a common proverb. In short it was the chief market town of the county in the middle ages, and the wool that made it so grew on the backs of the Ryland sheep, now a comparatively obscure breed but then most celebrated throughout England. Leominster claims to derive its name from Leofric, the West Mercian earl who like many other deserving men is better known as the husband of his wife, in this case no less a person than Lady Godiva. Like other border towns it spent much of its time fighting the Welsh, and our old friend William de Braose, who like other Marchers played the Welshman when it suited him, once burnt it to the ground. There are still a good many timbered houses in its streets but they do not show up very well. Entirely charming however is the beautiful arena of mellow turf at the side of the town. Used as a recreation space, and above all as a cricket ground, it is surrounded by a grassy terrace, and has for its single building a gem of a black and white residence contrived out of the old market hall. The occupant of another timbered house still standing, who in James II's time was member for the town, was fined the trifling sum of £100,000 by that vindictive monarch for incautious remarks on the Protestant succession. This I suppose was a playful formula for sending a man to prison for life, which would doubtless have been the incautious M.P.'s fate had not William III arrived and let him out.

But the church as already mentioned is the great glory of Leominster. The earliest part, its Norman nave, 125 feet long, dates from the beginning of the twelfth century. Its origin was a monastery founded here by Leofric, and outside its east end are the remains of the Saxon priory church, which was destroyed at the dissolution and consisted of an apsidal chancel with a processional path round the high altar and several chapels. The great central tower of the building, which was then cruciform, shared the same fate. The present church, imposing as it is, and of great width as well as of length, has been built at different periods, and was finally restored by Sir Gilbert Scott forty years ago.

DUCKING-STOOL IN LEOMINSTER CHURCH.

Two parallel roads run due north from Leominster to Ludlow, a matter of a dozen miles, both pleasant ones to travel in every sense of the word, particularly the more easterly of the two, which eventually drops into the valley of the Teme and runs up it through Wooferton and Ashford Bowdler. But I have already alluded to that group of villages, of which Weobley is the most southerly, whose timbered buildings call for especial notice even in this region of " black and white." Leominster would be the base for any curious pilgrim thither who used the railway, though for that matter a little branch line from thence to Kington goes actually through Kingsland and Pembridge, while the third of the trio, Eardisland, is near by. But by road the latter is the first you come to, lying like the others in a rich and gently waving country, through which those famous trouting streams, the Lugg and Arrow, ripple quietly after their noisy youth amid the Welsh hills.

Eardisland lies upon the Arrow—indeed the little river adds greatly to its charm : for gliding down between well-tended slopes of sward, and diving under the village bridge, a dam somewhere below forces back its waters at this spot into a broad and shallow lakelet, where ducks of strange plumage are skimming and the rising trout make rings on the still surface in summer evenings. Trees and flowering shrubs hang over part of the pool, and the rest is skirted by the village road and the old bridge under which the Arrow shoots as already noted into the mimic lake. On the nearer bank stands one of the hoariest and quaintest timbered houses in Herefordshire, known as the Old Vicarage. Beyond the pool and bridge a large Tudor pigeon house of red brick (I have only seen one other) rises in the centre of the picture, and scattered about on either hand on the edge of the pool and the velvety bank of the stream above are timbered cottages that lose nothing in some cases by having occupants that are conscious of the part their dwellings play in a quite idyllic scene. The actual village street straggles away behind for a brief distance and is unremarkable. It is this scattered outskirt which gathers about the pool and bridge and stream that gives Eardisland its modest fame. I have been here several times of late, and standing on the banks of the Arrow here it pleases me to think its limpid waters have

OLD VICARAGE, EARDISLAND.

made but a few hours' joyous pilgrimage from the remote hill villages of Radnor and the upland farms that lie under Brilley mountain and the heath-clad wastes of Squilver, where in former years I have spent pleasant hours in its merry company.

The " Old Vicarage " will speak for its exterior through our artist's pencil, and while the sketch was in progress the owner kindly showed me its hidden treasures, the immense oak beams and massive rafters that have bravely borne the burden of the heavy stone-tiled roof for over six centuries. The fact, too, that much old oak from elsewhere has been gathered in a lifetime within its low-pitched panelled chambers adds no little to its atmosphere.

Pembridge is a mile and a half away, and here you have a short street of timbered houses mostly of forlorn and uncared-for appearance which may or may not be in their favour. There is a fine old timbered hostelry in the village, and confronting it an equally ancient market house, consisting of a heavy roof resting on oak pillars and rafters. Pembridge was once a market town, like many of these ancient villages,

EARDISLAND. PIGEON HOUSE AND BRIDGE.

when England was a country of mainly rural habit and rustic people, and like the rest of the world without communications.

I should imagine that nowadays the market hall was mainly used to shelter the horses of farmers or waggoners from sun or rain, while their drivers found consolation in the inn tap-room hard by. The church is lifted high above the village street. It is a large cruciform building apparently of the Early Decorated period, with some striking lancet windows in triplets in the north transept, and recumbent effigies of a knight and three ladies, their feet on lions, lying in a row at the west of the nave.

But the feature of Pembridge church is its detached belfry of quite singular construction. The lower part is of stone and octagonal ; the main part above is of wood, supported by huge pillars composed of single tree trunks. Its outside appearance is of the pagoda type, and it is said to be of fourteenth century date. Happily some natives were working on the premises during my visit, and I did not have to search the parish for the keys of church or belfry, for

PEMBRIDGE BELFRY.

which I was thankful. The interior of this primitive structure was alluring. Full of time-worn beams and timber it was not unsuggestive of the inside of some ancient water-mill but for the pendent bell ropes, while in the chaos of woodwork above there was both a chime and a clock. The latter exploded the passing hour while we were inside with prodigious commotion, and reminded me that the sun was low, and that Ludlow, my destination, was fifteen miles away. My rustic guides, however, were properly patriotic about their belfry, and discoursed upon it in soft pleasant border Saxon with its odd touch of Welsh intonation and the inevitable " sure to be " that does duty as the indirect affirmative from Shrewsbury to Cardiff and as far into Wales as men can talk English.

It may or may not be advisable to keep churches locked, but it is a great trial to the curious stranger, and I could write a chapter on the hunts I have had after church keys. As often as not they are deposited at the remotest end of the village, and the functionary, usually of the feminine gender, who has charge of them, is just that type of individual who is naturally glad to turn an honest penny when harvesting and haymaking are in progress, and being very often not only a female but a lone one, you find yourself confronted by an empty house and a securely-fastened door. A trip into the country on these occasions is out of the question, but sometimes a neighbour pops her head out near by who thinks the keys may have been entrusted for the day to Mrs. Jones, who lives in the quarter you have just started from, and as directions from persons who have abode in one place all their lives are not always lucid, you find yourself knocking at the door of Mrs. Hughes, who is a fierce Dissenter and inwardly resents the imputation of guarding the key of a building whose interior, she thanks Heaven, she has never seen in her life. Occasionally, for in out-of-the-way villages I have noticed a praiseworthy sense of pride at the sight of a stranger evincing curiosity about the parish church, something approaching a hue and cry is raised when the keys are astray, which becomes embarrassing when a dozen different persons are laying you under a serious obligation. Then, again, when you have got them there are keys and keys. Some of them are fearsome weapons and do not readily work for strangers. I have had many anxious moments endeavouring to probe the mysteries of a yawning mediaeval lock with a Jacobean or Hanoverian key. For I admit at once that I do not like the company of the village dame in a church inspection. She is as a rule sublimely irrelevant and distracting. If uninterested she wears her silence with an air of resignation as if even the expected guerdon was as nothing when weighed against her abandoned soapsuds, and makes one feel uncomfortable. An eloquent dame is still worse, as her enthusiasm is apt to run wholly on things of to-day or yesterday. She drags you round to see the brass tablet just erected by the squire to a deceased and faithful gardener. She insists on disrobing the altar that you may inspect the new cloth worked by Lady Thingamy. She enlarges on the new warming apparatus, and cautiously but with no less redundancy on the virtues and defects of the present parson as compared with those of his predecessor and their respective families. If you endeavour to deflect the tide of her eloquence and ask her whether it is true that the church was built by William the Conqueror she will almost certainly reply "It was sure to be."

A sexton on the other hand is generally an acquisition, not because he has always any clear perception about the fabric of his church or its story, but for the manful and dignified way in which he supplies the void from his own imagination. Moreover he is often a character whose utterances are worthy of remembrance : nor again are you disturbed by any feeling that his time is of value. There are in his case no collars waiting to be ironed nor any children waiting to be spanked. And from a lower standpoint the prospective douceur may seem more cheering to him in the shape of a social pint or two imbibed with a conscience clear from the reproach of extravagance, and there is a familiar Welsh adage, *Allwyd calon cwrw da*, or, "The key to the heart is good beer."

Kingsland, the fourth of this quartette of villages, is the most northerly and lies near the Lugg, some three miles on the road from Eardisland to Ludlow. We are here still in a "plaine countrie," as the ancients have it, though fast drawing under the shadow of the Welsh hills. Kingsland is a long straggling village with some good blocks of black and white houses interspersed with orchards and other buildings, concerning some of which the less said the better. It has a further interest of its own, however, in having been swept over and over by the rush of battle on the bloody day of Mortimer's Cross. The natives point to a clump of oaks near the church as marking the spot where the victims of the great slaughter were entombed. But antiquarians hold that this is the site where Herewald, king of the Mercian South-saxons of Shropshire and Herefordshire, who lived and died here, had his stronghold ; hence the name of Kingsland.

Just apart from the village, its fine church, founded in the thirteenth century by the Edmund Mortimer of that epoch, lifts an embattled tower with much distinction above the surrounding country, and above a large graveyard bristling with headstones and monuments. Within it there is some old stained glass, a good stone screen, and in the nave some extremely graceful pointed arches springing from slender columns. One's attention is quickly arrested by a pathetic memorial tablet in the chancel of recent date, telling the tale of an entire family drowned at sea in the wreck of the *Drummond Castle* a few years ago. The name Gethin herein commemorated is interesting as one of the few rare and distinctive Welsh surnames. Indeed one may wonder at its infrequency

PEMBRIDGE OLD MARKET PLACE.

while Lloyd and Wynn are so common, for like these it was merely an adjective in common use formerly as a distinguishing soubriqet. Rhys Gethin, or Rhys the Powerful or the Terrible, suggests himself very naturally in the Mortimer territory as a leading instance of its use. For it was the warlike levies drawn from this very district by Sir Edmund Mortimer, its lord, that mainly choked the valley of the Lugg at Pilleth with their corpses in the first serious battle between Glyndwr and the royal forces commemorated by Shakespeare, and Rhys Gethin led the Welsh.

It was up its tributary too, the Arrow, but six or seven miles from Pembridge, that the fair Ellen Vaughan, or Ellen " Gethin," (" the Terrible ") of Hergest and of tragic memory lived with her sire, one of the lusty Bredwardine and Tretower stock so frequently alluded to. I have already told her story while telling of her country in another volume, and how she stabbed to death the slayer of her brother in the presence of the congregation during divine service. But there is another version, and as Kington and Hergest, which ancient mansion is still inhabited, would be easily visible from Kingsland church tower, the opportunity is a good one to give my readers that may recall the first the alternative of selecting the second, and quiet my own conscience. There is no disagreement whatever about the cause of the trouble, which was the killing of young David Vaughan, only son and heir of Hergest, by Shon Hir or Long John his cousin, son of a Breconshire Vaughan, the quarrel having arisen as to the headship of the Vaughan family. The fight, however, was a fair one as things went then, but David's only sister was passionately attached to him, and when they brought the lad's body back to Hergest, like Tennyson's lady though of a different mettle she neither spoke nor wept. But her silence was of a different import, for when in due course she heard of a forthcoming archery contest in Shon Hir's neighbourhood, at which he was a potential champion, she dressed herself in the garb of a man and taking her deceased brother's best bow and arrows traversed the intervening hills and put in an appearance on the scene of action just as her cousin had secured his expected victory. Posing as a youthful stranger from across the border, Ellen Vaughan caused something of a flutter by challenging the winner to a match, which he readily and somewhat comtemptuously accepted. So having fired the first shot with his usual precision, the unknown stripling next toed the mark and drew her bow with all her strength to the full length of the arrow and then played the trick that Howel Sele of Nannau had tried with such ill success upon the magic person of Glyndwr a few years earlier, but in this case with more fatal effect. For swinging suddenly round she planted the arrow in her cousin's heart instead of in the target, and in the confusion ensuing ran for her life and escaped. Ellen not unnaturally became a heroine, earned with good cause the sobriquet of " Gethin," and actually married later on a son of the Agincourt Vaughan of Tretower, who falling in the wars of the Roses left her a widow, while the bards, the celebrated Lewis Glyn Cothi among them, sang her praises in stirring verse which may still be read.

But there are many Saxon names among the Welsh on the

tombstones of Kingsland churchyard, and the countless admir-
ers of Mr. Stanley Weyman might be interested to hear that
several of the most conspicuous are, those of his immediate
and remoter forebears. The unique feature, however, of
Kingsland church is a curious " Volca chamber " adjoining
the north porch. It is thought to have been the cell of some
recluse, and contains what is apparently an open stone coffin
affixed to the wall.

Moving northwards out of Kingsland one is soon among
the level fields, where the followers of the Red Rose fell like

KINGSLAND.

the ripe corn which was falling when I was here before the
first rattle of the reaper, in the sore fight which made young
Edward, Earl of March, King of England. It is a particularly suggestive battlefield, for there, at the end of the level
tract of grain and pasture, the outer ramparts of the Welsh
hills rise in gently wooded slopes. Between them the road
winds up the glen towards Aymestrey and Wigmore Castle
five miles away, whence issued the Yorkist forces from that
last centre of Mortimer influence, as three distinct suns rose
on the second morn of the February of 1461.

> Three glorious suns each one a perfect sun,
> Not separated by the racking clouds,
> But severed in a pale, clear shining sky.

Two months previously the battle of Wakefield had been fought, with results disastrous to the House of York, followed almost immediately by a second defeat at Barnet, which once more placed the hapless Henry in the hands of his strenuous consort. The conflict had by now expanded from a mere barons' war, and had seized in some measure on the passions of the common people, and at the same time had taken shape to a certain degree, as a sectional struggle between the north and the south of the Trent. The interior Welsh, who still counted for something in military matters, and were to count for yet more a few years later, were mainly with the Tudors and the Red Rose, but the Welsh of the March and the English borderers were mainly Yorkist, as was natural enough when a representative of the Mortimers was making one more bid for the throne. Young Edward, Earl of March, was at Wigmore when the news came of the battle of Wakefield, the death of his father and most of his friends, the wholesale killing of distinguished prisoners, and the savage murder of his young brother, the Earl of Rutland, by the Black Clifford. He had started at once for the north with a strong force of borderers thirsting for revenge, when the news met him that Jasper Tudor, Earl of Pembroke, and his father, Owen Tudor, with an army chiefly Welsh and Irish, had appeared on the border and driven the Yorkist garrisons into Wigmore. Hastening back with all speed, he nearly surprised the Royalist army which lay here at Kingsland, but ultimately taking up a position at Mortimer's Cross under the hills, the two armies engaged in battle throughout the whole of the following day from nine in the morning till nearly sunset. Jasper Tudor charged one wing of the Yorkists with his Welshmen, and pushing them back fought a running and successful fight for nearly three miles, oblivious as those heady mediæval warriors so often were of the welfare of their partners. For Edward, opposing himself to Ormonde and his Irish, attacked them with his borderers, whose " brown bills " were too much, according to both the chroniclers and the poet, for the undisciplined Hibernians, who were driven into and through Kingsland village. Ormonde and Owen Tudor, with their knights and men-at-arms, made a desperate resistance, but deserted by their infantry they had nothing for it but to fall back. At this critical moment a band of Yorkists from Leominster arrived on the scene and intercepted Owen Tudor, who was taken to Hereford and executed with Sir John Scudamore and other leaders of distinction. And in the meantime, his son Jasper and his friends had struggled back to the field, only to find it covered with dead, mainly of their own people. They then effected a junction with Ormonde and the few who had remained with him, and a last desperate but futile effort was made to retrieve the day. The Earl Jasper, however, among others managed to escape and reached the continent in safety. In after years he achieved a fine revenge in the person of his nephew, Henry VII, whom he had watched over so carefully. Thirty-eight hundred Lancastrians bit the dust that day on these quiet pastures, where Hereford steers were now browsing and the hum of the incipient harvest rising above the hedgerows, while skirting the battlefield the Lugg murmurs among bushy alders over its gravelly bed, towards the orchards and

COTTAGES AT ORLETON.

the grey church tower of Kingsland. A month after the battle of Mortimer's Cross, a spot of such auspicious name and so appropriately adjacent to the great hill stronghold of the House of Mortimer, Edward was in London and on the throne. Roger Mortimer, the paramour of the she-wolf of France, had held the power without the honours of that exalted office. A young Earl of March again had been Richard II's heir, and his uncle, Sir Edmund Mortimer, as every one who has read Shakespeare (in this incident sufficiently accurate) will remember, essayed the division of England with Hotspur and Glyndwr. But a Mortimer, though only on the distaff side yet the holder of their honours and their great domains, had at last achieved the crown, and the Marches and the border no longer knew the great house that for three centuries had been famous, and for two had thrown a longer shadow over this corner of the kingdom than the king himself.

Mortimer's Cross is but a parting of four ways with a single ancient cottage hard by that might almost have witnessed the battle, and a roomy old-fashioned inn where those fortunate anglers who have rights on this prolific portion of the Lugg foregather, with an occasional wanderer perhaps who has a fancy for musing on forgotten battlefields. I admit a weakness myself for both forms of recreation, and Mortimer's Cross is a most alluring and secluded spot. The dominant woody hills, first promise of that upland arcady where Hereford and Radnor intertwine their confusion of leafy glen and fern-clad height and glancing waters; the green levels below so tempting for a wild charge of feudal cavalry or for the play of the long-bow then developed to its highest capacity, or for the free use of short sword, bill, and spear. How grimly silent these battles must have been to an onlooker, no smoke, no dust in winter, nor yet any great clamour, we may be quite sure after the first impact, for human lungs have limits, and men, I take it, had the sense to reserve their breath to save their heads if they had any superfluous store of it. The cries of the dying men and horses might well in such a fight as this have been the chief burden on the air to the timorous peasant who lurked in the heights above and was probably the sole spectator. Here, at any rate, in this sequestered nook a short-lived English dynasty was founded and the greatest of the border houses extinguished, not by the sword, but by promotion to a yet more exalted sphere. They will tell you in Hereford or Ludlow that there is nothing to see at Mortimer's Cross, but that there is a tolerable inn, where you can get lunch, which is perfectly true; but there is a good deal to think about if you have the wherewithal to stimulate your fancy.

We shall be at Wigmore later on, so I must cry halt before the pleasant five miles of road that leads there from Mortimer's Cross, following the limestone gorge of the Lugg to Aymestry, a somewhat idyllic hamlet with an Early English church, a bridge over the river and an old manor house (Yatton Court), with gardens and tall yew hedges sloping to the stream spread out just here in broad shimmering shallows. The road which carries the traveller hence to Wigmore is a section of the old Roman Watling Street; and I was almost forgetting that Aymestry is a classic name among geologists and furnished most valuable material to Murchison and Lewis in their valuable labours on the Silurian formation.

Pleasantly set amid the fields, a mile from Mortimer's Cross on the road to Ludlow, a large block of buildings provokes curiosity. This is Lucton Grammar School, noteworthy from its isolated situation, and not much less so from the period of its foundation, namely the unusual one of 1715, the founder being a benevolent London merchant by name Pierrepont. It owns property worth something like £2,000 a year, and close scholarships at Oxford and Cambridge, and gives a liberal education at a small cost to nearly a hundred scholars, who for obvious reasons are mainly boarders. Most of these old grammar schools, when detached from the support of a provincial town, have suffered either painless extinction or have been seized on by educational authorities for new departures. But Lucton would appear to have weathered the storm, and is as modern and up-to-date in appearance, in this sequestered spot, as if it were the recent experiment of some group of educational enthusiasts.

The direct road, however, from Mortimer's Cross to Ludlow, some eleven miles, traverses a country which has sufficient attractions, physical and otherwise, to fill a chapter of this book if space permitted. The first few miles are finely dominated by the south-western end of the great wooded ridge that runs out eastward from this border hill country and drops suddenly for almost a thousand feet on to the river, castle and town of Ludlow. Hereabouts it is known as Burcher Common, a fine untamed upland of steep, sheeny bracken wastes, sprinkled with birch and pine and oak, and merging anon into woodland; while white-timbered cottages glint here and there in the dells that break the rich drapery of the mountain side like the folds in some vast curtain. Spread out beneath are the parklands of Croft Castle, sprinkled with fine oak and chestnut timber. The castle itself is quadrangular with circular towers at the corners and crenelated front. But it has been so much altered and restored, first after the Civil War, during which it was dismantled, and then by Mr. Johns, of Hafod in Cardiganshire, that it would be too elaborate a subject, altogether, to grapple with here.

Mr. Johns married an heiress of the Knights, the great ironmasters, who purchased it from the Crofts. He was an ardent landscape gardener, as visitors to Hafod know, and the father of Colonel Johns, the scholar, antiquarian and poet. The Davies family have now been here for some generations. Within a few yards of the house is a quaint little church of ancient foundation, containing monuments of the Crofts, who lived here from the twelfth or thirteenth century till the reign of George III.

There are traditions here of Saxon thanes who survived the Norman Conquest and retained some measure of recognition, but they are hazy. In any case, for the centuries they were known to be here, the Crofts were prominent among the border houses, and produced warriors, statesmen and ecclesiastics of vigour and distinction. Sir John Croft married Janet, another daughter of Owen Glyndwr, and as it was after this period that the family chiefly distinguished itself, we may be permitted to fancy that the blood of the Welsh chieftain which coursed in its veins contributed in some sort to this result.

And so onwards to Burcher village, where some pretty timbered cottages and farmhouses, an ancient dovecot among them, fringed the highway, into the valley of the Teme. A prehistoric mound bearing a stately burden of great forest trees hangs high above the road, which undulates

YARPOLE BELFRY.

along the lower slope of the western ramparts of the vale. Wide outlooks over the latter delight the eye with a far-reaching landscape of pasture and grain field, of orchard, woodland and hop-field, of church tower and village. The hills beyond the Teme, spreading back to the ancient Chase of Wyre Forest, grow in stature till they reach the pointed crown of the Clee Hills, with their blue pale slopes and pinnacles of ruddy rock, some 1,700 feet above sea level. We leave Yarpole behind us on the right, where another detached wooden belfry makes its churchyard worth visiting to those who pass by it on the way to Kingsland.

Orleton lies just off our path, famous for its beautiful timbered Court, now occupied as a farmhouse by a well-known breeder of Herefords. Its panelled rooms are associated with Charles II after the Battle of Worcester, though he was never near here; while the room above the porch has unsupported traditions of Pope occupying it while courting Miss Blount, whose family owned the property. The best known of its members was that Thomas Blount, who lived and died in the seventeenth century, and left abundant and invaluable manuscripts concerning Herefordshire history now preserved at Belmont, near Hereford. The most famous native of Orleton, however, was Adam of that ilk, Bishop of Hereford, who was a fierce partisan of Roger Mortimer and the " she-wolf of France " against the hapless Edward II. When Queen Isabella and her paramour were at Oxford with their forces, Orleton preached a sermon before them and the assembled University from the text, " My head, my head acheth (2 Kings iv. 19), meaning the king's,

ORLETON COURT.

not his own, and suggested its removal by way of a cure. When Edward was at Berkeley Castle in his enemies' hands,

NOTE.—Since writing the above, and about the time of the urgent appeal of Oxford and Cambridge for funds, the whole Orleton estate was bequeathed by its late owner, the Rev. — Blount, to the wealthy American University of Yale.

Orleton is said to have conveyed his patron's order for his destruction in the well-known line, the purport of which depended on the situation of a comma, and thus left the bishop a ready loophole in case of after-difficulties : *Edwardum occidere nolite timere bonum est.* He was afterwards ambassador to France and Bishop of Winchester.

Orleton is a scattered village lying about a prattling brook threaded by devious ways, rich in pleasant nooks and corners,

DOVECOT IN RICHARD'S CASTLE.

and possessing another large timbered house, besides the Court above mentioned, of seven or eight gables. A mile or two nearer Ludlow is Richard's Castle, high perched upon the crown of the western ridge, its fine old church with detached belfry cutting the skyline. The view up and down the Teme valley from its wide-spreading graveyard, so singularly rich in handsome and ancient monuments, is among the treasures of recent memory to the writer. Adjoining the precincts. a densely-wooded mound and moat still hold a few smothered fragments of the once powerful castle, which was originally built by those pre-conquest Normans, whose settlements and doings at Ewyas Harold and here we discussed so fully in the second chapter of this book. Rank underwood and briars riot over the crumbled walls and choke the encircling moat, while the tall oak and ash trees which spring high above out of the tangled chaos are clothed to their topmost limbs with thick mantles of ivy. In the Civil War, too, the acquisitive Roundhead, Colonel Birch of Weobley, gained a little victory here over some local Royalists. There is also near by a curious and noted well, which remains perennially full of minute bones of fishes, or actually of frogs, and was thus noticed by the industrious Drayton:

Of that prodigious Spring he
   wondering as he passed
That little fishes bones continually doth cast.

This fine old church, so curious within and so nobly placed and full of memories, has been recently displaced as a regular centre of worship by a large modern me-

AT ORLETON.

morial church, to a recent purchaser of the property from its former owners, the Salweys, whose ancestor, a Roundhead officer, in turn acquired it from the Lyttletons. The village below the long slope contains many more timbered buildings, notably a very fine farmhouse with a beautiful sixteenth century dovecot. Skirting the grounds of Moore Park, the road drops down to the valley turnpike from Leominster: a mile or two further it dips with another short pitch to the Teme, and crossing the long stone bridge into Shropshire climbs the steep streets of the most beautiful and distinguished country town in England.

CHAPTER VIII

LUDLOW

The towne doth stand most part upon a hill,
Built well and fayre with streats both long and wide,
The houses such where straungers lodge at will,
As long as there the counsell lists abide.
Both fine and cleane the streates are all throughout
With condits cleare and wholesome water springs,
And who that lists to walk the toone about
Shall find therin some rare and pleasant things.
Churchyard.

THE position I ventured to assign to Ludlow in the closing sentence of the last chapter was no mere fervent expression of local patriotism, for I was never seriously in Ludlow till this past summer in my life. Nor is such unqualified appreciation of the south Shropshire town stimulated by any of those prolonged holiday associations which are apt to make men and women lose sight of the perspective, even when describing mere homely scenes. There are towns of its size perhaps as quaint and boasting as many ancient buildings, but they do not in all probability crown an eminence amid really striking scenery, nor yet again share such distinction of site with one of the finest mediæval castles in England, and one possessed of a military and political history unique in the annals of British castles. It is this combination of natural and architectural charm with its intense historical interest that gives Ludlow such peculiar fascination. Other great border fortresses were centres of military activity from the conquest to the battle of Bosworth, but when Ludlow laid aside its armour and burst out into the graceful embellishments of Tudor architecture, it became in a sense the capital of fourteen counties, the seat of the President and Council of Wales and the Marches, and remained so for nearly two hundred years.

Let us take a bird's-eye view of the town and castle before

endeavouring to tell their story. To this end I would drop down to the wide hurrying river on the south or west side, crossing it by the old Norman bridge at Ludford, or by the later one at Dinham, and climb three hundred feet or so up the grassy slopes of Whitcliff towards the fringe of the forest, which spreads hence to Mortimer's Cross, over high hills and deep vales an unbroken mantle of foliage. Thence look down for a moment over Ludlow and you will not grudge the trifling climb. A clean old town of red and grey complexion, with roof and gable and even the lines of its steep streets showing clear in the smokeless air, covers the larger half of the outstanding ridge, while on its crest rises the finest parish church in Shropshire, if not in England, where sonorous chimes fling familiar melodies far and wide over the surrounding country with the passing hours. On the western and highest portion of the ridge the noble fortress, with its long array of hoary towers and curtains, crowns the steep slopes where lofty trees seem straining upwards in vain efforts to soften with their topmost foliage the grim outlines of the battlements. In the gorge at the foot of the town and castle on the hither side, and expanded here into broad and rapid shallows the river races under the massive arches of its two stone bridges, to vanish from view behind the ancient church and Court of Ludford, perched high above it on the Hereford shore. Away behind and high above both town and castle the Titterstone and Brown Clee lift their green slopes and quarried summits to almost the height of mountains, and being but a few miles distant dominate the landscape with singular distinction. Far to the northward from the castle rock spread the green levels of wood and pasture through which the Corve and the Onny urge their bright streams over beds of gravel and red sandstone to meet the Teme; and all about and far up this trio of valleys are clustering hills, densely wooded for the most part, even to Wenlock Edge, till the dimmer heights of rugged Caradoc and the wild uplands of the Long mynd give a mountain background to a view that does not readily fade if you have beheld it almost daily for many weeks.

I purpose to give some outline of Ludlow's story before taking note of such monuments as survive to remind one of it, and it is a little singular that even the local chroniclers, in whom Ludlow has been fortunate, have nothing but conjecture to offer upon its condition prior to the Norman Conquest. The late Mr. Wright, the most exhaustive historian of Ludlow, is

LUDLOW.

uncertain upon the subject. Mr. Eyton, the most able historian of Shropshire, thought that a Saxon town named Luda stood here and even contained a mint, for Saxon and Anglo-Danish coins bearing its stamp are extant. But the ruin caused by constant incursions of the Danes up the Severn was complete in this corner of England, and whole districts are described in Domesday as desolate that had been previously populous and cultivated. The Conqueror sent his ablest commanders to settle on the Welsh border, for the obvious reason that it had to be held against a warlike and as yet unvanquished foe. And it is significant that the Welsh became far more aggressive, and remained so after the Norman advent than in the days of the Saxons. The common peril of the Danes had probably acted on both nations. And furthermore the Saxons had limits to their land hunger, being by then perhaps agriculturists first and warriors afterwards, not as the Normans, soldiers and land-grabbers by profession, nor like the latter could they build the stone castles necessary to permanent occupation had they seriously sought it. Tribute was readily paid when convenient by the Welsh princes even to the king, sometimes by request in the curious form of wolves' heads, as the notion of an island suzerain in London was an old tradition devoid of offence. It was after the conquest, when the Welsh were goaded by Norman aggression, or what was worse were tempted for the sake of beeves and loot or revenge, to take sides in Anglo-Norman quarrels, that they became such a scourge to the neighbouring counties and turned out such a relatively large number of men inured to war and ready for any devilment.

But of the great families founded by Norman soldiers sent to look after the Welsh, the Mortimers and the Lacys were most concerned with Ludlow, and Roger de Lacy of Ewyas in the time of Rufus made a first beginning of the castle from which the town sprang. The constant strife between kings and barons, the confiscations and the restitutions ensuing therefrom, unless probed with almost antiquarian zeal, are a purposeless relation, and would, I feel sure, be skipped by the gentle reader. It is enough that Ludlow played an animated part in Stephen's wars, and the only incident worthy of general note is when that valiant soldier, if he were nothing more, in vain efforts to recapture his own castle, saved the person of the Scottish king's son whom he was carrying about with him as a hostage. This young man was not denied the luxury of taking a hand in every form of warlike diversion that was afoot, and being over-venturesome it seems that on the occasion in question he was successfully hooked by a grappling-iron flung from the walls, and was in danger of being ignominiously hoisted up to a change of domicile that might or might not have proved less indulgent. But the king, from what motives it would be ungenerous to inquire, rushed valiantly forward at great personal risk, as he saw his guarantee of Scotland's goodwill in the act of being torn from his protection in such fantastic fashion, and prevented the mishap.

But before Stephen's death he had captured the castle, and mistrustful, as well he may have been, of both Mortimers and Lacys he confided it to a favourite and doughty warrior, one Joce de Dinan, a knight, some suppose, of Brittany, but others that he took his title from Dinham, as Ludlow was then called. Joce may fairly be styled the second founder of Ludlow, seeing that he so greatly enlarged and improved the castle, and in fact made it as regards military details very much what we see it to-day. This enterprise, no doubt, was due as much to self-preservation as a taste for architecture, since the Mortimers and Says, the one at Wigmore and the other reaching south as far as Richard's castle, were both unpleasantly near, and entertained a cordial hatred for the interloper. Joce and Hugh Mortimer, then head of his house, were soon at open war, and the former, too weak in men for the moment to meet his enemy in the field, found himself unable to venture out with hawk or hound in safety. This became intolerable, and so getting a clue to Mortimer's movements he laid an ambush and captured the redoubtable borderer while taking his rides abroad unattended, and shut him up in the tower of the castle which still bears his name. He was soon after allowed to purchase his liberty by the payment of 3,000 marks, all his plate and horses, and possibly by some agreement to leave Joce alone for a time. The Lacys, also represented by a Hugh, then took Joce in hand, and the strife waxed hot in the valley of the Teme, its motive being the time-honoured one of estates to which both parties laid claim. Many of the incidents in this bloody and protracted strife have been preserved to us in a lengthy and curious family history known as *The Romance of the Fitzwarrenes*. It is supposed to have been written by a minstrel of that family early in the thirteenth century, and relates not only some incidents concerning Ludlow, which passed about that time to the House of Fitzwarrene, but

a whole store of much less credible adventures in which members
of the family took part.

Now Fulke Fitzwarrene, born to the castle and honour of
Whittington in Salop, was seven years old, when, according to
current custom, it was thought well to place him in the household of some valiant lord who would train him up in those
arts of war which he must cultivate if he would hope to hold
his own in the turbulent world of the twelfth century. Joce
de Dinan, it so happened, was the instructor selected by his
father for young Fulke, and the boy had been some ten
years with him when the De Lacy troubles broke out, and gave
him his opportunity. Early one summer morning, says the
Fitzwarrene chronicler, Joce mounted the highest tower in the
castle to look out for enemies, and had not to look far, far just
to the south of the " town of Dinan," or Dinham, he saw the
gleam of armour and the banners of the De Lacys and a great
array of their following hastening to attack him. The alarm
was sounded instantly, and Joce despatched in haste a part
of his knights with arbalisters and archers to defend the bridge
over which I conducted the reader into Ludlow in the last
chapter. In a short space he followed himself with five hundred
knights and men-at-arms and the burghers of the town, and
after a sharp conflict beyond the river put the enemy to
flight. But Walter de Lacy, who was apparently commanding
for his father, then absent in Ireland, was cut off from his men
in the *mêlée* and presumably also from his shortest road home, as
he was presently espied by Joce riding at hot haste by himself
up the river bank towards Bromfield. The lord of Ludlow,
without waiting for support, dashed off at once in pursuit of
his enemy, and overtaking him within sight of the castle found
him already disabled by a wound, and was in the act of taking
him prisoner when three of De Lacy's knights, seeking
no doubt the same line of flight, came suddenly on the two
chieftains and at once set upon Joce.

Now it so happened that Joce's lady and her two daughters
Sybil and Hawyse, who had anxiously watched the fight from
the castle walls, became also witnesses of this last incident, a
thing by no means improbable to any one familiar with the commanding prospect obtained from the castle over the fields
below upon the Bromfield side. When the ladies beheld the
imminent peril of their lord they filled the castle with their
shrieks, which quickly brought Fulke Fitzwarrene on the
scene, for though the young man was seventeen he had not

been considered of sufficient experience to take part in the morning's entertainment. To his anxious queries Hawyse replied with hot scorn, "Hold thy tongue, thou resemblest little thy father who is so bold and strong; thou art but a coward and ever will be. Seest thou not where my father who has cherished and bred thee with so much care is in danger of his life for want of help, and thou art not ashamed to go up and down safe without paying any attention?" Stung to the quick by the maiden's speech, Fulke rushed into the great hall, covered his head with a rusty old helmet that was lying there, and seized a Danish axe, the only weapon to hand. He then ran to the stable and appropriately completed his outfit by snatching a draught horse from its stable and leaping on its back. Thus provided, Fulke lumbered across the meadow on his awkward mount at the best pace he was able, and arrived at the scene of conflict just as his guardian was being overborne by the numbers of his opponents. To quote the original, "Fulke had a foul helmet which covered his shoulders and at the first onset he smote Godard de Braose, who had seized his lord, with his axe and cut his backbone in two parts, and remounted his lord. Fulke then turned towards Sir Andrew de Reese and smote him on his helmet of white steel that he split it down to the teeth. Sir Arnold de Lys saw well that he could in no manner escape, for he was sorely wounded and surrendered to Sir Joce. The Lacy defended himself, but he was soon taken. Now is Sir Walter de Lacy taken and Sir Arnold de Lys and they are led over the river towards the castle of Dinan." Then spoke Sir Joce, "Friend burgher, you are very strong and valiant; and if it had not been for you I should have been dead before this, I am much bound to you and shall be always. You shall live with me and I will never fail you." Then the lad answered and said, "Sir, I am no burgher, do you not know me, I am Fulke your foster-child." "Fair son," said he, "blessed be the time that I ever nourished you, for a man will never lose his labour that he does for a brave man."

The distinguished prisoners were treated with kindness and courtesy, particularly by the ladies, and most particularly of all by a very gentle damsel "Marion de la Bruere," or "Marion of the Heath," who fell a victim to the fascinations and fair promises of Arnold de Lys, for Arnold was *jeuene bachiler e bele grantment* even to her own undoing. Under such conditions, and as he promised to marry her directly he was free, she was easily persuaded to connive at the escape of Arnold and his chief, which was effected by the time-honoured method of tying sheets and napkins together and dropping out of a window. "Then Sir Walter and Sir Arnold all alone went their way on foot, and at the dawn of day came to Eyias to the castle of de Lacy. But Joce De Dynan rose early and went to his chapel within the castle and heard the service of God, and then mounted the highest tower in the third ward of the castle, which is now called by many Mortimer's Tower. Joce surveyed the country and saw nothing but what was well. He descended from the tower and caused the horn to be sounded for washing, and sent for his prisoner Sir Walter, for he honoured him so much that he would never wash or eat before he did the same. The prisoners were sought everywhere ; it was in vain, for they were escaped."

Sir Joce does not seem to have taken the matter much to heart, but De Lacy's good treatment had not mitigated the bitterness of his defeat, and he sent for more troops to his father, who was engaged with Strongbow in that Norman-Welsh invasion of Ireland for which the innocent Saxon of to-day receives the curses of his Hibernian contemporaries. So Sir Walter de Lacy continued the war with Joce de Dinan till the business became such an intolerable nuisance, even for those times, that their neighbours put pressure on the combatants and brought about a reconciliation. The sequel to this part of the story will be obvious even to those who do not read novels, though the brilliant wedding between young Fulke and Hawyse in the wonderful circular chapel just built by the bride's father, and still partially standing in the castle, which took place immediately, has the disadvantage of being an historical fact. The Bishop of Hereford, Robert de Betune, came all the way to tie the nuptial knot, and the ceremony was followed by a fortnight's carousal.

After these auspicious events the whole family party left Ludlow for a visit to Berkshire, Joce entrusting the castle to thirty of his knights and seventy soldiers "for fear of the Lacy and other people." The fear was well founded, and Joce had left a lady in the castle who more than neutralized the thirty knights and seventy soldiers. For our very gentle maiden, Marion of the Heath, had shirked the journey with her friends by feigning illness, and at the first opportunity sent word to Arnold de Lys, hinting that the window she had let him out of was at his service for re-entering at any time he liked to visit her. Arnold must have held her in light esteem, for the opportunity took a practical rather than an amorous shape in his eyes, and he at once suggested it to De Lacy as a means, though a shabby one enough for both of them, according to modern ethics, of capturing the castle. He played on De Lacy's fears, too, by telling him he had learnt through Marion that Joce had gone to collect more soldiers for a great attack on Ewyas.

Lacy was nothing loth, and a moonless night was appointed for the atttempt. Maid Marion had been advised of her lovers

LUDLOW CASTLE.

coming, and had sent De Lys a silken cord representing the exact height of the fatal window from the ground. Arnold kept the assignation with a ladder of leather, but with a thousand men at his back as well, some of whom hid in the castle pleasaunce by the river, and the rest in the woods of Whitcliff on the further bank. The unsuspecting lady was punctually at the window, and dropping a cord to her lover the ladder was soon hauled up and made secure and its owner within the tower. But while Arnold repaired to his lady's chamber the ladder remained, and before daybreak a hundred armed men were climbing stealthily up it. To curtail the Fitzwarrene chronicle, the sentinel was hurled from the wall, the knights and soldiers were slain in their beds, and " many a sheet which was white at even was all reddened with blood," the gates were opened and the main body of De Lacy's men took possession of the castle. But the gist of the story remains to be told, for the Maiden of the Heath, when she realized the havoc she had wrought, was seized with remorse and shame and anger, and belied the gentle character ascribed to her in the chronicle. For snatching the treacherous Arnold's sword she plunged it into his undefended body, and then threw herself from the window and brake her neck.

The window from which this hapless lady leaped is described as looking down on " Lyneye," a name still retained by the quarter immediately below the highest perched and north-western wall of the castle, which here drops on to a steep wooded slope and faces the open country away from the town and all sign of humanity. Nearly every midnight or thereabouts for a month it fell to me to traverse the quarter of a mile or so of dark lonely lane that leads beneath it to the falls of the river, and a spot more calculated to invite the restless wanderings of a despairing and guilty spirit, and to demand the presence of a spectral visitant of some kind I never saw. But though the savage grey towers far above shone betimes in the moonlight, and the tall trees below rustled weirdly in the night breeze, and the rush of the river over the weir rose and fell, as is the wont of falling water, in the silence of night, I looked in vain for the wraith of the hapless Maiden of the Heath and finally gave up the quest.

In the meantime the feelings of Joce and Fulke, who were enjoying themselves at Lambourne in Berkshire, when they heard the news, may be left to the imagination. But what actually happened was their arrival with 7,000 men before Ludlow, which De Lacy had strongly manned, not only with his own forces but with subsidies sent from Ireland. The besiegers were encamped at Caynham, then a small castle, now a well-known seat, two miles from the town. A series of vigorous attacks were successfully repulsed, but when De Lacy attempted sallies he was badly worsted. Joce's people, however, contrived to burn down the massive door of the outer ward with a fire of bacon grease, and thus made good their footing within.

De Lacy, now driven to despair, fell back on the usual resort of the border baron, and called in the Welsh, who responded cheerfully with twenty thousand men, and duly reached Ludlow. This turned the tables altogether on Joce de Dinan, who, after an obstinate resistance at Caynham, made a desperate attempt to cut his way through the Welsh. It was useless, however, for he himself and most of his knights who remained alive were captured and cast into the dungeons of their own castle. Fulke Fitzwarrene made another attempt to rescue his foster-father, but was himself attacked and wounded by no less a person than Owen Cefeiliog, prince of Powys-Ucha, a famous Welsh warrior, an astute politician, and author of that immortal poem, *The Hirlas Horn*. Fulke escaped, however, with Owen's broken lance point in his body and managed to reach Gloucester, where King Henry was staying. The king received him cordially, made his wife Hawyse a lady of the Queen's Chamber and sent peremptory orders to De Lacy to set his prisoners free and evacuate Ludlow. Henry II was generally obeyed, even by border barons, and Joce soon joined his son-in-law at court. He died soon afterwards, however, at Lambourne, and Fulke, who though he lost his father in the last conflict had by now a son of his own name, was endowed by the king with the castle of Ludlow and the honour of Corvedale. He distinguished himself greatly in the ceaseless Welsh wars, and was created lieutenant of the Marches, and through Richard's brief reign remained in high favour. At his death the young Fulke, the eldest of his five sons, maintained the family honours untarnished till the ill-conditioned John came to the throne, when all was changed.

For it seems that when children together at King Henry's court, John smote Fulke one day over the head with a chessboard in a passion at losing a game to him, whereupon Fulke knocked him senseless. On being restored to consciousness John went whining to his father, who curtly intimated that it served him right. So when the prince came to the throne he proceeded to strip Fulke of some of his possessions, whereat the other repaired to Westminster and spoke his mind before the court with remarkable candour, a proceeding which, followed by still more strenuous action impossible to relate here, left him in time a landless man and an exile in Brittany. Fulke had managed, however, to carry some of his mother's movable treasures with him, and now he and his brothers and several cousins crossed over to England, and gathering round them, mainly from the Welsh borders, other venturous spirits ill-used by the king, or the world, began a serious career of outlawry in the active and aggressive sense of the word.

Their adventures as related in the Fitzwarrene Romance are of a most stirring and really entertaining kind, and are illuminated by much practical joking at the expense of the king, who was sorely tormented by this high-born gang for several years. They lay in woods, and their operations were mainly in Shropshire, but being constantly pursued by swarms of knights sent out by the king, they frequently changed their venue to places as remote as Kent and the New Forest and the Scottish border. They entered castles, treating the owners with courtesy or harshness according to their politics. They plundered merchant trains, and sometimes even assumed oriental disguises, and went to court either to achieve the escape of some captured friend or for the mere sake of out-witting King John, who is represented as in a state of perpetual frenzy at his inability to catch Fulke and his troop. Twice, indeed, they actually caught the king in their turn, making him swear on each occasion to proclaim their pardons as soon as liberated. The first oath he broke, the second he kept, and ultimately restored Fulke to favour and to the Whittington estates. The famous outlaw baron served afterwards in Ireland and died blind and in the odour of sanctity at Whittington, being buried in the priory that he had there founded. Much of this singular tale was doubtless written for the honour and glory of the Fitzwarrene family, but curiously enough frequent entries in the Rolls corroborate the main fact of the outlawry of Fulke, the position he assumed, his pardon, and finally the restitution of his estates in 1204. On the same Rolls are the names of his companions included in the pardon. Fifty-four of these are entered, many of them scions of noted houses.[1]

The Mortimers and De Lacys would seem the natural owners or custodians of Ludlow, but as a matter of fact it was generally held by the Crown as a defence against the aggression of those powerful houses. All sorts of sturdy warriors filled this critical post, or failed to fill it, till the Mortimers, in the person of the most famous of their many Rogers, absorbed Ludlow by marriage with its heiress in the reign of Edward II. Just prior to the Wars of the Roses, Richard Plantagenet, Duke of York, successor to the now extinct Mortimers through the female line, lived chiefly in Ludlow, till Parliament elected him protector of the kingdom on Henry's mental collapse.

[1] See note at end of chapter.

In the ensuing struggle Ludlow was of course a great Yorkist centre. Early in October of the year 1459 the fields by Ludford Bridge, where Joce de Dinan and other heroes innumerable had engaged so often in deadly pastime, which was the business of their lives, were within an ace of becoming the scene of one of the greatest battles in the York and Lancaster wars. For the Yorkist forces had actually entrenched themselves with cannon in the meadows, where agricultural shows are now held, and the king's army, numbering 60,000 men, were encamped in front of them burning with revenge for their recent defeat at Blore Heath, in Shropshire. But a certain Sir Andrew Trollope, a veteran soldier with a body of veteran troops from Calais, was the hope of the Duke of York and his army. A council of war, held in the evening, decided that an attack should be made at daybreak on the king's army. But Sir Andrew and his veterans changed t h e i r politics and their side in the night, which created a situation that left nothing for it but an i m m e d i a t e *sauve qui peut* of the Yorkist leaders and a stampede of the Yorkist army. The duke

THE CASTLE CHAPEL.

and his son, the Earl of Rutland, made for Ireland and got there. The Earls of Warwick, Salisbury, and March fancied the continent and got there also, landing at Calais. Ludlow thus lay at the mercy of the Lancastrians and was shown little, being sacked of everything but " the bare walls." There was the usual carnival of blood and executions, and the ensuing excitement to the victors of confiscations.

But we must not get further involved in the Wars of the Roses. It will be enough to say that Ludlow, being Edward's own town, was conspicuous as a combatant and a sufferer, and reaped rich reward when the good time came in the way of favourable charters and franchises. Edward IV made the first attempt to bring that outside legislation to bear on the turbulent Marches of Wales which Henry VIII perfected. For he created his eldest son Prince of Wales in 1472, and sent the child and his younger brother with their half-brothers, the Marquis of Dorset and Sir Richard Grey, to Ludlow castle under the guardianship of their uncle, Anthony Woodville, Lord Rivers. Here a council was appointed of which Alcock, Bishop of Worcester, was president. This little court and government sat at Ludlow till King Edward's death in 1483, when the lads were brought to London, and as every schoolboy knows, done to death by that wicked uncle of our Mrs. Markham period, Richard the hump-back.

Whether the Ludlow government and council had much effect upon the Marches of Montgomery, Brecon, Radnor, Monmouth and Glamorgan, deprived by the late war of so many of such heady chiefs and barons as had administered rough and capricious justice there, it is hard to learn. But Henry VII at any rate thought the plan a good enough one to follow, and sent his son Arthur, as Prince of Wales, to Ludlow soon after his birth in 1486. Here this promising youth remained till his lamented death sixteen years later ; for much of the time under the guardianship of the wealthiest and most distinguished Welshman of his day, Sir Rhys ap Thomas, a noted leader in the battle of Bosworth and supporter of Henry VII. The king himself came frequently to Ludlow in these years ; the castle was kept up in semi-royal magnificence, and altogether it was a place of high renown. Prince Arthur's untimely death, however, within its walls in 1502 terminated the period of thirty years, during which Ludlow was not merely the residence of the Prince of Wales but his official seat of government. The young prince's death, just after his marriage with Catherine of Arragon, was a deep grief to his father, and doubtless had much to do with that decline of interest in his native province which caused Welshmen and the March folk to accuse the first Tudor king of ingratitude.

But in ceasing to be a royal residence, Ludlow did not lose the substance of its official dignity, for the Prince's council was continued as a court of jurisdiction for the government of

Wales under a lord president who sat in the castle. Successive prelates occupied this distinguished post, but there is no evidence that Welshmen or borderers stood much in awe of it, till the advent of Bishop Lee in 1535, a date only less famous than that of 1282 in the annals of Wales. For it was now that, importuned by petitions from Wales and urged by Lee and others, Henry VIII enacted those vital ordinances which obliterated Marcher rule, turned the Marches into Shires, like those of north Wales and England, and for the first time gave Wales regular representation in Parliament. In short, Henry by a stroke achieved the complete political union of the two countries. This may seem a small matter compared with the number of wives he made away with to persons who think carelessly in modern figures, and reck nothing of what Wales

THE WEIR, LUDLOW.

and the Marches meant to an England not yet united to Scotland, with a thinly peopled north and with Ireland a distant war-smitten colony. It was a propitious time too, for dethroning the forty odd Lord Marchers, most of them Norman with a strong strain by now of Welsh blood, and a few of them native Welsh with a strain of Norman blood.

The Wars of the Roses had broken the thread of many an arrogant hard-hitting line. Their people had got out of hand, and such lawless chaos prevailed that not only the average Welshman or borderer but these privileged Palatine nobles themselves were not wholly averse to relinquishing honours that in former days they would have defended to the death. Moreover a Welsh Tudor was on the throne, and Celtic Wales felt that now the ancient prophecies were fulfilled. The motives for racial hate and strife had ceased, and peace and union had come to them as it were with honour, and they now prayed to be made in every respect an integral part of the kingdom ; for even the old Edwardian shires of the north were not yet represented in parliament. The further fact that the Tudor king had personally inherited the great Mortimer and Lancaster interests on the March and the Palatinate of Chester, still further facilitated the reform. Another mitigating circumstance was the general distribution of church property that was then impending, and there was proportionately more of this upon the border than in any part of England.

Bishop Lee was the first President of the council to take his coat off and face the cleansing of the Augean stable of the Marches. Shropshire, Cheshire, Hereford and even Worcester were all under the jurisdiction of the Ludlow court, for their western portions were as lawless as Wales. The well known Shropshire family of Kynastons, for instance, had recently demanded a special act of parliament " for the great abbomination as well of murthers as of robberies and other greate and inordynat offences commytted by them." The Crofts for similar reasons called for special legislation. While combating the licence of the border aristocracy, Lee and his council did not overlook the misdeeds of the proletariat. A beggar was thrown into prison for declaiming in a village alehouse that " he wished the King's head were boiled in a pot and he would be the first to drink of the broth." A farmer was charged with attributing the bad weather to his Majesty, having doubtless heard from his grandfather the achievements of Glyndwr in this particular. " Yt ys long of the Kyng," remarked this rash bucolic, " that this wedre is so troublous and I wene we shall nevir have better while the Kyng reigneth and therefore it maketh no matter if he be knocked or patted on the heed." As the pronouncement in question was delivered on the road home from market, and the orator no doubt in that beatific condition known to-day on the border as " market peart " his arrest would surely seem a somewhat harsh proceeding. One Robert ap Roger's accusation, let slip at Wigmore, that the king was out of the pale of the holy church as he put down holy days, robbed saints and churches of their due, was the more treasonable as the more logical and he doubtless suffered for it.

If Henry's reforming zeal helped to soothe the ruffled dignities of the greater people with substantial sops, it proportionally irritated the poor of the border, who lost their alms-givers and the sheet anchors of their faith and gained nothing. Carrying away widows and heiresses and making forced marriages with them seems to have been another popular form of escapade as it was in Ireland much later. But when Bishop Lee died in 1543, the Duke of Northumberland and Herbert, Earl of Pembroke, broke the ecclesiastical reign in the Presidential chair of the Ludlow court. Then more bishops followed, till in 1559 the famous Sir Henry Sidney came and remained in office twenty-seven years. The middle portion of these years he spent in Ireland as Lord Deputy, retaining however his office and his interests in the Ludlow government. But all the earlier and the later ones he worked hard at Ludlow, expending his time, his talents and his money without stint, like the great gentleman and able ruler that he was. Among other things he brought pure water by pipes into the town and castle, and his provisions for it are still in use. Many of the Tudor additions and embellishments are his work, for which as well as for many other expenditures in his government, he was only partially reimbursed. It was the scanty thanks as well as the unpaid debt which inspired the somewhat pathetic inscription placed by the great Elizabethan over the gate of the inner ward a few years before his death:—

HOMINIBUS INGRATIS LOQUIMINI LAPIDES ANNO REGNI REGINÆ
ELIZABETHÆ.

In a letter written from Ludlow to Sir Francis Walsingham in 1583 concerning the marriage which was to connect the two families, Sir Henry Sidney, after recounting his services rendered to the queen, concludes in this pathetic fashion :—
"The Queen will not be moved to reward me. I have not now so much ground as will feed one mutton. My lady is gone with small pox which she got by continually nursing her Majesty in that sickness. I am now fifty-four years of age, toothless and trembling, £5,000 in debt and £30,000 worse than at the death of my dear King and master, Edward VI."
Sydney died at Ludlow in 1587, and his body was carried with great pomp to Worcester and thence to his home at Penshurst. He found on taking office that matters in the council and in the regions it governed had fallen back since Lee's time. Monmouthshire oddly enough was the worst offender : " So many manslaughters, robberys, theftes :

such fighting and quarrelling and manifold offences that no county within the commission is so much misliked." It seems to have been the old story : masters and magistrates and sheriffs upholding the misdeeds of their own servants and retainers and turning every groom's quarrel into a family feud. It is a curious story, this protracted taming of the Marches ; this last protest against settling down to the humdrum, secure, uneventful life which had characterized most parts of England for generations, save for interludes of civil war. The larger and at least more logical issues on which these men had fought

LANE'S HOSPITAL, LUDLOW.

almost uninterruptedly for centuries had been left by now a hundred years behind. But the habit of partisanship of the sword and of adventure seemed ineradicable. Even Merioneth and Carmarthen had almost quieted down by the end of the sixteenth century, while remoter Cardigan and becastled Pembroke seemed to have peaceably subsided into horsebreeding and the importation of pheasants and interparish matches at Knappan, which ferocious pastime was perhaps a safety valve against more serious conflicts.

But by the seventeenth century even the borderers were tamed and the work of the Court of the Marches grew less arduous and less necessary. One argument for its retention as a court of appeal was the saving of time and expense to litigants, who would otherwise have been compelled to go to Westminster. As the century advanced, though the court officers under an always distinguished president still sat at Ludlow Castle, it became unpopular, expensive and cumbersome. The four English counties particularly objected to its jurisdiction, and even carried their cases elsewhere in defiance of its authority. However, its story now becomes one of legal rather than general interest and would be out of place here. Richard Baxter, who resided in youth with the chaplain of Ludlow, describes the castle as a place " occupied by many idle gentlemen who had nothing else to do but gamble and the town as full of temptations through the multitude of persons, councillors, attorneys, officers and clerks all much given to tippling and excess."

It will be enough to say that after being suppressed during the Civil War, the court was restored again at the Restoration to a brief and feeble existence, which was finally terminated by Act of Parliament in 1689. With the abolition of the court the glory of Ludlow departed, and the grand old building sank gradually into decay.

On entering the precincts to-day through the arched gateway leading from the top of the town the great outer ward or court, spreading over two or three acres of level turf and suggestive of the varied throngs that must have gathered there through so many centuries, makes a fine approach to the castle itself. In the far left-hand corner are some old insignificant buildings that are the remnants of the actual Court of the Marches, and exact our respect and touch the fancy on that account alone. Close to them is a tower of odd semicircular shape and great antiquity celebrated as the prison of that Hugh Mortimer who, it will be remembered, Joce de Dinan found it necessary to capture and lock up. A deep dry moat hewn out of the rock on which the castle stands divides its stately front from this outer court, and a Tudor portal built near the original one, now obvious enough though walled up, is reached by a small wooden bridge very unlike the great drawbridge that swung up and down close by it in the days of Joce.

As one passes through Sidney's gateway under his arms and his inscription, already partly quoted, leaving his graceful

Tudor buildings to line the moat upon the right, and enters the interior court of the castle, all that may be within you responsive to such influences goes out at once to the imposing vista of roofless but roof-high towers and walls that here display themselves. To the left rises the great square keep, the original work of the first De Lacy founder. Further on to the right is the remarkable circular nave of the chapel, the only instance of its kind similarly placed in England. In front is the main pile of buildings containing the great hall and the state apartments erected for the most part by the Mortimers in the four teenth century. The banqueting hall in the centre is sixty feet long and has some beautiful pointed windows looking out from a great height up the valley of the Teme to the north and west. It was here in 1635 that the *Mask of Comus*, written by Milton and suggested by the youthful adventures of the children of the lord president was performed. To the right of the hall are the state apartments, the armoury and the rooms traditionally occupied by the two princely victims of Richard III's brutality, and a tower supposed with good reason to be that of Pendover where Arnold de Lys and Marion of the Heath loved and died. On the left of the great hall are the apartments relegated by tradition to Prince Arthur, though the best opinions see no sufficient reason why so illustrious a resident should not have occupied the state apartments.

The outlook towards Bromfield from the lofty battlements of these northern buildings has been sufficiently indicated at the opening of this chapter, and as I do not hold that going through a castle or any ancient building in lengthy detail is a sane proceeding on the pages of a book not technical in character, I shall only say that the minor alterations in Ludlow have been more than usually numerous owing to its continuous occupation for six centuries by personages who had the means to make it both comfortable, beautiful and secure. Sir Henry Sydney's Tudor buildings at the Gateway and to the east of it are of course a contrast to the rest, but they are eloquent of a great man and of a great period in the castle's history, and in any case the Tudor embellishment of a feudal building is never inharmonious nor unacceptable if only for the link between past and present it typifies. It was in a room over the gateway, too, that Butler, who was steward of the castle under Lord Carberry, wrote the first part of *Hudibras*. One singularity may perhaps be noticed, namely that the well of the keep, nearly a hundred feet deep, is twenty or thirty yards away, instead of within the tower as usual, and one would imagine as vital, to every defensive stronghold. This is a sore trial to antiquaries, and will remain so to those yet unborn.

Ludlow now belongs to the Earls of Powis, and it seems a pity that these great landmarks in the nation's history cannot be taken over by the Crown. There are lofty portions of the State apartments which to say the least of it are dangerous, while alterations of a utilitarian kind, destructive of artistic harmony, are proceeding on the eastern side of the outer court. On the other hand successful work has been recently effected by antiquarian zeal in tracing the foundations of the vanished chancel of the circular chapel within. The outer gate of the castle opens appropriately on to the central ridge of the town and looks along it, a broad pleasant space with market house in the middle and bordered with good residential buildings of varying periods. Some of these are ancient and highly ornate timbered structures, while sheltering rows of trees without the castle walls give the finishing touch to a spot which looks worthily conscious of its historical responsibilities.

Further along the ridge amid more cramped surroundings and at the junction of many streets and wynds leading from every quarter of the world below, stands the Butter Cross, the heart and rendezvous of the town, a Renaissance building with a bell turret dome and cross, and an open basement for foot traffic to wander through and for loitering groups to shelter in from rain or sun and take note of every wight who comes or goes in Ludlow. A short way on at the end of the ridge is the bull ring and the celebrated *Feathers Hotel*, one of the finest old black and white buildings on the March. All the streets of Ludlow climb by steep gradients to this central ridge from the valleys either of the Teme or Corve, and those from the former which are wide and perfectly straight have rather an effective appearance, being of ancient construction and displaying so many old gables along either front. Broad Street, which runs up straight as a dart from Ludford bridge to the Butter Cross, is blocked in mid ascent by a large, somewhat modernized building of ancient origin, which leaps right across the street, the latter burrowing under it through a narrow archway dating to Henry III.

Ludford, with its house and church on the further side of the bridge, is one of the notable features of Ludlow, not because the spot was so often the point of attack on the

town but for the buildings themselves. The appearance
of the fine old house would give any one pause, ascending from
the bridge into Herefordshire. An archway leads into a
large open quadrangle laid out in carriage sweeps and shrub-
beries, three sides of which are stables, domestic offices and
such like, while the fourth adjoining the church is the residence
itself. This last is spacious and rambling, full of tortuous
passages and fine old rooms, many of them panelled and
hung with valuable family portraits. It also boasts a dungeon,
into which I have descended with the kind assistance of the

BROAD STREET, LUDLOW.

present occupant, for I should add that it is a private residence.
The story of the house is interesting. The manor, which
belonged to St. John's Hospital, was appropriated by the Crown
and sold to John, Earl of Warwick, from whom it was purchased
and the house converted into a mansion by William Foxe, who
had obtained a previous grant of it from the Master and Brethren of the Hospital. His son Charles was secretary to the
Court of the Marches and accumulated in that capacity a handsome fortune. In 1607 it was bought by the Charltons. The
church, whose graveyard the irregular steep-roofed main block
of the building overlooks, is uncommon and possesses a Charlton

chapel, built by William Foxe and divided from the nave and chancel by two arches. In this transept are some interesting and quaint monuments, notably a large brass representing William Foxe himself, who died in 1554, his wife and fifteen children, and an altar tomb with full-length figure of Sir Job Charlton in scarlet robe and black skull cap. Sir Job was Speaker to the House of Commons, and entertained James II here in 1687, who created him a baronet. There is also a tablet with the head of a lady, of which family I forget, but her virtues are represented at sufficiently fulsome and inordinate length to have much more than neutralized them all in the eyes of a more cynical and less guileless generation.

Among the other treasures of Ludlow is a chapel outside the castle walls now used as a warehouse, which was dedicated to St. Thomas à Becket, while there was another inside the castle that the great and wicked Roger Mortimer erected in gratitude for his escape from the Tower in 1323. Lane's Asylum in Old Street is an interesting building, and then there is the Grammar School with its dormer windows, which is one of the oldest in England and is quite useful and flourishing at the present time.

Next to the castle, however, the glory of Ludlow is its church, which has not only the advantage of a commanding site, namely the opposite end of the ridge from the castle, but as already mentioned is held to be the finest in the county of Salop. To those who know Shrewsbury, with its abbey and St. Mary's, this estimate will be significant. Built of red sandstone and cruciform in shape its graceful and lofty tower is a landmark over miles of country and beautiful in the near approach. With nave, choir, side-aisle, transepts and two chapels, the church covers a large surface, while the north side of its graveyard rests on a section of the old town wall with adjoining gate tower, and looks up the Corve and over to the Clees, which fill the sky upon this side. Like nearly all old churches, this one of St. Lawrence covers the site of a still earlier fabric, a Norman one unquestionably, as neither church nor town were here at their advent. The present building, however, is thought to have been finished early in the thirteenth century with additions by the Verdons and Mortimers a hundred years later, and still further alterations in the Perpendicular period which have stamped that style upon its general appearance to-day. The nave is supported and divided from the aisle by fine pointed arches springing from graceful clustered pillars, with a clerestory above. The church was collegiate ; and the stalls in the choir, with their miserere seats, fancifully carved, bear eloquent testimony to the fact. The canopies above them though of beautiful design are modern work. There is a great deal of modern decorative work both here and on the rood screen. The large choir contains five pointed windows on each side, and there is a very large one at the east end filled with scenes from the life history of St. Lawrence, a Spanish saint of the third century. This curious window, I am told, has been much defaced and patched up at various times. It contains twenty- seven scenes from the life of the saint and three hundred figures. The glass of one of the choir windows bears singular evidence of its pre-reformation date, its subject being the Almighty handing the table of stone to Moses. For the latter is depicted in the guise of the Pope and the commandments are numbered in the Roman fashion, an almost unique instance, according to Mr. St. John Hope, of such singular provocation to the Puritan conscience surviving the Puritan hammer. In St. John's chapel, cut off from the chancel by a finely-carved screen, is some beautiful old glass : one window depicting the curious progress of some Ludlow burgesses as pilgrims to the Holy Land in eight scenes, including at the same time a not unfamiliar legend in which the king, St. John the Evangelist, a beggar, and a ring are the chief actors. In the seventh scene the returned pilgrims are being embraced by an elderly official, who might be the mayor, in the presence of the citizens, who throng the battlements. The last scene represents Ludlow *en fête* in honour of its pious and adventurous sons. In the Lady chapel there is a large Jesse window. While there is a great deal of fine modern work in the interior, as is natural in a church that possesses such abundant and far-reaching family attachments.

The monuments are numerous, and as might be expected flavour much of the Court of the Marches. Here in the chancel, beneath a tomb supported by heraldic shields, lies Ambrosia, the daughter of Sir Henry Sidney, who died at Ludlow in 1574. Near by are alabaster figures of Edmund Waller, " Chief Justice of three shires in Wales and one of his Majesties council in the Marches of Wales " ; and of Mary his wife, a Hakluyt of Eyton. The judge wears a long cloak and the lady long loose sleeves, the Tudor ruff and a French hood, while their children in strange garments march in dutiful progress round the tomb. Across the way are two figures kneeling opposite one another :

THE READER'S HOUSE, LUDLOW.

the gentleman wears a red gown, a cap and ruff, the lady is in appropriate costume of the period, and was a Foxe of Ludford. Her husband, who erected the structure in his lifetime, was " Edward Waties one of his Majesty's councill in the Principality and Marches of Wales." In the south transept another lady attired in the height of Tudor fashion, with hooped petticoat and pointed stomacher, leans on her left elbow as if momentarily expecting the " joyful resurrection " she looks forward to in her epitaph. This is another great personage of Ludlow's halcyon days and wife to the " Right Honourable Ralphe Lord Eyere, Baron of Malton, Lord President of the Principalitie and Marches of Wales ; " who was buried himself in the church, being the only lord president who lies there. And here in the chancel is another functionary of that luminous period, chief justice of the council in the Marches of Wales, etc., with his wife beside him and twelve children, " lawfully begot," grouped around. This is Sir Robert Townshend, who is in plate armour with his head on a book and his feet on a stag. This tomb is of earlier date, and Dame Alice wears a quilted gown and a cap, and in deference perhaps to her husband's learning wears a book attached to her by a chain. There is no inscribed monument to Prince Arthur, though something of the sort might be expected, seeing that he lived, ruled and died here. Some recessed arches in the north aisle, with two altar tombs beneath them, but bearing no name or date, are sometimes erroneously believed to have been erected in honour of the prince. Sir John Bridgeman and his wife, another justiciar of the Marches, boast of the highest sepulchral honours, for he lies carved in white marble on a fine altar tomb within a railing in St. John's chapel, supposed to be the work of Francisco Fanelli. And as a last word on Ludlow there is the curious six-sided south porch resembling that in St. Mary Redcliffe, Bristol, and a most beautiful little timbered building of the Tudor period standing adjacent to the east end known as the " Reader's House."

[From the chronicles of Stanley Abbey, near Calne, Wilts (Marsh): " Fulke Fitzwarine took refuge July 2nd in the Abbey of Stanley in Wiltshire, and was there besieged, together with his followers, for fourteen days by almost the whole county, and by many others who had flocked to the place. But he came out safe in the peace of the Church, and was reconciled in the following year, 1202."]

CHAPTER IX

WIGMORE, BRAMPTON BRIAN AND CLUN

MY purpose in this chapter is to thread the devious and hilly ways that wind south-west and west by Wigmore, Brampton Brian and other scenes of ancient fame to the remote land of Clun, thence to work back by the more direct route that carries Clunnites to the outer world and *Craven Armes*, which last creation of the London and North Western Railway lies eight miles north of Ludlow on the great road to Shrewsbury. With this in view we must pass over Joce de Dinan's bridge, which binds Ludford to Ludlow and Hereford to Salop, and in so doing may take note that there are not many large bridges in use to-day which we know to be Norman, and furthermore that this particular bridge is almost unique in the singular breadth of its piers and parapet angles, which have withstood the mountain floods of Teme for seven centuries. I have made note in the last chapter of the unforgetable prospect which Ludlow offers to those climbing the steep heights of Whitcliff, a feat the Wigmore road easily accomplishes by much judicious grading. But when these giddy heights are surmounted you have only in fact begun the ascent of one of the biggest "banks" that any important border highway is called upon to face, and that is saying much. The people of Ludlow, before the Mortimers eventually gobbled them up, must have been upon the whole thankful that this tremendous barrier lay between them and Wigmore, for the ridge in question, commonly known as the Vinnal, is nearly 1,300 feet in height, and where the highway tops it can hardly be less than a thousand.

The ascent, however, is lengthy rather than steep upon the hither side ; for the second millstone is left well behind before the strain is off the collar. For more than half the distance the way lies through the edge of a thick forest, which opens almost at the moment the ridge is gained, and you seem of a sudden to be looking out over all the kingdoms of the earth. As a matter of fact it is only the March of Shropshire and Hereford, with Radnor filling in their background, that tumbles so far and in such fine confusion towards the west. Ridge upon ridge of hills of every shape and every stature from a thousand to two thousand feet toss hither and thither like the billows of a troubled sea. Far down the narrow vale beneath, where some four miles away its course is barred by a lateral ridge, and readily visible if you know where to look, the fragments of the great stronghold of the Mortimers lurk with grim significance in the shadow of "The Rolls of Wigmore." It is not only this noble outlook over the deep furrowed region where the Lugg and Teme collect their waters, and generations of Mortimers gathered their men, that keeps one lingering on the top of the Vinnal, but the forest itself blowing immediately beneath and around us, with its miles of woodland wall so different from those gentle undulations of stately timber and bracken glades that in England one chiefly associates with the term.

Here we have a long range of hills rising in places considerably over a thousand feet, and densely wrapped from base to summit with woodland of every age and every variety. As you stand on the apex of the pass, a deep gorge hundreds of feet below splits the main ridge, and opening out a distant glimpse of the rich Hereford lowland leaps up again on the further side, an immense curtain of verdure, to trail away along the sky-line at a great height over Yatton and Bircher towards Mortimer's Cross. And as you descend the valley road leading to Wigmore, you find the same mass of upland forest hanging high above your right shoulder and clothing the lofty spur which stretches north-west to Downton and presses down upon the valley of the Teme, forcing that river to renew its boisterous youth amid contracted channels of cliff and boulder. All through these miles of sylvan wilderness, of which Lord Windsor and Mr. Boughton-Knight are the chief owners, fallow deer range in a more or less wild condition, after the manner of roe in Scottish woods. It was down yonder, too, in the bosky gorges of Hayswood and at the foot of High Vinnals, that the young sons and daughter of the Earl of Bridgewater, then just appointed president of Wales, were benighted on their way to Ludlow and met with those mild adventures which prompted Milton to write the *Mask of Comus*. It was first acted with much pageantry at Ludlow Castle, the young heroes of the adventure taking the principal part, together with Henry Lawes who wrote the music.

Wigmore stands on the old Roman road which carried a big traffic even through mediæval times. Its name is derived from a Danish camp that once stood here and signifies with remarkable appropriateness, " The Moor of the Sons of War." Once a little bustling town on terms of frequent intimacy with crowned heads, and all the blood and glory and pageantry they brought in their train, it is now a sleepy and in part dilapidated village, far from the busier haunts of even rural man. In the hollow on the highway the *Castle Inn* and a few other modest dwellings wear a contented whitewashed face; and indeed

WIGMORE CASTLE.

a town which received its deathblow about the reign of Henry VII will have had ample time not only to resign itself to the situation but to acquire complete oblivion to its ancient glories. Collie dogs doze in the sunshine, and a brewer's dray, suggestive of thirsty harvest fields, now full of life, slides its barrels into the cool vaults of the inn. But as

you climb the single lateral street up the hill leading to the
church and castle, and have regard to the habitations of the
citizens which line it, you will possibly be reminded of a back
wynd in some seacoast fishing village. So great is the variety
of patchwork and makeshift in the low one-storied cottages, that
this was at any rate my first impression; and I was interested
to learn afterwards from a clever young artist in the neighbourhood, who paints marine subjects among others, that he had
found Wigmore invaluable in this particular. The old church
with its embattled tower stands boldly out upon a lofty ledge
looking down over the roof trees and gardens of the village
and the vale below. A few furlongs onward, and yet higher up
the narrow ridge, one enters the grassy precincts, which trend
upward again to the ivy-hooded gateway in the massive broken
walls that still partly encircle the castle mound.

Mr. Round has rudely shaken of late some time-honoured
beliefs. He has not only driven a coach and four through
many famous pedigrees, but has propounded the theory that
the tumps and mounds on which the Norman invaders erected
their keeps were not always the work of their more or less
remote predecessors, till lately an article of faith, but that in
some cases they actually threw them up themselves. And
furthermore, that they were often contented for the time
being with wooden palisades like any ordinary Saxon, Briton
or Dane, till there was leisure and opportunity to build those
familiar square stone keeps that mark their earlier efforts.
Wigmore is an immense tump, and seems almost certainly to
have carried the wooden fortresses of the Mercian guardians of
Offa's Dyke as well, no doubt, as those of their Danish enemies.
To-day its sides are strewn with the fragments and the still
upstanding masonry and foundations of the Mortimer
castle, and scarred by the constant trampling of youthful Wig-
morians, who seem to make these scenes of departed glory
their particular sporting ground. Large trees, however, keep
a firm footing upon the slopes and twine their branches lovingly
among the still surviving fragments of masonry that have
seen, no doubt, their predecessors sprout from seedlings and
grow to old age and decay. The shell of the keep, however,
holds out bravely and crowns the top of the steep towering
far above the foliage and still looking proudly out over
the three vales that meet below. And the church tower springs
boldly up in the foreground, while the continuous forest ridges of
Bringewood, Vinnal, Leinthall and Yatton fill the sky beyond.

The grasp of the Mortimers spread far and wide over Britain before they had finished and merged through the female branch into the royal line. But this secluded and romantic eyrie was the true nest and stronghold of the breed. The castle was dismantled in the Civil War as too dilapidated for a profitable defence and yet solid enough to give some footing to an enemy. Silas Taylor, writing soon afterwards, calls it "a melancholy, dejected prospect of stately ruins." At the Norman conquest all Shropshire had been given to Montgomery, King William's kinsman, who afterwards upon his own account

COTTAGES AT WIGMORE.

annexed the March which bore and still bears his name. Herefordshire was parcelled out in portions by Fitz-Osborne among several knights, of whom Ralph de Mortimer was one. Ralph had been an active factor in driving out the Saxon Edric, who though left in possession of his old earldom of Shrewsbury had not shown the sense to remain quiet within it, and was granted Wigmore, Cleobury, and Caynham as a reward.

To deal in any detail here with the long dynasty of this mighty race is out of the question. But a succession of Hughs, Rogers, and Edmunds followed one another, till the child who was nominated Richard II's successor was put out of the race by Henry of Bolingbroke, and bearing no grudge died childless, fighting under the victorious banner of Henry's son in France, the last of the male stock. The Mortimers are described by old writers as the most consistent "haters of the Welsh," and certainly they intrigued with them less than any of their neighbours. They improved their fortunes, too, by frequent and judicious marriages with the greatest Marcher families, and their devotion to Henry III in his wars against the barons left them after the victory of Evesham more potent than ever. But when the introduction of the second Edward's favourites to place and honour on the march stung its great families into active protest, Roger Mortimer went out with the rest, and at the defeat of Boroughbridge was taken captive and immured in the Tower of London under sentence of death.

How he drugged the constable who was good-naturedly entertaining him at a final carousal, bribed the jailor and escaped to Queen Isabella in France, and what came of it afterwards, is a matter of common history. It is a familiar story, too, how he meted out twofold vengeance on the hapless king, by annexing his queen and compassing his ruin even if he did not actually order his murder, as rumour had it. He entertained Queen Isabella and Prince Edward in regal state at Wigmore as well as at Ludlow, which had by then become a Mortimer possession. But he gave such rein to his immoderate ambition and love of display that even his own son dubbed him "the king of folly." The turn of fortune when it came, as it generally did in those days sooner or later, was complete. For Edward III was not satisfied with meting out an honourable death to the gentle Mortimer, the late ruler of England and his mother's paramour, but he hung him high on a common gallows at Tyburn, the very first victim to suffer on that notorious spot. His remains, like those of most of his line, were brought back to Wigmore and laid in the abbey. His grandson, Roger, after a long minority, fought so doughtily for Edward in France that by a process of logic, not very obvious to a modern intelligence, he obtained a declaration of Parliament affirming that his grandfather had been unjustly executed on false charges.

The young Roger was restored to the Earldom of March, and acquiring many other high honours died commanding the English army in Burgundy. He also was buried at Wigmore. His son Edward developed the family talents so precociously that at eighteen he was commissioned to treat for peace between England and France. He was lord lieutenant of Ireland under Richard II, and it was he who by his marriage with the daughter of the Duke of Clarence brought the family into the line of royal succession. Dying early, his son, another Roger, was also viceroy in Ireland and fell there fighting, leaving the little boy who, as ex-heir to the throne, fell childless in the French wars as already related. One may also, perhaps, recall the fact that the last Roger's sister married Henry Percy (Hotspur), and figures on the Shakespearian stage with her unfortunate brother Edmund, who as acting head of the Mortimers was captured by Glyndwr's Welshmen at the battle of Pilleth, where half the Wigmore vassals fell.

Bolingbroke saw small advantage in sanctioning Mortimer's ransom, for though he had fast hold of the nephew, the uncle might well have proved troublesome. So Hotspur, Mortimer's brother-in-law, went up to London, had stormy passages with the king on this and the matter of the Scottish prisoners, and after shaking his fist in his face, left the royal presence with the threat that he would meet Bolingbroke on the field of battle, which we know he did at Shrewsbury and got killed. Edmund Mortimer in the meantime revenged himself by marrying Glyndwr's daughter and espousing his cause, which was useful to Owen if only for the effect it had on the Mortimer tenantry ; but hardly otherwise, for this particular Edmund made no showing whatever in the war and finally died of privation in Harlech castle during the siege. The final glories of Wigmore were in those occasional visits which Edward IV paid to the home of his ancestors when it became his property. From this time forward it was only occupied by deputies, and was finally sold by the Crown in Elizabeth's reign to the Harleys of Brampton Brian for £26,000.

Wigmore Grange is now a large farm of familiar name among border stock breeders. It lies low, within easy view of the castle, set pleasantly in the flat of the valley, which winds northwards to Leintwardine. A good many portions of this old abbey of the Mortimers still survives among the farm buildings, and the story of its founding is given at great length in a thirteenth century MS. reproduced in Dugdale's *Monasticum* ; not an embroidered tale like that of the Fitzwarrenes, but a plain unvarnished narrative infinitely instructive of the manners of the time and district. It seems that some Augustinian monks from the abbey of St. Victor at Paris had been imported and settled at Shobden by Sir Hugh Mortimer's steward, a man of some birth and property, Oliver de Melimond, who had made their acquaintance during a pilgrimage to some foreign shrine. Thence they moved to Aymestry, and had just begun to build when Mortimer's friends called his attention to the fact of how useful stone buildings in the narrow south entrance to Wigmore might prove to his enemies, Joce de Dinan, for instance, for this was the Mortimer that Joce waylaid and locked up at Ludlow. So Sir Hugh, thinking this sounded reasonable, removed the settlement, which had been further recruited from France, bodily to Wigmore, allotting quarters in the town to the brethren. But with these the holy men were anything but satisfied. The buildings, they complained, were rough and narrow, the water supply deficient, the pull up to the church too steep, the language of the neighbours unfit for their pious and fastidious ears (*vileines paroles et deshonestes*). Sir Hugh saw reason in their complaints, and told them to look round his territory and see if there was any particular spot they fancied. As for himself, he had a little unpleasantness with young King Henry on hand, to say nothing of local quarrels, and had no time at the moment to look into the matter.

In the meantime, the climb to the church grew no less arduous and the language of the Wigmore citizens no more parliamentary, but the brethren had found nothing eligible in the way of a building site, till one of them, Walter Agameth, while seated during harvest amidst the reapers in the field of Beodine, had an inspiration that this was the very spot for their purpose. His brethren being of the same mind they repaired to Sir Hugh on his return and stated their wishes. The baron was in the best of humours, and gave them the land ungrudgingly, as well as some practical advice to the effect that they should erect small wooden huts on the site for habitation while they were engaged in building the abbey. He gave them, moreover, the church of Meole Brace, just outside Shrewsbury, whose parson had lately died, and also the church and manor at Caynham, and shortly afterwards he went down himself and marked out the site of the church and laid the first stone, gilded with a further subscription. His neighbour, Brian de Brampton, and his son laid the second and third stones, but only with good wishes and privileges, so the chronicler tells us.

The zeal of Sir Hugh for his abbey slacked in no wise, and he heaped lands, benefices and mills on the canons with lavish hands. He took great personal interest in the building of the church and found most of the money, and when the bishop came to dedicate it, he solemnly confirmed all his grants in presence of the abbot and canons and assembled populace. He next presented cups, chalices, and candle-sticks of gold to the church, while the bishop thundered sentence of excommunication against any wight born or unborn who should be tempted to alienate them, and himself gave a cape of purple leather, richly adorned. All these ceremonies satisfactorily completed, the noble benefactor, now full of years, was gathered to his fathers, in good hopes of reaping somewhat in heaven of what he had sown on earth—that is, of what he had latterly sown. Having worn armour to some purpose all his life he was received into the brotherhood on his deathbed by Abbot Randulph ; and his corpse, attired in monkish garb, which must have startled his old friends, was carried in state to the abbey and buried beneath the high altar. And if Sir Hugh had laid about him all his life without much regard to the virtues, he died in the very odour of sanctity. Masses and special offices were to be performed daily and weekly for his soul, and periodical distributions of bread, ale and meat were to be made for ever and ever, in pious memory of the pious founder.

But his son Roger did not share the enthusiasms of monks and people. He seemed to think that his father's generosity in his old age had been somewhat at his expense, and in his anxiety about his own soul—for the unfilial youth put it this way—he had disregarded the interests of his successor. The latter, however, was prevented from attending the funeral, since Henry II had him at the moment under lock and key for killing a Welshman, an absurd pretext for the period, of course, but the real cause of offence does not transpire. Roger was released and arrived at Wigmore, where he was received with great joy, particularly at the abbey. Here he was led up to the high altar with much ceremony by the abbot, and after worshipping there, embraced the brethren all round and promised to walk in his father's ways, so far, at least, as the abbey was concerned. But the kisses he distributed so lavishly were those of Judas, for no sooner was he out of the church than he began to challenge in bitter language their right to Caynham Manor and commanded them to disgorge forthwith. But the abbot stood firm, and refused to yield a single foot of land, whereat young Roger was greatly enraged, and as Caynham was the reward of services rendered to the Crown by his ancestor one cannot withhold some measure of sympathy from the young man, whose time for insuring his soul's welfare after the current fashion was not yet within measurable distance. So he began to sorely persecute the holy men, till most of them retired to their ancient haunt of Shobdon, leaving two or three only to look after the church.

When the king heard of these doings, however, he sent intimations to Roger, who was out, so to speak, on good behaviour, which resulted in the return of all the brethren to Wigmore. They even squeezed out of him a further grant of the manor of Smytton, a concession which brought upon him the gibes of his worldly companions, who pointed out what a convenient half-way house it had always been between Wigmore and Cleobury, his other castle, whereat Roger repented and cancelled the gift, a proceeding of which he had some cause to repent. For when his devout wife, Isabella de Ferrers, was shortly after journeying to Cleobury, she was prematurely confined at Smytton, and lost her child, a boy. This judgment was unmistakable, and the pious lady prayed her lord with tears in her eyes to restore the property, and with such an argument behind her did not plead in vain, even with a young man, " gay, changeable, headstrong and fond of light company," as we are told was Roger. The monks, however, wanted their lord's sympathy as well as his good offices, but he would have none of them, and all that remained to the abbot and canons was to pray for the conversion of this worldly youth.

Constantly brooding on the pious but as he thought selfish alienations of his father, Roger was particularly provoked one day at the sight of a beautiful piece of young wheat growing on some land that had been recently granted to the abbey. " See, fair lords," cried he to his companions, how my father entirely advanced himself and forgot me, his eldest son and heir, to the advantage of these boors of the abbey." But soon afterwards all the bells of the church began to ring funeral peals, and Roger, calling his chaplain, who was of the party, asked the meaning of it ; whereupon the latter reminded him that it was the anniversary of his father's death, and told him of all the good works that were done upon that day. When Roger heard this he was abashed, and the " Holy Spirit seized him." and he commanded that they should all go forthwith to the abbey. And when the abbot saw him coming he met him outside the church with his whole company in full procession.

The canons then proceeded to chant the masses and afterwards
to distribute the food among the hundred poor people speci-
fied in the charter. By all these ceremonies, the unstable Roger
was profoundly affected and humbly begged the abbot on his
knees to pardon him for his untoward attitude towards the
brethren, and once more he kissed them all round and became
regenerate so far as the abbey was concerned, and as good a
friend to them as his father had been " to the joy of good men
and the spite of the wicked." His steward (not Oliver) was
among the wicked, for he told his master bitterly that he might
as well give them the " Treasure of Mortimer," a productive
field near the abbey, at once, and then the monks would possess
all the land round them. But the reformed Roger was not a
man of half measures and dismayed his officious bailiff by taking
him literally : " By my head, fair friend, you have said and
advised well, and since that place is called the Treasure of Mortimer, I will deliver it to such treasury to keep for my use,
where no thief will steal it nor moth eat it, but it shall bear
fruit to my soul," and forthwith he inspected the field and
repairing to the abbey gave it in perpetual alms to the house
for ever, for the souls of himself, his ancestors and his successors,
and confirmed it by charter sealed by his seal before all the
people.

Travelling northwestward and passing through the centre
of the fertile basin, which the monks thus wrung piece by piece
from Hugh and Roger Mortimer, there is a striking retrospect of
the castle perched on its high promontory with the church no
less conspicuous on the upstanding ledge beneath it. There is
a good three miles of valley road before the parting of
many ways brings us in sight of Leintwardine, the ancient
Bravinium of the Romans.

At the further side of a wide sweep of level meads the village
nestles picturesquely at the foot of high hills, and the Teme
meanders towards it in wide and chastened current between
meadowy banks, while the Clun comes hastening down to join
it from the north. Famous among border anglers, familiar
by repute to most anglers, is the name of Leintwardine. For
several miles a very close corporation here control one of the
best stretches of trout and grayling water in the whole
country, not surpassed by the best of the Monnow or the
cream of the Lugg. And indeed, Leintwardine is in other
respects an ideal fishing station, with its ancient church rising
in the background and the large scattered village spreading

down the slope to the tall trees that line the river bank, and the picturesque hostelry where anglers gather, standing exactly in the right spot at the end of the high stone bridge which crosses the stream. But the course of the Teme from here to Ludlow is by no means always so peaceful as amid these far-expanding meads, dimpled with Hereford cattle and bereft of timber or hedgerow. For two or three miles below this the lofty steeps of Tatteridge Hill on the one side and of Bingewood Chase on the other, press their feet so close together that after many twists and turns the river is forced into the character of a Highland stream and rushes through such a beautiful gorge, for the space of a mile or so, that almost you

LEINTWARDINE.

might be on the Conway about Bettws-y-Coed, or on the Dee above Llangollen or the Towy at Ystradffin. A fine confusion of limestone cliff and crag and luxuriant woodland here hems in the lusty river which rushes downwards in a glorious succession of rapids and rockbound pools to the outlet of the gorge, where the park lands of Downton open out and the waters cease from troubling and ripple gently onward to another and a final riot through the woods of Oakley.

Downton castle, an imposing pile of towers and battlements, built in the eighteenth century, stands on the ridge of the long slope by which the park rises from its bordering river. The Knight family, who built it and still own the property, were great iron-masters at the end of the seventeenth century. For the abounding woodland of this country made it profitable in those days to bring ore on horse- or mule-back from Staffordshire and smelt it on the Teme. The remains of one of the forges is still standing. But when the smelting of iron had ceased as an industry in merely forest countries, the Knights became distinguished in other lines. Richard Knight, who built the castle in 1774, was celebrated throughout England for his skill in landscape gardening, and his denunciations of the stiff French style of that day. One prevalent fashion of the period, that of lengthening the approach to a house from its park gates as much as possible for reasons unnecessary to elucidate, was a favourite object of his satire. As he wrote extremely good verse among other accomplishments, he naturally turned to rhyme in lighter matters. So after suggesting that a coat of arms should be erected at every mile of these superfluously tortuous drives he offered another alternative :

> But why not rather at the porter's gate
> Hang up the map of all my lord's estate
> Than give his hungry visitors the pain
> To wander ore so many miles in vain ?

Richard Knight presented a valuable collection of art treasures to the British Museum, of which he was a trustee. He was also M.P. for Ludlow, and a conspicuous figure in his day. His brother, Thomas Andrew Knight, who succeeded to Downton in 1821, was the most distinguished horticulturist of his time, and president of the Royal Horticultural Society.

His name still lives, in that of many of the specimens he introduced, and the woodlands of other Herefordshire demesnes besides Downton, owe much to his taste, zeal and knowledge. Nor should it be forgotten that Downton is rich in traces of the Roman settlements at Leintwardine. For in the gorge of the river described above are some curious passages cut in the rock known as the Roman Caves.

From Leintwardine it is a matter of some three miles to Brampton Brian with its pleasant village green and big lime trees and bowery cottages, and the stormy memories that would seem inevitable to such a sonorous and suggestive name. The feudal castle of the Brians held under the Mortimers, and of the earlier Harleys, who fought at Tewkesbury as Yorkists and at Crecy, Poitiers and Flodden as Englishmen, stands united with the Jacobean house built by the later Harleys on the ashes left by the Civil Wars. The brick mansion and the castle ruins stand together amid pleasant lawns and flower beds, and are now known as Brampton Hall. The park lies across the road from the house, and is said to contain some of the finest timber in England. But the castle, though the continuous ownership of such an illustrious stock as the Harleys would confer distinction on any place, is chiefly notable for the two sieges it endured during the Civil War, above all the first and the successful one of which Lady Brilliana Harley was the heroine.

Now when the Civil War broke out the Harleys were almost

IN BRAMPTON BRIAN VILLAGE.

alone among the great families of Herefordshire in espousing the cause of the Parliament. Sir Robert Harley, as member for the county, was compelled to remain in London, and leave his property in charge of his spirited wife. Lady Brilliana, though a delicate woman, was more than equal to the occasion, serious though it was. Her friends, for her own sake, and her political enemies for theirs, tried to persuade her to remove with her children to a safer place ; but she decided to remain, and was well assured that " the Lord would show the men of the world that it is hard fighting against Heaven." For the first year of the war no action was taken against

Brampton Brian, but continuous rumours of attack kept the brave lady and her garrison in a state of prolonged suspense that was almost worse, for the chatelaine at any rate, than action. In the midst of neighbours, once friends, but now growing more inimical to the house of Harley with the progress of the war, her situation was trying enough. First it was reported they would burn the farms and blockade the castle. Then rumour had it that Brampton was to be blown up, and next, that the sheriff of Radnor with his train bands was on the march against it. " They have taken away all your father's rents," she writes to an absent son, " and then they will drive the cattell. They have used all means to have me leave no man in my house and tell me I should be safe but I have no caus to trust them." So like a valiant woman she put her house in order and prepared for the worst. The lead was recast, the timber renewed and the moat filled. She was sent a sergeant from Colonel Massie's division, " abrave and abell soulder " who had served abroad, a Hakluyt, whose name speaks for itself. The family doctor, Wright, proved also a tower of strength, and the Tudorized fortress, which had long abandoned its martial character, was called upon, like so many others in England, to renew its stormy past.

On July 26 the crisis came, and Sir William Vavasour with 600 men laid regular siege to the castle. At the end of a month he had accomplished nothing, and being summoned himself to Gloucester, left Colonel Lingen in command, a neighbour of the Harleys who bore them grudges much older than the war. The attack was pressed with much activity, but Lady Brilliana with her doctor and her trusty sergeant, who was captain for the occasion, repelled it with the utmost valour. The church and village were burnt, but at the beginning of September no impression had been made on the castle, and Lingen raised the siege. No great loss was suffered by the defenders, but a cook was shot by " a poisoned bullet which murdered him with great torment and poysomness to the whole family." The strain, however, had been too great for the gallant Amazon, and she died a month after it was over.

In the following spring the castle was attacked again by Sir Michael Woodhouse, and defended with the same gallantry by Wright and Hakluyt, the Harley children being still within the walls. This time the siege train was too strong, and the buildings were knocked about the defenders' ears and they were forced to yield.

The sequel of the story is admirable and quite characteristic of that chivalric feeling one gets so many glimpses of in this struggle, which would have been incomprehensible to the mailed warriors of former days. For after the triumph of the Parliament, the bereaved and half-ruined Sir Robert was placed at once in a position to retrieve in part, at any rate, his material fortunes, though his brave wife was irrecoverable, and in the general settlement, as was only right and natural, his bill of costs, which his steward estimated at £12,990, was drawn by the Parliament on his malignant fellow-countryman, Lingen, who had been a leading instrument in the damage. Sir Robert, however, died before the moment of compensation came, and it fell to his son Edward to present the account at the gate of his enemy. The latter, it so happened, was himself in prison or in exile, and his lady alone remained in occupation of his estates. Upon her, therefore, young Harley waited, and presenting the account of the property assigned to him, inquired if the details were correct. On receiving Lady Lingen's answer in the affirmative he presented her with the schedule, and with splendid magnanimity made her a present of it, waiving all claim to the assignments which were his legal due. England had surely travelled far since the War of the Roses ! The items of loss at Brampton are instructive, the cattle being valued at £940, the furniture and fittings of the castle at £2,500, the library at £200, while 500 deer are set down as having been killed. The library, which contained the earlier Harleian collection, is thought by antiquarians to have been over-modestly valued. This magnanimous Sir Edward Harley was afterwards Governor of Dunkirk, and died at Brampton, and his descendant, the first and great Earl of Oxford, was born in the house, which was altered to much its present condition by the fourth Earl in the middle of the eighteenth century.

Some half-mile beyond Brampton we leave the main road to pursue its westward way by the Teme valley and under lofty hills to Knighton. Brampton Brian, like so many of these villages in the middle March, holds a time-honoured horse and pony fair, where the hardy stock from the Welsh hills comes out to woo the favour of dealers and private buyers from all quarters of the land. Knighton, however, is nowadays the most important of these gatherings. I encountered that important function unawares last August, and could hardly persuade the booking-clerk at the crowded station of Craven Arms to give me a ticket to Carmarthen, or various friends and acquaintances whom I encountered on the platform from diverse parts, that on such a day there could possibly be any other point of pilgrimage. Knighton, to be sure, is a gathering of old renown, but I fancy its pre-eminence just now is due to certain enterprising spirits in Radnorshire who have read the signs of the times more clearly than elsewhere, and have kept the standard of the polo ground and one or two other needs of recent development in their eye. For no one of middle age who can remember the prominence of the pony in ordinary life in the days of their youth, would need telling that the demand for small mountain ponies or even of cobs has shrunk amazingly. Practically no one rides nowadays except hunting people, and they only behind the hounds, always excepting, of course, the tailors and schoolboys, who ride in front of them for brief and stormy periods. Even the more guileless lady novelist has ceased to make her Apollo, crowned with the triple laurels of Lords and Putney and a double first, pursue his arcadian amours on a glossy thoroughbred. The cycle alone must have swept thousands of ponies and hacks and trappers out of use; and now the motor has arrived, with its unfathomable possibilities and its lengthening shadow over the equine race, as well as its terrors to the peaceful wayfarer. The true horse lover is prone to draw hope for the future from the well of his own fervour and count too much on sentiment. Yet no one knows better than he, that three-fourths of those who keep the market alive for good class horses are not really horse lovers and have no horse knowledge, and utilize them for various reasons which would crumble in a moment if the social position of the noble animal were seriously affected. It should be a vast consolation to breeders, too, that such a multitude of persons hunt who would much rather not, if the truth were known, and they could achieve the same end with less trouble and risk. As to the pony business, when the Raleigh and governess cars that still thread the roads of prosperous suberbias all over England in fair abundance find their equivalent in some cheapened automobile, as they surely will, the Welsh pony fairs, it is to be feared, will feel it sorely. It is quite conceivable that to the next generation of Britons, driving may be a lost art as riding is gradually getting to be now to all but returned colonists and those who can keep

studs of hunters or a string of polo ponies. But all this is
à propos of the fact that pony breeders in Wales, who are in
touch with the outer world, are specializing on lines that are
not so nearly threatened by the revolution now in progress,
for it is nothing less. Moreover, dealers nowadays more often
get wind beforehand of likely animals, and seek them out on
their owners' farms, thereby lowering the standard of the fairs.

As we leave the Knighton road, cross the Teme and head
for Bucknell near by, the classic hill of Coxwell Knoll, of modest
height but rugged contour, rises in the rear of Brampton.

BUCKNELL.

For if the spot where the last blow for liberty was struck by the
British tribesmen against the power of Rome is not classic
ground, I do not know what is. It is true that the claim is made
for other places in the neighbourhood, which is full of both Roman and British camps. Tradition has fixed on Ambrey Croft,
the south-western extremity of the high Vinnall ridge, looking
down on Croft castle, Yatton and Aymestry as the chief strongholds of Caractacus, and it is generally thought that the last
retreat of the Silures, as described by Tacitus, was by way of
Wapley, which is strongly fortified, and thence by Wigmore

to Coxwell, where the final struggle took place between the British chieftain and Ostorius Scapula in the year 52 A.D. Spearheads as well as stone balls, evidence of Roman engines, have been freely unearthed throughout the district. Still there are some who incline to the Breiddon Hills, near Welshpool, as more completely answering the description of Tacitus. Others contend that the evidence of a deadly strife are more continuous here, and that the lofty camp of Caer Caradoc, in the old forest of Clun close by, is a further point in their favour.

We are now again in proud Salopia, and, crossing the Central Wales branch of the London and North-Western, which carries travellers from Craven Arms to Llandrindod and other delectable haunts on the Upper Wye, may pause a moment in the peaceful hamlet of Bucknell, which spreads along the banks of the Redin brook as it babbles joyously towards the Teme. A couple of miles of tortuous lane, with the south-eastern heights of Clun rising here and there above the trammels of the Enclosure Act, to crests of verdant sheep pasture, which touch the scale at fourteen or fifteen hundred feet, and the old tower of Hopton confronts us in its once swampy glen. Hopton took my fancy greatly. It is unlike any mediæval fortress known to me in Wales or in the Marches, and suggests at once the Pele towers of the Scottish borders, among which I rambled for a summer a few years ago. Planted on a mound, it is a simple quadrangular building, three stories high and about fifty feet square, with walls ten feet thick, and a deep-moulded Gothic doorway, lifted a few feet above the ground; it had also a ridge roof, now vanished. Hopton figures in Domesday as a fief of Clun, and the family of Hopton seemed to have held if from the Norman to the Tudor period, and to have built the castle at the time of those abortive risings of the Welsh, which followed the Edwardian conquest.

It stands at the mouth of a sequestered glen, wandering up into the hills of Clun, and a small rivulet issuing thence washes the foot of the castle mound, and no doubt fed its moats. There is an austere simplicity about this simple tower which holds the fancy, more particularly as it seems to have filled for centuries the ambitions of the same family, who must have taken their full share of all the hard knocks that were going. There is no suggestion here of the pageants and the splendour of the Marches, though it was apparently modified within to suit the more comfort-loving and peaceful times of the Tudors, by the Corbets or Wallops, to whom it successively passed. The outside shell is eloquent of nothing but the grimmest border strife, and of a stock who neither founded abbeys nor aimed at upsetting dynasties upon their own account. In the Civil War, however, it was too good a position to overlook, and was stoutly defended throughout by Samuel More, of the Linley family, for the Parliament, but in vain, the garrison being mostly put to the sword.

Passing through the neighbouring hamlet, a mile or so of uplifted and somewhat lonely road but for the constant whirring of startled cushats, brings us to the banks of the Clun river, and a short pitch beyond climbs to " Hundred House," and the main highway between Clun town and Craven Arms. At the four crossroads here is an old and roomy inn, which you might well pass without special notice, unless stimulated by hunger or thirst. At any rate I did so, more than once, till in a good hour it happened to confront me at the right moment for legitimate refreshment, when I passed with some surprise right into a large low-pitched hall with a fine oak ceiling, and eloquent all over of some former distinction. The landlord happily was eloquent also, and as he was just completing the hundredth year of the family occupation, he had much to say of the house, and mainly to the point. It was the old manor house of Purslow Hundred, where the Courts were held, till the Enclosure Act altered the conditions of the district and made them superfluous. This large ground floor chamber was where the court sat, and still contains some of its fittings. I was conducted upstairs to a still larger hall, from whose walls various Earls of Powis and other Shropshire worthies looked down upon wooden tables and benches where Petty Sessions are still celebrated monthly. Down in the meadows by the Clun, overhung by Clunbury Hill, the village of that name clusters picturesquely round its massive church tower. For we are now within the mystic circle whose drowsiness inspired a Salopian bard to the immortal quatrain ;

> Clunton and Clunbury,
> Clungunford and Clun
> Are the quietest places
> Under the sun.

If he had lived in the reign of Henry III, let us say, or had been a contemporary of the two Llewelyns, or Owen Glyndwr, he would have sung another tune, but of that anon. As a matter of fact " quietest " is a modern interpolation for " drunkenest," in deference to the susceptibilities of Clunites and their reformed habits. Clun is a limb of south-western Shropshire, thrust far out into Wales, and is practically Welsh of the modified East Walian kind, and mostly Celtic in blood and place names. The outer world have, I think, caught at times vague echoes of Clun as a romantic, secluded kind of Arcadia, for Shropshire has made herself heard both in prose and verse to a moderate extent, though very much the finest achievement of her sons is one of the best county histories extant, to wit, the seven volumes of Eyton. The worst, probably, and almost the latest, curiously enough, is the single volume on the county written by that most agreeable and cultivated writer, the late Augustus Hare, a work into which he put none

CLUNBURY.

of his virtues, except his sketches, and most of his vices, eliminating by almost guide book compression, without guide book accuracy, all opportunity for the talent that has gained him such a wide following. Nor was he, I think, at all in touch with Shropshire.

The younger Mr. Houseman is identified with the Shropshire atmosphere in a different way, and is, I think, a native. The county is fairly strong in antiquaries, while the average Salopian, not being more interested in history than most other people, picked up a little of his own, when Shrewsbury celebrated the quincentenary of its battle, 1903, with prolonged fervour, in a week of instructive entertainments. Till then I fancy the conviction was general that Glyndwr had watched the battle from the branches of the Shelton Oak, and that

Prince Henry slew Hotspur, according to Shakespeare. There was a good deal of perturbation and some after-murmuring, I remember, when a representative local audience was confronted with scientific history in the person of the greatest living authority on Henry IV's reign, mounted on a tombstone in Battle church graveyard, who was very humorous as well as learned. Nor did any one appear to see the joke, when a gentleman from America, owning a not uncommon placename, posed very seriously, and I am sure honestly, as a lineal descendant of the Norman baron who built the castle, and made a long speech, quite unworthy of his eloquent nation; but how should they, not suspecting for a moment the simplicity of American genealogical procedure as regards British ancestry?

" We are kin to Lord Mayo," once observed a lady acquaintance of mine in Virginia, bearing that name. But, said an ungallant Irishman present, " Lord Mayo's name is Bourke." The lady bore up bravely and pulled herself together. " Well," said she, " I reckon it must be through the Burkes (small farmers of peasant origin in her neighbourhood)—my grandmother was a Burke." It was particularly superfluous, as the Mayos are an old Virginian family, and have an admirable record, though not noble ancestors.

Shropshire is strong in genealogy and its landocracy is probably less bourgeois in origin than that of almost any English county. Some statistics compiled a few years since allotted to it very much the largest number of families who have owned the same estates for five centuries. The county has produced, at least, its share of notable men, conspicuous among whom are the great Lord Hill, of Peninsular fame, and his relative, Rowland Hill, the preacher, Lord Clive, Charles Darwin, Alison the historian, Churchyard the poet, Bishop Percy, Wycherley and Richard Baxter.

The wide open valley of the Clun, up which the highway winds from Hundred House to the Metropolis of Clunites, is none the less pleasing because it resembles so many border valleys, which follow a trout stream up into the heart of the hills. The vale is noted for the quality of its soil. Its low-lying pastures furnish the heaviest cattle; its slopes produce more than average crops of grain and roots. The river shimmers here and there through its alder screen amid the meadows as you ascend its course. The rounded hills of old Clun forest fall back against the skyline, still thrusting here and there some remnant of their ancient wildness above the lines of the early Victorian survey, which between 1837 and 1852 enclosed some ten thousand acres. We have left Clun, Clungunford and Clunbury behind and only Clunton remains ; a mere road-side village within sight of the mother church and town, which latter looks well as you approach it perched on the left bank of the river, while on both sides and beyond it a waste of bare hills rolls far away to the south and west. Clun is indeed no ordinary market town. The fact of its being nine miles from a station by no means expresses the measure of its aloofness and originality, neither of which are interfered with by the regular service of an omnibus which daily rumbles back and forth to Craven Arms. I am quite sure a very fine book could be written on Clun, if fate had decreed that some antiquary with human and humorous instinct had, by good fortune, spent his life there. But there is nothing particular of a superficial kind to engage the pen of a visitor ; an old-fashioned whitewashed townlet of little more than a single long street, neither wholly Welsh nor wholly English, but eloquent of the March, with the grim remnants of a border fortress spring-ing high above its western limit, and breathing defiance over wide and windy wastes of Wales. The lofty keep of Clun, set high on the sharp slope of immense grass-grown earth-works, with the prattling river washing two sides of them and the western sky for a background, fills a distinct place in the memory, even though the latter were imprinted with every castle in Wales and the Marches. I was fortunate in having the peaceful hour of a gorgeous sunset for my first introduc-tion to it, with nothing more inharmonious to disturb it than some full-uddered milk cows crunching greedily at the grass-grown moat on their way to the pail. An early owl hooted somewhere, and there was a murmur of the stream below. The towering square keep, bereft long since of its inner wall, blackened gradually against the fiery sky, and its ragged win-dows blazed like furnaces ; while far away over the folding hills of the still wild upland of Clun forest to the distant heights of Kerry, the shadows deepened into the gray of twilight.

Clun castle is generally accounted the scene of the *Betrothed*. Scott visited friends or relatives in the neighbourhood and thus made its acquaintance, and few border ruins, from their pose and situation, at any rate, could have been more calcu-lated to inspire him. Great, however, as Sir Walter was, he was an alien here. The *Betrothed* is admittedly one of his mediocre productions, though it has the merit of being the only recognized romance in existence treating of a subject which should have such infinite possibilities for the historical novel. The Norman, the Pembroke-Fleming, the Welshman and the Saxon are all duly represented, and as one would expect in Scott, there is not a line that jars for a moment with historical truth or perspective. Yet somehow the work seems thin and uninspiring. One feels that the author could not resist the temptation of this other border influence so like and yet so unlike his own, and did all that even a great genius could do, who had only drawn a few draughts of the atmosphere and made no pretension to be steeped in its story. The very authorities quoted in the footnotes, if irreproachable,

CLUN CASTLE.

seem a trifle elementary and the references laboured, and the note struck is so different from that which rings out so spontaneously from his pen on Scottish soil.

Powys castle is sometimes introduced by editors and illustrators in the usual vague way as the possible scene of the story. The centenary edition has an impossible engraving of Harlech for its frontispiece, a castle on the north Welsh sea-coast that never had the faintest connection with border wars or Marcher interests. But there is every reason to believe that Clun was the original of "Garde Dolareuse," and one takes one's hat off to Scott for his own sake as one stands beneath its ruined keep, and feels grateful to him, at least, for his quick recognition of what it typifies and for a memorable tribute to it, The late Mr. Jasper More has written several pages in the visitors' book at the *Buffalo Inn* to prove that Scott actually slept there, and if this is open to question it in no way affects the situation. The stars were out and the far shadowy bounds of Melineth and Elvael and Arwystli, names familiar enough to the defenders of these walls but long lost to usage, had sunk into the night before I descended from the castle steep and sought mine inn. The grim old keep, still eighty feet in height, was wrapped in silence as well as darkness and every note of the river broke on the ear with flute-like clearness :—

> And far beneath where slow they creep
> From pool to eddy still and deep,
> Where alders moist and willows weep
> You heard her streams repine.

Scott was naturally in one's thoughts, and if his mental perch on this occasion was the rampart of a Lothian castle, and the music in his ears that of a Lammermuir stream of remote and somewhat cherished memory to the present writer, the inscribing of this melodious fragment, which sprang not quite irrelevantly to my mind, may, I hope, be pardoned.

Readers who have not been under the spell of Clun castle at sunset and nightfall will not tolerate its long story, so I will content myself with saying that it was the stronghold of the Fitz Alans, who built it in Stephen's reign, and became Earls of Arundel, and the continuity of ownership has been remarkable since it passed in remote times to the Norfolk family who still own it, and indeed boast Baron Clun as their first title. It was dismantled by Glyndwr and blown up by the Roundheads, for whose pious and political services the antiquary has to pay so fearful a price. The Fitz Alans were among the Marcher barons who claimed the particular privilege of supporting the canopy at coronations with silver spears. Its sieges by the Welsh were many and fierce, but as that luminous authority on mediæval castles, the late Mr. G. T. Clarke, observes, more injury has been done to Clun, as to other similar strongholds, by wanton moderns, from Roundheads to barn and stable-building iconoclasts, than by all the sows and battering-rams of the ancients.

The entrance to a secret passage between the castle and the old court-house, which lies in the flat several hundred yards off, was discovered in the eighteenth century. There is a tradition too that the castle was built of material from a neighbouring quarry, and that the stones were passed from hand to hand by a chain of men a mile long. While the castle and High Street of Clun occupy one ridge, the fine old church and rectory and other buildings are set on the other, the Clun running between them under a curious stone bridge of the same age as the castle. This bridge, by the way, and Clun gener-

CLUN CHURCH.

ally, is the scene of Goodall's well-known picture, " Raising the Maypole," and many illustrious Clunites figure on the canvas. There was an old saying in the neighbourhood that those who crossed Clun bridge came back " sharp." So keen were the trading faculties of the citizens, that a stranger from Knighton or Presteign, or Bishop's Castle, had only to encounter them once to become a changed man, and himself too much for his comparatively guileless neighbours.

After a comfortable night at the *Buffalo*, not upon the wooden bedstead where Scott is supposed to have reclined, I had a walk with the rector, whose spiritual jurisdiction extends over a vast area and includes three churches. There are scarcely any country houses in this immediate neighbourhood and no resident gentry, nor has anybody yet satisfactorily derived the name Clun, which has, I believe, no sort of equivalent elsewhere in England or Wales. The natives in Georgian times were a wild set. If Clun and her satellites were as quiet as the bard makes out, it was not for lack of drinking or fighting. The present youth of Clun, I am told on the best authority, takes the keenest interest in the doings of its forefathers, not the Georgian anes, but those ancients whose fortunes were more or less involved with those of the castle. This is rare indeed, and should more than neutralize the shortcomings, if such one may call them, of the intervening epoch. Clun was a corporate town till recently, and had its bailiffs, but the silver maces plone remain of its civic glories. The church is finely blaced high on the opposite hill slope. The tower is low but of a great strength, and doubtless was of much service in times of strife ; the nave is Early English, but the whole fabric has been well restored by Street. In the large grave-yard the sonorous border names are thick : Cadwalladars and Merediths, besides the inevitable Hughes, Pughes, Prices, and Watkinses, which with Brunts, Gilleys and Gittoes make a curious variety. One, Robert Luther, lies here, and a friend who is much in Clun tells me among other things that he was a famous sportsman and Master of the United Pack, a farmer's hunt that still flourishes in these parts. Luther left implicit instructions that he was to be buried " as a sportsman." These, I am told, were carried out to the letter, and after a fashion which may be left to the imagination of those who knew Clun fifty years ago, which I did not. There also lies in Clun church-yard another enthusiastic sportsman, one Charles Dyke, who died in 1825 at the early age, for this part of the world, of forty-five. And on his tombstone is written a pathetic but not unfamiliar story :—

> Joyous his birth ; wealth on his cradle shone.
> Generous he proved, far was his bounty known.
> Men, horses, hounds were feasted at his hall ;
> There strangers found a welcome, bed and stall.
> Quick distant idlers answered to his horn,
> And all was gladness in the sportsman's morn.

But evening came and colder blew the gale ;
Means overdone had now begun to fail,
His wine was finished, and he ceased to brew.
And fickle friends now hid them from his view.
Unknown, neglected, pined this man of worth,
Death his best friend, his resting-place the earth.

A gem among epitaphs surely is this ? Humanity accepts such general truisms about itself with much complacency, but this personal application of it to a particular neighbourhood from a dead man's tomb must have made some of the early Victorians of Clunton, Clunbury, Clungunford and Clun feel extremely uncomfortable. The ill-treated and open-handed sportsman, however, lived most of his life in Mainstone,

FARMHOUSE NEAR HOPTON CASTLE.

a parish just north of Clun, though he died at the latter place. So we may perhaps believe that the rector and churchwardens of the moorland metropolis felt that their flock were not seriously implicated in the moving tale, and indeed may even have composed the verses as a slap at a neighbouring community, for Clun was ever clannish. Though old houses are plentiful enough here, there is little of architectural interest with one striking exception, and that is the small hospital for old men, founded in 1617, by Henry Howard, Duke of Norfolk. It consists of two quadrangles, one inhabited by the fifteen veterans, who besides their rooms receive a blue cloak and hat and ten shillings a week apiece, and a second containing a cloister and the subwarden's house. The low-pitched picturesque old building, profusely covered with varied creepers, its chapel and dining hall and its quadrangle gay with well-trimmed lawns and flower-beds, is an almost more seductive spot than the Conningsby Hospital at Hereford. The rector of Clun, who introduced me to it, is ex-officio warden, and a curate as sub-warden occupies the cloistered chambers sacred to that office.

Prehistoric camps lie thick upon the surrounding hilltops, and there is a noted Druidical circle on Pen-y-wern just above the town. Seven miles to the north is Bishop's Castle; equidistant upon the south is Knighton. You may travel westward, however, for fourteen or fifteen miles to Kerry, through the pastoral holdings of the old forest, whose summits roll about you at the elevation of Dartmoor and Exmoor, though more enclosed nowadays even than these. Clun sheep have been so mixed with the Shrop as to lose their individuality. Clun Forest mutton is still advertised in London butchers' shops, but a local friend tells me that the salesmen may invariably be put to confusion by merely asking them where Clun Forest is ? The land of Clun or rather its population have vastly changed in the last generation or two, The daily omnibus to Craven Arms has not affected this social revolution, but rather suggests the old order of things. But the world moves, and Clun like other isolated districts has moved too, at any rate sufficiently to shed its belief in witches or "over-lookers," as they are called in this part of the country. Its graziers no longer fight or drink much beyond the stage of "market peartness." But you may yet see groups of men, and even women, jogging along the road on ponies or cobs in Welsh fashion. It is an easy pilgrimage of nine miles from Clun down to Craven Arms, past Hundred House again, and Clunbury, and so by Aston to the famous junction of the North-Western Railway, an active centre both of highways and railways, and an excellent beginning for our next chapter.

CHAPTER X

CRAVEN ARMS AND CHURCH STRETTON—THE LONGMYND, —WENTNOR AND PLOWDEN

THE eight miles of highway from Ludlow to Stokesay and Craven Arms affords very different travelling from the circuitous and hilly route which we compassed in the last chapter. The former stretch is almost level, and is a section of that main road from Hereford to Shrewsbury so deservedly popular with motorists and cyclists, not only for its easy gradients, but for its admirable surface of Clee Hill stone which so greatly lessens the evils of wet weather and minimizes the terror of the skid. Much umbrageous timber, too, waves above either hedgerow, and though the way is easy, pleasant hills encompass it about, and cool trout streams ripple anon beneath it or shimmer in the bordering meads.

I have said nothing of Oakley, the beautifully wooded park of Lord Windsor; which, reaching nearly to Ludlow, encloses the Teme for many a mile within its sylvan bounds, and is open at all times for those who like to follow a by-road through it. Bromfield, three miles from Ludlow and conspicuous from afar by its row of lofty poplars known as the "twelve apostles," is the first village on this northern road. An open green, with old-fashioned cottages fringing one side of it, an ancient church tower set high on a wooded knoll upon the other, and the Onny rippling towards the Teme beneath an old stone bridge in the centre, makes a pleasing scene. Many uncanny things however have happened even at Bromfield in olden times. Just to the westward up the Teme on the Oakley property there is a long stretch of pasture known as Crawl Meadows, and the country people derive its name from a source unexpectedly romantic. For once upon a time, it seems, the daughter of the then proprietor plighted her troth to an impecunious knight, an imprudence that so incensed her sire that he swore she should have no more land for dower than she could crawl over on her hands and knees between

229

STOKESAY CASTLE

sunset and dawn. But the maiden, borrowing a pair of leather breeches, started at dark on her painful and inglorious pilgrimage, and covered no less than four miles before daybreak, thus marking out with the suffering and toil of her body a handsome provision for her future husband. Let us hope he treated her well.

I said somewhat, when at Skenfrith Castle, concerning the belief of mediæval rustics in hidden treasure, stimulated no doubt by the frequent discovery of Roman coins or "Fairy money." These deposits in the border country were often thought to be guarded by dragons. Thomas of Walsingham tells us that in 1344 a Saracen mystic came to the lord of Ludlow and asked permission to slay a dragon at Bromfield, who not only guarded a hidden treasure, but was a terror to the neighbourhood. Having received his commission, the Oriental proceeded to encounter the monster, not after the martial fashion of St. George, but with incantations which proved quite as effective. Unfortunately, however, some peasants overheard the performance, so when the dragon was disposed of, they undertook upon their own account the second and safer part of the programme, and dug out and appropriated the treasure, leaving the poor Saracen to his barren victory with nothing whatever to his share but the hide of the dragon, whatever that may have been worth in the local market. These mean spirited villagers however met their deserts, for the earl's retainers, hearing of the discovery, promptly relieved them of their hoard and incarcerated them into the bargain ; we do not gather, however, that the meritorious Saracen profited anything.

A pleasant four-mile journey from Bromfield, which by the way had once a priory of Benedictines, up the valley of the Onny, brings us to Stokesay castle, so called, standing between the railroad on one hand and the road and river on the other. Stokesay must have astonished many a traveller on the main line, being so plainly visible and but a stone's throw distant. For the merest tyro would recognize at a glance a type of building that he had probably never before encountered. Stokesay is not in truth a castle but a fortified manor house of the thirteenth century, for in 1291 one Lawrence de Ludlow was granted permission "to crenalate his house at Stokesay," and there it is to-day still virtually perfect, and our sketches will be more effective than any description of its exterior. The half-timbered gate house leading into the courtyard will be also noticed. The banqueting hall is over fifty feet in length, and its long windows are of Early English design and tracery, while the house is entirely surrounded by a moat over twenty feet wide. The tower at one end of the building and the far projecting timbered windows at the other are a curious blend of the military and domestic, dating from so remote a period. There are very few fortified manors

STOKESAY CASTLE.

of the thirteenth or fourteenth century left in England of such size and state of preservation, for the entire roof of this one is intact ; the rooms are floored and contain some good fireplaces. The drawing-room, which has two peep windows looking down into the banqueting hall, contains also a most beautiful Jacobean mantle, while each storey of the great tower is for all practical purposes as it originally was. It is

quite a unique building in my experience, and I have seen
at one time or another almost every old fortress in Wales and
the Marches. It is fortunate too in an owner who not only
keeps it up but throws it open to, let us hope, an appreciative
public at a trifling fee. Lawrence de Ludlow seems to have
been one of the very earliest instances of a local trader developing into a great landowner and founding a family.

Adjoining the castle is the small church and graveyard,
the former worth entering if only for some handsome carved
pews and a canopied pulpit therein. My first inspection of
it was prompted by the vague hope of finding traces of the
Baldwins, who held the manor, but I only found Onions ! a
worthy name no doubt, but not of itself suggestive of plate
armour. There is, however, a most eccentric epitaph on a tombstone near the churchyard gate, erected to an old gentleman who
died quite recently at the age of ninety-four, and in its lowly
way as unique as the manor house itself. It reads thus :—

> Autumn came, and Thomas had
> Nuts and apples for the lad,
> He to manhood having grown,
> Determined to erect this stone,
> The soul of Thomas having flown.

This stimulated my curiosity, and I returned to the caretaker
of the castle in his mediæval gatehouse, and learned that the
lad thus worthily and modestly immortalized at his own
expense, together with his ancient friend, was moved by
grateful memories of the venerable soul who had been wont
in this simple fashion to minister to his boyish appetites. If
the tribute is not quite Tennysonian in form, it is at least
idyllic in spirit and sincere beyond cavil

Craven Arms is hard by Stokesay, and like New Swindon,
though on a far smaller scale, has within my own recollection
arisen from a station in a meadow into a populous settlement
of railway operatives. Nought therefore need be said concerning it unless to make mention of a comfortable little
hotel on the banks of the Onny, where visitors to Stokesay
refresh themselves and some few others given to the pursuit
of trout and grayling or the investigation of an interesting
neighbourhood make more prolonged sojourn. I must not
overlook the fact, however, that immense auctions of stock
are periodically held at this now important railroad entrepot,
when the loud clamour of Hereford and black bullocks, of

Radnor, Cardigan, or Shropshire sheep, of collie dogs, and drovers from Cambrian Hills, and March land meadows fills the air for brief interludes. A mile beyond Craven Arms we again cross the Onny, where its upward course vanishes for good amid enfolding hills, and the valley of the main route is filled by a little tributary not nameless but unknown to fame. Wenlock Edge, that long high wall of dense foliage, broken only by its stone tower, fills the sky upon the east, while upon the west ahead of us the Stretton Hills are looming into view. Rolling cornlands and meadows are all about on either hand, and Felhampton with its roomy brick Georgian homestead fronts the road. Many a Hereford bred on these pastures crossed the Atlantic in the eighties to impress their

GATEHOUSE AT STOKESAY.

virtues on future herds in the Western States or the Argentine. I well remember what a time we had, some twenty years ago, in these very yards, trying to persuade a famous bull, well named *Merry Monarch*, to sit for his photograph, of which I have yet a faded specimen.

Beyond Marshbrook, road and railroad enter the glen between the main range of the Stretton Hills and their outworks, that striking pass so well known to travellers between Lancashire and Bristol or Cardiff. High up on the right hand near by, though not visible, is the interesting Tudor manor house of Acton Scott, which has been for several hundred years in the Acton family, one of whose members, Mrs. Stackhouse Acton, in the last century was a well known contributor to Shropshire lore, At Little Stretton we get on terms of intimacy with the real y imposing masses of the Longmynd, which with their steep sides and wild surface look fully more than the 1,700 feet allowed them by the ordnance map. On the other side Caradoc leaps up to a somewhat similar altitude with its fine rugged crest and rocky profile, so familiar a landmark from every part of Shropshire; while between them the popular summer resort of Church Stretton nestles cheerfully in the narrow wooded vale. To the northward and beyond lies the village of All Stretton, and a familiar local legend attributes the distinguishing title of this ultimate Stretton to James II, who once followed the route to Shrewsbury. Having passed through Little Stretton and Church Stretton, he in-

LITTLE STRETTON.

quired the name of the next village, and being informed that it too was Stretton he remarked petulantly that all was "Stretton" in these parts, and I never heard a more impossible derivation for a name. Watling Street runs up the valley, a hillside lane swerving eastwards towards the buried city of Uriconium, and no doubt is responsible for the derivation *All*, which in this case is a corruption of "*old.*"

Caradoc is the finest isolated hill in Shropshire, bolder as well as higher than the Wrekin. Popularly known as Querdoc it has played its part in the folklore as well as in the rural festivities of the county, for when legendary events have provided a suitable occasion it has risen to it and burst into a volcano, and the caves where Caractacus hid after his defeats are still obvious on its steep face. Wakes were very important functions in Shropshire till the middle of the last century, and some of them were held on hilltops, notably on those of Caradoc and the Wrekin. The former associated itself since remote times with Trinity Sunday. Barrels of ale were then broached, refreshment booths erected, hawkers went to and fro, and rough sports, notably wrestling, were engaged in, and much fiddling and dancing, with other evidences of old-world heartiness, as late certainly as 1830. The Wrekin wake, held on the first Sunday in May, was renowned for the annual fight between the mining and the agricultural interest, which became at last so bloodthirsty that the feast was abolished. The tradition, however, has by no means died out, for young people, I am told, still repair, though in demurer and more peaceful mood, both to Caradoc and the Wrekin on the old fête days, and make love no doubt in board school English. It seems strange that the "continental Sunday," as some call it, should have trenched so close upon the intervening period that made Sunday in England a day of pious dread to most young people of normal vitality. Indeed the conflicting views on Sunday deportment held by Britons since the Civil War should of themselves justify much personal liberty of the subject in this particular without offence. What, for instance, can be said for the inconsistent wights who deliberately break the only distinct Biblical utterance on the subject by driving a hard-worked horse to church or chapel, and yet regard their neighbour who rests his cattle and proceeds thither on a bicycle with the long upper lip of Calvinistic disapproval? Yet thousands of such people are still roaming at large.

Church Stretton has swollen within the last twenty years from a village frequented by a mere handful of border people to quite a little town of lodging houses and private residences. There was a good hotel there when I first knew it, and also a lunatic asylum. Indeed it was then so inconsiderable a place that a visitor had to make up his mind to be gaped at as a mental patient, and suffer the curious and sympathetic gaze of the rustic when he took his drives abroad. All this is now changed : both hotel and asylum still flourish, but there is quite a large summer population, and furthermore a fine hydro set high up amid woods on the spur of the hills, which caters for the most fastidious taste. Seeing that this occupies the prettiest site of the prettiest spot in accessible Shropshire, whence roads lead in every direction, not only to places of historic interest and physical beauty, but are themselves among the best in England for motor or cycle, it should prosper. Of its interior arrangements I can only give the opinion of friends, which is entirely favourable.

There is a fine cruciform church at Stretton with a Norman chancel, a thirteenth century roof and some curious panelling. In regard to its restoration, however, one cannot help thinking that the craze for ruthlessly exposing the naked stone of church interiors has often a most gloomy and depressing effect. Why should architects in pursuit of past ideals real and imaginary resort to methods that were rarely intended or followed by the original builders of parish churches. There are exceptions, beyond a doubt, when the stone is warm and ornamental, but the result of the modern craze seems not infrequently to suggest the interior of a barn or a cowshed, and surely some measure of disrespect to the Almighty. The bells of Shropshire churches seem mostly to have something to impart to wayfarers. Those of Stretton exclaim " Roast beef and mutton " ; those of Clun, " Hop, skip and run " ; while Acton Scott suggests the Sunday dinner more pointedly with " Pudding in the pot." Lebotwood, a parish north of Stretton, invites its parishioners to " lay a bottle in the wood," and the remoter village of Llanfair chimes inconsequently of " Roas' goose an' gander." This was a merry part of the county in olden days, for not only was there Caradoc wake in Stretton parish, but the church dedicated to St. Lawrence held a revel on the Sunday after its saint's day, as did All Stretton and the little hill church of Mintown. Many of these ancient functions date back no doubt to pagan times, when primitive Christianity was grafted on pagan stocks and gathered naturally round the sacred spots of the earlier worship.

The last three decades have been terribly destructive of legends, folklore and dialect. Miss Jackson and her editor, Miss Burne, were just in time to enclose a good deal of the old Salopian atmosphere in a volume of some six hundred pages, but in this, as in so many folklore collections, the purely local and national legends and customs are blended somewhat confusedly together. The folklore of west Shropshire, though the latter is so close to Wales and physically akin to it, has mainly a Saxon flavour The dialect is a variety of the Saxon vernacular

LOOKING UP WATLING STREET TO CHURCH STRETTON.

238

common to the border counties south of Cheshire, with more observable peculiarities in it than the kindred tongue of Radnor, Hereford or Monmouth. The H is conspicuous by its absence, but the Welsh intonation is always present along the March, in some parts unmistakable, in others only noticeable to a sensitive ear. The " Shanna, willa, would na'," suggestive in print of the far north, seems even more typical of west Shropshire than of Radnor and Hereford, and the voice loses in softness as you move northward up the March from the last-named counties. Save for an old-timer here and there it is idle to pretend that any serious belief in fairies, giants, witch cures and such like still lingers. It is enough to catch their echoes and to hope that their memories at least will not be lost.

Education and cheap railway trips have turned the attention of country lads and lasses to more practical interests. The parish is no longer the limit of range for either action or fancy. Farm servants do not now gather at nights round the mysterious half-light of the farmhouse kitchen fire, keenly sensitive to every uncanny influence, but they live in their own cottages and read *Tit Bits* by an explosive oil lamp. A good many wonderful things happened in this Stretton Valley before it took the fancy of the outer world, and indeed it is just the spot to accumulate legends. It was one of the many places in Shropshire where rustic plays were regularly acted a century or more ago. These performances were promoted and conducted almost entirely by the peasant class, and were in themselves quite innocent functions, boys taking the female parts. The stage was usually laid on a couple of wagons placed alongside a public house into which actors retired between their parts. On this rude platform the chairman was seated with the book of the words in the double capacity of prompter and call boy. The performance lasted about three hours, and over a thousand people sometimes collected to see as much or as little of it as they could. The actors found their reward in all the meat and drink they could stow away and in the applause of their neighbours, and the piece was usually acted in several different villages. At the close of the performance fiddling and dancing lasted well into the night, and indeed these plays seem to have been often the leading item of a parish wake. From a paper on the subject by a well known Salopian I find that the best known plays in this district were *Prince Musidorus*, *The Rigs of the*

Times, Valentine and Orson, and *St. George and the Fiery Dragon.* The dragon was contrived of wood and manipulated by a pole from behind, and squibs of gunpowder in his mouth gave a realistic effect to the encounter. In the last scene he was made to rear up on his hind legs so that St. George could more conveniently cut his head off, amid the cheers of the audience. Here is the advertisement of a wake in the *Shrewsbury Chronicle* of date August, 1777.

Notice is hereby given that Shawbury Wake begins on the eleventh of August, when there will be the usual diversions of stage plays on Monday, a horse race on Tuesday, and Wednesday for fifty Pounds each day. No one will be allowed to bring any kind of liquors on the Racecourse for sale that dont subscribe five shillings towards the Plate.

N.B.—There will be an Ordinary for the gentlemen at the *Elephant and Castle,* and for the ladies at the *Squirrel* each day. Dinner to be on the table at two o'clock.

There will be an assembly each night. A stag to be turned out on Monday morning exactly at two o'clock.

Nunc est bibendum, nunc pede libero pulsanda tellus.

Come, cheery damsel, come away,
Nice dress your hair for Shawb'ry Play
Then to the Ball and Dance till day.

Shawbury, which must surely have been an aristocratic type of wake, is far out of our beat, being a village to the north-east of Shrewsbury. If the reminiscence may be pardoned, though I have never been there since, the idea has flashed across me since writing the above, that I may have unconsciously assisted as an alien of tender age in the waning glories of Shawbury wake. What old cricketer does not remember the momentous occasion when, as a small boy, he was first deemed worthy to engage in a regular match, and the dreadful joy of striving to look unconcerned and happy with a full-sized bat on his first anxious trip from the crowded tent to the wicket. There were no garden party boys' matches in those days to break the plunge, but a great deal more rustic cricket of a serious and hearty description, if on wickets not conducive to forward play. Under the hospitable roof where I sometimes found myself in summer holidays, "the Shawbury match" was the cricket event of the season, and the object for which grooms and gardeners bowled fast underhand at one another and at us in the park for days previously in the perilous dusk of summer twilight, for alien experts were not imported for such occasions in those days, and the local talent was on its mettle. The grown-up sons of the house were horsemen first and cricketers afterwards, and the putting together and manipulating an improvised four-in-hand for the occasion was their prime care and provided a further excitement for the day. This was over forty years ago, which is my only excuse for the interpolation, except that the date

CHURCH STRETTON

about coincided with that of Shawbury wake, and the fixture may have been an incident in what was left of it. For I remember that the natives demonstrated in force amid the long grass outside the pitch, which was responsible everywhere in those days for so many " lost balls " off indifferent strokes, while the fieldsmen stamped impotently round in circles and the onlookers yelled encouragement to the batsmen who ran their ill-deserved six in spasmodic, nervous and half-guilty fashion.

But we will leave the highway at Church Stretton and mount the steep spurs of the Longmynd which rise immediately behind the straggling village. A tolerable road leads right over the mountain top, used for all time by the folk of the back country, but improved no doubt for the benefit of the weaker members pleasuring in Stretton, whose legs are unequal to carrying them to one of the finest prospects in England. The Longmynd is a broad-backed lofty ridge ; true moorland, not down, running north and south for many miles and throwing out high precipitous spurs into the vale below. The deep combes with which its sides are thus riven are partially clad with fern and gorse and watered by mountain brooks, and have all the quality and the mystery of a mountain country. The summit of the range and higher slopes on both sides is one continuous grouse moor, the heather being so deep and thick that the ordinary wayfarer is virtually confined to the green drives that cross and re-cross the wild. One of these traverses the summit of the range for its entire length from Robin Hood's Butts, near Lebotwood, to Plowden in the Onny valley. It is known as the Portway and is an ancient British track, used a good deal probably in the middle ages when the valley, even though threaded by Watling Street, had its drawbacks and is recorded in ancient charts as " the King's hie way." I have myself taken a cycle over the Longmynd for use in the country beyond without the slightest difficulty, for though the track crosses the range near its highest points, 1,700 feet, the rise from Stretton, which itself stands high on a valley watershed, is not much over a thousand. A beautiful ascent it is, too, with the deep bare glen of the Carding Mill and its threadlike riverlet winding far below, and the British camp of Bodbury springing high into the air on the far side, clear cut and defiant on the verge of its almost inaccessible steep. While midway between earth and heaven golfers may be descried flitting from green to green like specks upon the waste. Caradoc and Lawley rise finely to our own level beyond Stretton, which as we ascend the Longmynd gradually subsides from view, into its deep bosky trough. There is little danger nowadays of sharing the fate which overcame so many returning revellers from the latest of the Stretton wakes, as to earn for it the ominous title of Deadman's Fair ! A blood-curdling account, however, of a night spent in a snow storm up here by a former vicar of Ratlinghope while following a call of duty in the sixties is a sort of classic in the neighbourhood,

and though well worth reading is quoted with somewhat wearisome reiteration by every local author.

CARDING MILL VALLEY, CHURCH STRETTON.

Now the Longmynd enjoys a quite unique association with
the uneasy spirit of a Saxon warrior. For the old heroes of the

border, both those that in the local phrase "come back" and those that lie in peace, are mostly of Norman or Celtic origin. But over the wastes of the Longmynd and the crest of Caradoc wild Edric and his men were firmly believed by past generations to ride upon the gales, bursting in times of coming import from the depths of the old lead mines, where they lay entombed like Arthur and Glyndwr, awaiting their hour of vengeance.

Edric has been already alluded to as that Saxon Earl of Shropshire who retained his honours for a brief space after the conquest, and then engaging with Welsh allies in a fierce struggle with the Conqueror and his lieutenants, harried the Norman grants and was finally subdued by the first Mortimer who, it will be remembered, received Wigmore and other of his estates for this service. Edric then became the Conqueror's man, and bearing apparently no malice fought with him against the Scots. After a record more strenuous than that of Hereward the Wake, though fiction has not adopted and popularized him, it ended mysteriously, a fact not disconnected by tradition with the uneasy habits of his wraith. He was more often of course heard overhead in the dark of the night than actually seen by the light of day, showing himself, it seems, only on the eve of great wars. A young woman of the neighbourhood told Miss Jackson that she and her father had both seen him distinctly just before the Crimean war. On this dread occasion while on the hill she heard of a sudden the blast of a horn, and her father told her to cover her face all but her eyes lest she go mad. Then the wild cavalcade swept by, Edric leading it on a white horse and his wife Lady Godda (*sic*) riding at full speed over the moor. Edric had short dark curly hair and bright black eyes; he wore a green cap and white feather, a short green coat and cloak, a horn and short sword hanging from a golden belt, and in the girl's language "something zigzagged" here (touching her leg below the knee). The lady had wavy golden hair falling to her waist, and round her forehead a band of white linen with a golden ornament on it. The rest of her dress was green, and a short dagger hung at her waist. The girl watched them ride over the hills to the north, for the direction taken on these occasions was always that where war was impending. Her father had seen this same thing before the final struggle with Napoleon, and then the ghostly train were galloping to the south.

Wild Edric was supposed to have married an elf maiden. For one day, hunting in the forest of Clun, he came at nightfall to a large brightly-lighted house, where were a number of most beautiful women, larger than is wont with the daughters of men, clad in shapely linen and dancing with a swinging motion and singing softly in a language Edric could not understand. One of them surpassed even her companions in loveliness, and while watching her the fires of love extinguished the awe which Edric had felt before this mystic, uncanny scene, and the heady Saxon rushed into the group of dancers and seized the syren round the waist, with the object of carrying her off. The others attacked him with teeth and nails, but helped by his attendants he succeeded in bearing away his prize. For three days the maiden sulked in silence, but on the fourth relented and promised to make a good wife to her abductor, provided that he never allowed her sisters' names or any allusion to the place where he discovered her to pass his lips : this she said would prove fatal. Edric promised readily, as did the Carmarthenshire farmer in the case of his water-wife from the Van Pool. There was a smart wedding attended by all the countryside, and William the Conqueror was so interested that he invited the happy pair up to London, who brought with them a cloud of witnesses to attest the supernatural affinities of the bride. But her unearthly beauty, the Londoners said, was quite proof enough for them, and the Conqueror sent them home again with his blessing. After some happy years, on Edric returning one night from hunting, tired and cross, he missed his wife from her usual place, and when she appeared, upbraided her with having been detained by her sisters. Then the blow which hung over all men who married elfin wives fell, and she vanished never more to be seen or heard of by Edric, to his grief and despair.

The first time I was on the Longmynd during the past summer was the eleventh of August. It was noontide, and the atmosphere under the clearing breath of a light north breeze and a tempered sun was in a condition of quite marvellous transparency. It is hardly too much to say that the greater portion of Wales lay at my feet. Mere clearness of detail over a vast outlook is not, to be sure, the most complete form of beauty in landscape ; but for me at any rate it has a great fascination, above all when every point is familiar, and most are full of associations personal or otherwise. It was an extraordinary day and an extraordinary spectacle, rarely I should imagine vouchsafed to an appreciative mortal on this height. There was little light and shadow, for there was no sun shining over

Wales. The ten counties, which to this westward outlook alone revealed more or less of their surface, were wrapped in almost a monotone of pale grey. I could not be sure of Snowdon, but Cader Idris, the Arrans and the Berwyn Ranges stood out boldly. Then came Plinlimon with its smooth swelling outline, and thence the low grey ribs of the long wilderness rolling south from it for fifty miles to some dim shadowy humps, that I recognized as Carningly and the Precelly uplands of north Pembroke. Clun and Radnor forests, the Black Mountains, the sharp peaks of the Brecon Beacons, and the familiar summits of the Carmarthen Vans just hid, Glamorganshire the only county in Wales but Flint and Anglesea that contributed nothing to this remarkable panorama. It might have been a cast of Wales raised upon grey paper for the benefit of a physical geography class, so utterly unresponsive was it to any elemental influence.

Yet immediately over our heads the sun was shining sufficiently to light up the miles of purple bloom that covered the lofty platform on which we stood. By the solitary cottage which up here breaks the waste, I found the keeper who inhabits it scanning with his glasses the purple sweep which was to yield its tribute of grouse upon the morrow. He told me their bag in the previous year had been about fifty brace upon each of the two first days. So the Stretton visitors can be no great hindrance to the moor, for if memory serves me right these figures are an increase on those when tourists were not an item worth considering. As a matter of fact on this glorious morning, though Stretton was crowded there was not a soul to be seen on the whole waste of purple hills, but a group of whinberry gatherers, a dozen stalwart females working their way through the deep heather under the keeper's nose. But this is, I believe, an inalienable privilege, and as something like five hundred pounds' worth of these berries are gathered here every season, I felt that my instinctive sympathy with this lonesome official was misplaced, though the grievance from his point of view was only human. I have hardly mentioned what a fine appearance is made by Caradoc and its satellites, with the Wenlock Edge lying low on the east, or by the distant Wrekin which shapes best at this angle, or by the Malvern Hills in the further distance, because the marvel of the Welsh outlook on that occasion somewhat lessened the interest of the other.

But turning westward again, and to the foreground this

time, the deep valley of Ratlinghope lies tucked beneath the Longmynd, and rising immediately behind it is the almost parallel range of the Stiperstones, of about equal length and altitude. But this other range is of an appearance unique in England, according to Murchison, for the strange outcrops of rock that spring at intervals from the summit of its long hog back. It has been compared to the back of a monster fish with an undue complement of spinal fins standing erect, and is one of the familiar objects in that wide hill-girdled panorama with which citizens of Shrewsbury and all dwellers in the western plains of Shropshire are upon terms of daily intimacy. The great geologist above-mentioned and the country people take naturally divergent views of this fantastic freak of nature, which has something of an equivalent in the lower ranges of Pembrokeshire—Trefgarn, to wit. The rustics have it that the devil was on his way from Ireland to the Wrekin with an apron full of stones, but being overcome by the heat when he arrived here, which considering the traditional temperature of his own quarters seems a weak supposition, he spilled his load and there it is, the highest of the chief outcrops to this day being called " the devil's chair," and it is said still to smell of brimstone in hot weather.

Having wandered thus far into the realms of mystery and folklore, I am going to crave indulgence and dally somewhat longer in them. The fascination of these things is in their ancient origin, and in the thought that generations innumerable have believed or half believed in the weird properties of familiar objects that we regard to-day with the proper scepticism of a higher civilization so-called. And for most of us, this detracts nothing from the pleasure of dwelling on these bygone superstitions that so harmonize with one's mood when wandering in lonely places. Plenty of us even now have our doubts, and though they no longer take the shape of giants or wild huntsmen. All this is à propos of the fact that from the top of the Longmynd here I could see, far away, beyond the Welsh border-line, a dim grey hill which marks the spot where my own scepticism, a fairly robust one on these matters, has been once at any rate most rudely shaken. At the risk of being more discursive than is perhaps seemly, even in this unfettered narrative, I shall tell the story exactly as it happened, and I think it is worth the telling.

Perched at a considerable altitude, with its back to a waste of wild half-enclosed Welsh moorland and its front looking down over a wide expanse of the neighbouring county, and remotely removed from the madding crowd, stands a small manor house of a reasonable antiquity, though this matters nothing to the story. It lies adjacent to an old church, a hamlet of some half-dozen dwellings and the ruins of a border keep. These items, too, though a harmonious setting for an uncanny incident, are not otherwise relevant to it. For a couple of generations the house and shooting has been let on short leases to many different tenants of that numerous leisured class who take small places in the country. In the summer of 1901 some intimate friends of my own had occupied it for five years, their lease was expiring, and they were giving it up for no reason connected with the place, to which they were much attached. I visited them twice in the above-mentioned summer in the months of June and September, and it was between these dates the following strange things occurred. My hostess, whom I will call Mrs. A——, and her guest of a week or two, an old friend from the other side of England, who shall be Miss B——, are the only members

SHROPSHIRE COTTAGES.

of the small household concerned in the story. It is necessary to state that neither of these ladies had any particular psychological tendencies, or were afflicted with a neurotic or hysterical temperament, though had they possessed all these

characteristics the fact would not help one iota towards the solution of this particular mystery. Now, it so happened that Miss B—— had a planchette board in her travelling trunk, which she was incidentally conveying as a present from some friend in the south to some others for whose house or neighbourhood she was bound in the north. By way of passing half an hour one evening the two ladies suggested bringing it out, and for the fun of the thing see how it worked, as it was somewhat different from the ordinary board used by children and others as an evening game. This one was of Swedish make, and known I believe as a Vega. The covering board with a marker under it does not trace on blank paper in the usual way, but runs over an arrangement of printed letters. On putting the question usual in the game, in this case addressed to any former inhabitant of the house or room, whose ghostly presence might favour them, the answers, which were written down, were of such a curiously pessimistic and gloomy description as to make some impression on the operators, the most realistic of those decipherable being, "Jealousy is stronger than death." A quite unlooked for interest had been aroused, and as a climax the name of the speaker was called up.

Now the answer made by the pointer, which I may not give literally for obvious reasons, was the name of a woman.

The first was actually Catherine, as to the second it was a surname that, though simple in construction, is as a matter of fact remarkably rare ; appearing for example only twice in the Army list and Clergy list respectively. I have never myself come across any one bearing it, nor had either of the ladies in this adventure, which is more to the point. I will call it " Fallow," as it is similar in length, type and singularity to the other. Catherine Fallow, then, spelt with sufficient accuracy to be inscribed at the moment without hesitation as the name of the spiritual visitant, was written down on the paper beneath her communications. To neither of them had it the faintest significance. One was a total stranger to the country, the other had neither knowledge of nor interest in any of the numerous tenants who had formerly occupied the house. The name, however, being both so definitely spelled out by the pencil under their hand and so singular, together with the curious nature of the previous communications, made just that amount of impression on them as it would have made on nine people out of ten, and Mrs. A——did what most of us would have done, and asked one or two of the people about the place if they had ever heard of an individual bearing it. They shook their heads, and there was apparently an end of the matter.

A few days later, however, she happened to be in the little post office of the adjoining hamlet, whose presiding genius was a dame well up in years who had been there all her life. A still lingering and most natural curiosity prompted my friend to repeat the question in what after all was the most promising quarter. To her astonishment, and I may venture to add her dismay, the old lady did not shake her head like the others but rubbed it thoughtfully, with the result that she recalled the fact that a Miss Fallow used to visit as a guest at the Lodge, a matter of twenty-five or thirty years back. She couldn't recall her Christian name, or for the moment what she was like, but the letters that used to come for her were quite clear in her recollection, as was her frequent presence in the place, and I must repeat that this is a most isolated spot, the Lodge being the only gentleman's house in the entire district. This sounds exhilarating in narrative, but it made my friends feel extremely uncomfortable, as well it may have. Still there was just the chance the old lady might be mistaken, so a few days afterwards, when the agent for the property came over in connection with some repairs, Mrs. A—— asked him at once if he had ever heard of a " Catherine Fallow " in connection with the Lodge. The agent, a lawyer of old standing in the nearest country town, replied : " Kate Fallow (*sic*)—I should think I had. I knew her quite well when I was a boy. She used often to visit here when the ——— rented the place (mentioning tenants of some thirty years back, of name unknown to the others), and she frequently came to our house in ——— to see my mother." The lawyer was able to recall her as a young woman of perhaps twenty-five, of ordinary looks and ordinary personality. He remembered, however, that she was supposed to be engaged to a young officer who was about in the neighbourhood at that time, but that the affair was broken off. All he had ever heard afterwards of Miss Fallow was a rumour of her death. He remembered also the name of the young man, for which Campbell will well serve. Nothing was said to the agent, nor for that matter to any one, of what had happened.

Miss B—— in the meantime left Wales for other visits, and in the next few weeks occasional strangers turned up with " orders to view," as my friends were shortly leaving. In August, a few days before my own final visit, a trap drove up one afternoon with a middle-aged military-looking man, bound on this errand. Mrs. A—— met him in the hall, and after asking permission to see the house he dropped the remark that it would seem strange to be shown over a place which he had known quite intimately as a young man and spent so many pleasant days in. The visitor's respectability being evident, Mrs. A—— had not noticed his card or " order to view," which he had placed on the table, and requesting the parlourmaid to show him round, returned to her occupations. When he drove away she happened to be out of the house, and on returning later through the hall, noticed the card or order lying on the table, and read thereon, " Lieutenant-Colonel Campbell."

There is the end of the story, which I was the first to hear, as I arrived on the scene a few days afterwards. As a matter of fact, however, almost nothing was said of this business outside for quite a long time. The impression it made on the two parties concerned was wholly unpleasant, and of that kind which makes for reticence. For there was no explanation possible. It was not like a rumbling floor or a black dog or a grizzly hand. Predisposition, indigestion, hysteria, optical delusions were of no help here whatever. Nor was it even a single but a double incident; everything was most uncannily simple and happened to the minutest detail as I have set it down. The actors in it know no more to-day than the reader now knows. We talked it over and over at the time, we talk it over and thresh it out now when we meet, which is very often, though as a matter of fact there is nothing to be threshed and there is absolutely nothing effectual to be said. The Vega board was a mere instrument. Its spelling of the name was practically accurate : if it had not been it matters nothing, as the ladies in a room by themselves copied out the fortuitous vagaries of a pencil on a covered board, and wrote down a name they had never heard, thinking nothing of it one way or another at the moment. And then came the second business a few weeks after ; a coincidence this last, if you like, but what a strange one ! Colonel Campbell to be sure might have been followed up in the interests of psychological research. He came, I think, from a house agent in a border city. But at the moment any such enterprise, for reasons sufficient but irrelevant here, was utterly out of the question, even if inclination to pursue an incident by no means relished at the time had been present.

I spent some days with both the parties to the incident quite recently in another county, and the mystery is as fresh, as inexplicable, and as hopeless to them as ever—and likely to remain so. It has created an extraordinary interest, however, among the intimates of those concerned in it, who like myself feel the force of it more than could be expected of a stranger reading it in cold print. Indeed, I feel the risk of telling the reader such a plain, unvarnished tale. However, if he can suggest a solution it is a great deal more than anybody actually or nearly concerned can, and we have had exactly four years to think it out and have nothing for it but to recognize something outside human ken.

It is a beautiful descent by a rough lane down the western slope of the Longmynd to the deep, secluded Vale of Ratlinghope, or " Ratchop " as the vernacular has it, where is a shooting box and an old church, once a monastery of Augustine monks and attached to Wigmore. The uncanny monoliths on the Stiperstones looming high above give much character to the uplook, and at such close quarters with their Satanic associations should have served to keep the zeal of the holy

WENTNOR.

men below at high pressure. Immediately above their heads, too, hung the well defined remains of an oval British camp, which may have served to remind them if reminder was needed that the ancient British had not yet ceased from troubling, for the Welsh were very hard on these frontier monasteries. More passable lanes carry you down through steep valley meadows to a tortuous road leading from Bishop's Castle to Shrewsbury, where I have encountered few objects more animated than the milestones which would seem to have somewhat outlived their utility. The Stiperstones range rolls away to the south-westward upon the right. More sparsely heath-clad than the Longmynd it is also more broken, leaping up and down in the sugar-loaf fashioned heights of Corndon and Linley.

Wentnor lies prettily on a ridge sloping to the valley, as it opens wide where the two ranges spread apart. The infant Onny runs near, and away ahead Bishop's Castle may be descried clustering on the hillslope with the northern ridges of Clun rising behind it. Linley Hall lies high on the breast of Linley hill. The house is comparatively modern, but the Mores, who still own it, are an ancient stock, and Samuel More distinguished himself as a leader of the Parliament troops in the Civil War. The last squire, Jasper More, was well known both in Shropshire and in the House of Commons, where he sat for a long period. They derive their name from the neighbouring village of More, and their representative in the time of Henry II is said to have been expected to provide 200 men-at-arms when the king fought in Wales, and to have had the right to carry the king's standard with his own hand in the front of the army. A fine oak avenue a mile long leads up to the house, and there is another of beeches which climbs the hill. A queer tale is told here of a couple of men who were hung in this same avenue for killing a tax collector. The noose was ill adjusted, and they remained alive on being abandoned to the crows, as was the custom of the day. Indeed they could not have been greatly inconvenienced, and must certainly have retained a healthy appetite as they consumed candle ends which a poor widow living close by brought them at night by way of nourishment.

From Wentnor the road runs to Asterton, a hamlet tucked close under the western lea of the Longmynd. Thence a delightful lane, hugging the heather and bracken-covered steeps on the one hand, and looking down through woods on the other to the Onny valley, brings you to Plowden station on the little single-track line which runs from Craven Arms to Bishop's Castle. Through all this upper portion the little Onny pursues a lovely course. The southern extremity of the Longmynd rises bold and high above the verdure that fringes its northern bank, while beyond the narrow meadows, where it sings among the alders, high slopes of wood and park and pasture shut in the view. Here, while renewing an acquaintance with the trout of Plowden, after an interval of fifteen years, I found a group of cloggers with their white tents busy among the alders, familiar folk enough to those who haunt the smaller streams of Wales and the border.

There would seem some spice of romance about the clogger's trade. He pursues it in the pleasant places of the earth, in sequestered glens where silvery streams dance beneath the shade of the timber on which he makes discrimating and no wanton on-

THE ONNY AT PLOWDEN.

slaught. Indeed he is a friend to the angler as to the landowner rather than otherwise, unless it be for the tribute he can take from the stream with such impunity if he chooses,

On one hand is his pile of blocks, on the other his heap of clogs, shaped so easily and deftly out of the soft white wood, and ready for shipment to the northern towns where a passion for wooden shoes seems still to flourish. Sometimes he and his hands lie gipsy-like of nights in their tents and sometimes in neighbouring cottages. He knows most of the streams on the border and in Wales, and rates them by the quantity and quality of their alder timber. My Onny clogger informed me that hard winters and the plunging of the ice was the worst enemy to the trees from a business point of view. It is pleasant to note at any rate one old-fashioned local industry that is beneficial all round and seems to defy the concentration of modern commerce.

It is eight miles from here to Craven Arms, and a sound broad highway, side by side with the harmless little railway, follows the twisting of the stream around the folds of steep, wooded hills for most of the way. But in the meantime the beautiful old manor house of Plowden, which the family of that name have owned and mostly occupied almost since the Conquest, lies in a richly timbered gap on the high ridge to the west of the stream. The house is reached by a gradually ascending drive over a mile in length, and is justly famous for its picturesque blend of Tudor and Jacobean architecture, and the panelling, tapestry and valuable pictures within; while surrounded by timber on three sides, its back windows and lawns command fine distant views of the Montgomery hills. The immediate forbears of the present owner for two or three generations lived on another property, but that is, I think, the only break of occupancy since the days of the crusades, when tradition says that a Plowden who was captured at the siege of Acre vowed to build a chapel if he recovered his liberty. Being fortunate in this he erected the chapel at Lydbury church a couple of miles off, where the Plowdens have been buried ever since. It is a curious thing that there are three adjoining estates here whose owners bear or bore till lately the respective territorial name Plowden of Plowden, Oakeley of Oakeley and Walcot of Walcot. Their ancestors are said to have fought side by side in the crusades under Cœur de Lion. The Walcots lost Walcot in the eighteenth century by sale to the Earls of Powis; the Oakleys have only sold within the last few years. The Plowdens are still here. The family is notable as having always held to the old faith, and there is a chapel in the house containing many interesting treasures. The family and other portraits are numerous and valuable, Lely, Vandyke and Kauffmann being among the painters of fame represented. But the house is perhaps unique for its secret hiding-places and escape-holes, which must have proved of much practical utility in periods when priests ministered at the risk of their lives or liberties. One escape-shaft runs down at the side of a chimney from an upper story, and looking through the trap door you can see the turf of the lawn at the bottom. Several members of the family have been distinguished in law as well as in arms. Plowden is supposed by many to be the place that inspired the opening chapters of *John Inglesant*. Near Plowden at the north-western foot of its ridge the fragment of an old castle clings to a more modern homestead. This is Lea, whither the Corbets of Caus repaired in the reign of Edward III and afterwards built a manor which was burnt by the Royalists in the Civil War. Two

PLOWDON HALL.

miles from Plowden, at the southern foot of the ridge, stands Lydbury North, whose ancient and important church, bound up with Plowdens and Walcots, would demand description if space admitted, while over against the foot of the Clun range close by is Walcot, already mentioned, whose large but not ancient mansion and wide-spreading park and extensive lake make a great feature of the neighbourhood. Two or three miles on a level road from here north-westward, and you are climbing the steep old-fashioned street of Bishop's Castle, my goal for this chapter and starting-point for the next.

CHAPTER XI

BISHOP'S CASTLE—CHIRBURY—MONTGOMERY AND WELSHPOOL

THE little town of Bishop's Castle is of no high distinction, either historically or architecturally. Such fame of the kind as it enjoys is derived from the fact that it was once, together with a large tract of the surrounding country, the appanage of the Bishops of Hereford, who on that account were themselves Lord Marchers. They do not seem, however, to have been very efficient in this pre-eminently secular position, and more than once had to be sharply reminded that a border castle carried responsibilities in troublous as well as a rent roll in peaceful times.

There is nothing left now but a few fragments of this episcopal fortress at Bishop's Castle. Its site is occupied by a beautifully placed and spacious bowling green surrounded by a pleasant screen of foliage, through which the burghers of the little town, when engaged in this most eminently civic pastime, might look out over wide sweeps of hill and dale. From this pleasant apex narrow streets descend on three sides between houses of old-fashioned but generally undistinguished aspect, and at a sharp gradient to the vale below. Here a church with ancient tower and more modern nave occupies an unusually detached and lowly attitude towards the town it serves.

Often enough in past years had I beheld Bishop's Castle from afar, but was only privileged to make its more intimate acquaintance during this late summer. By an incredible oversight, however, I found myself on the road thither from Montgomery on the very evening of the border townlet's great annual function, its agricultural show, when the needs of the casual visitor in the one hostelry adapted to them had small chance of adequate recognition. The untimeliness of such an advent dawned upon me slowly and painfully as I encountered trap after trap, raising the dust of a not usually much travelled road, and some of them requiring more of it perhaps than their fair share. Then suspicion ripened into certainty as the foremost of those curious processions, only to be seen on such rare occasions, hove slowly in sight. The most intelligent townsman, whose holidays were spent mainly by the seaside or on the continent, might readily be excused if, at the first glimpse, he prepared himself for encountering the menagerie of a circus travelling at large. A shire cart-horse gaily decorated, a Shetland pony, a yearling bull, a mare and foal and a Shropshire ram, with coloured placards swinging on their breasts proclaiming them as first and second or third prize winner, do make rather an uncanny showing in the distance. And indeed they are queerly assorted fellow-travellers, these mixed companies, wending their triumphant but laborious homeward way. Many of such convoys, not all prize-winners, however, I met on that warm August evening. If the clouds had not been banking so ominously in the southwest, I should have headed for Ludlow and deferred my introduction to Bishop's Castle, knowing well by experience how heartily these gatherings are celebrated in remote places.

I soon found that Bishop's Castle was no exception, for both the interior and the yard of Mine Inn exhibited as cheerful a pandemonium as the occasion could possibly demand. Traps of all varieties stood waiting their turn in serried ranks, while distracted and perspiring ostlers and grooms struggled with chaos. Flushed young farmers in sporting garb shouted protests as the right horse was being backed under the wrong shafts or the reverse, while their blooming wives and sisters in smart attire huddled in corridors from the rain that was already lightly sprinkling. It was quite obvious that to discuss bed and board with such distraught functionaries as laboured within would have been fatuous as well as unkind. So having extracted the fact that the main question of bed presented no difficulties I deferred the other indefinitely, and resigned myself to tobacco and the humours of the scene.

The middling farmer makes up in hearty fashion for the comparatively unsociable life of his normal but not unpleasant lot when the occasion serves. And who would grudge him those mellow moments when, to a congenial audience, he airs his pet hobby, his pet grievance, or the quality of his last young horse, and emphasizes them with his great reserve of lung power and sturdy fist upon the jingling table. Times do not change much in the bar parlour of a farmers' inn. The same boisterous tones and racy vernacular, uncontaminated as yet by the cockney schoolmaster, the same abiding topics of interest and style of humour fill the misty atmosphere. Board schools and county councils, cheap trips and the great slumps in grain are all innovations since I first made acquaintance with the British farmer. But in these old-time haunts the hand of the clock has almost stood still. The fly-specked prints of ancient Derby winners, the curled and whiskered portraits of lord lieutenants and county members and masters of hounds long bald or dead seem no wit out of date or keeping with the unaffected hilarity that makes their frames rattle on the walls. Even the costume of the average farmer has not altered greatly in thirty years, the skin-tight cord breeches that he almost alone, except hunting men actually in the field, so often affected, has given place it is true to the baggy article which he now shares with prosperous week-enders at Brighton or Eastbourne who have never crossed a saddle. The blue bird's-eye tie has vanished, or at least lost its significance. But the farmer would seem to have changed less than almost any other class, and still retains some character of his own, even in those externals that with his social superiors or town equivalents are always shifting.

These cheerful Salopians were very distinctly English and not Welsh, though virtually sitting upon Offa's Dyke, which is not, however, in these parts of much modern significance. The majority had Welsh names and were doubtless strong in Celtic blood, but its evidences have long vanished, and most of them, robust in the ancient prejudices derived from border strife, would greatly resent the soft impeachment of Celtic nationality. Indeed, on this very eventful evening an incautious dealer from Birmingham, who had a brief hold of the floor, remarked, during a peroration on cattle trucks, " Now you Welshmen think, etc., etc." " Don't Welsh me," shouted half a dozen indignant listeners in a breath.

When the last farmer's dogcart had safely eluded the posts of the inn yard gate, and the passages were clearer and it seemed no longer heartless to claim the attention of the exhausted staff, I discovered a comfortable sanctuary where a commercial gentleman and a London cyclist of the badge-wearing, pace-making type were consuming poached eggs on toast in such matter-of-course fashion that I felt quite aggrieved and lost no time in getting even with them. The former was a bit of an antiquarian, the latter so little of a topographer that he did not know how he had got here from Bangor, where he had apparently breakfasted, being obviously content with the fact that it was 110 miles and a good road. But the great occasion of the local calendar had yet to be discussed by the citizens of the town, who mustered in force a little later in the bar parlours and congratulated one another on its exceptional success over the cheerful tumbler till the remorseless stroke of eleven scattered them and closed this memorable day. I sat them out, and on wending my way bedwards along the corridor of this typical old posting inn, felt as if I had lived in Bishop's Castle all my life and knew the idiosyncrasies of every man, woman, and child within it and for ten miles round. Morning, however, relieved my memory of this

RUINS OF MONTGOMERY CASTLE.

load of superfluous acquaintances and irrelevant gossip, and by the time I had threaded the Onny valley to Craven Arms, not much more was left of it than is set down here.

It is some eight miles from Bishop's Castle to Montgomery, and the road heads north-westwards through the valley, which, after parting the southern end of the Stiperstones and Corndon range and the northern walls of Clun forest, expands into the wider country whose corners are occupied by Churchstoke, Chirbury and Montgomery. This is a fair stretch of corn and grass country, nearly surrounded by hills of from a thousand to seventeen hundred feet in height, while the great rock carrying the fragments of Montgomery castle rises on the open side to the Severn and the north. Not many little tracts of a few miles square are richer in associations than these three compact and hill-girt parishes. The county has the unique distinction, too, of being named from a Norman family, and possessing probably the smallest county town in Britain. The sleepy village, lying on a gentle slope at the foot of the castle hill and facing the south, is not, however, without dignity. The main and better part of it lies round an open space, in the centre of which stands the court house, while the fine old church rises on a bold knoll facing the castle. Montgomery makes a most creditable effort to look like a town, and only fails because there are really not buildings nor people enough to make it successful. But it is a quaint and quite alluring place, and sufficiently visited by discerning folk in summer as to support a capital hotel. Even some few Americans come here. Most Americans of the not very uncommon name of Montgomery who are able make the pilgrimage, cherishing the astounding legend that they are descended from the Norman founders of the castle. By what process of deduction they arrive at this conclusion the British genealogist may well ask,' but it is in fact the very simple one of identity in name which suffices for so many Americans in quest of old country forbears. There is a good opening, I think, for a course of lectures in the United States on the origin of British surnames. It would not be always palatable, but I think it might be financially profitable if delivered in sprightly and entertaining fashion. It would serve to dissipate much widespread and elementary misapprehension, though it deprived a few thousand otherwise intelligent souls of baronial and knightly ancestors. And after all a revolutionary great grandfather is so much more effective in the social circles of America.

The rocky ridge rising behind the town, on the eastern point of which the castle stands, is 350 feet in height and about a quarter of a mile in length. Slopes and summit are sprinkled with well-grown trees, sycamore, ash, and wych elm, and the ridge is traversed by three ditches quarried in the rock, dividing the outer and inner portions of the castle. Of the latter there is little left but just enough of the tower to illustrate the superb position in which the fortress stood, the north-eastern point of the ridge falling perpendicularly from its feet. This district was claimed and partly held by the Saxons, Offa's dyke running within a mile of the castle. It was occupied by the Conqueror's man, Roger de Montgomery, and is registered as his fief in

Domesday, being there reckoned as in the county of Salop. It immediately confronted the Welsh, and the first castle built here by the Norman Roger was deeply resented by the men of Powysland, who in 1095, just after his death, stormed it successfully and destroyed the garrison. This brought down William Rufus, who made the first of many inglorious experiments by Anglo-Norman kings in Welsh invasion. He penetrated to Snowdon, and no doubt roughly measured his success by his mileage. But then his commissariat gave out, and he had to retire precipitately, fighting small rear-guard actions to the border, where he found himself worse off than when he started like so many of his descendants engaged in a like venture. Roger also built the castle of Kerry ten miles higher up and just south of the Severn valley. This stung the Welsh to fury, and in his son Hugh's day they managed to destroy it. I don't think a list of successive Norman owners of Montgomery would prove very light reading. How much they held as Marchers and how much as ordinary vassals of the king, is a trifle involved even to those familiar with the surrounding country and interested in March lore, a combination not likely to prevail among the most enlightened readers of this little work. The Welsh call Montgomery Tre-Valdwyn, as one, Baldwin, is said to have held the post for Earl Roger before he erected the first castle, and a more impregnable perch for a fortress would not have been easy to find. It will be enough to say that Henry III is generally credited with the building whose remains we now see. He moreover granted a market to the town, which was also walled and ditched, and made over the whole property to his son Edward.

Fighting was almost incessant, till the latter's reign, around Montgomery and up the Severn, on which river about a mile distant there was a much-used ford, though it was still more famous as a meeting-place for the discussions relating to peace or war. Montgomery was so fiercely attacked in Henry III's time by the Welsh that he had to come himself to its rescue. According to Matthew of Paris, who tells us so much of these times, the cause of irritation was an attempt of the garrison to clear the neighbourhood of woods which favoured the tactics of those ill disposed towards them. Indeed Henry seems to have played havoc with the indigenous oak forests of Montgomery and other parts for strategic purposes, and furthermore he made yet another attempt to build a castle at Kerry. But the Welsh were altogether too much for his men and his masons combined, and about this time he made his somewhat ignominious treaty with Llewelyn, which seems to have contained an agreement not only to cease from pursuing this design, but to actually destroy what had been already completed.

But standing up here on the rock of Montgomery and looking out to the tower of Chirbury church two miles away, and over the deep wooded dingles of the Camlad brook and the fine mass of Corndon rising behind them, a personage much nearer our own times than Henry III or Llewelyn seems an even more appropriate subject for invocation. For the grass-grown ruins around us, and nearly all of the inspiring prospect they command, were the property, and here was the home, of that remarkable Lord Herbert of Chirbury, who, in the reign

TOMB OF THE EARLS OF MARCH, MONTGOMERY CHURCH.

of the first two Stuarts, cut so unique a figure. Who that cares for such things at all has not read that delightful auto-biography. I can just see the house from here in whose library shelves the little old edition no doubt still reposes which ages ago first introduced me to his Lordship's fascinating memoirs; you may now buy a little pocket reprint for two shillings, and a most judicious investment it will prove to those who have yet to make the acquaintance of this remark-able person.

Just below, the beautiful timbered house of Lymore, where the autobiography was mostly written and first deposited, is plainly visible, with its dark August woodlands and twin pools glittering like jewels amid the surrounding greenery about a mile distant.

Edward, Lord Herbert of Chirbury, was great-great-grandson to Sir Richard Herbert of Colebrook in Monmouthshire. His grandfather was the first Herbert of Montgomery, to which Chirbury, as I have before mentioned, is the neighbouring parish, the one in Shropshire, the other in Wales. He was a great enemy to the outlaws and thieves of the Montgomery mountains, seeking them out in their lairs, and dragging them to summary justice, and such a power in the country, says his grandson, that "divers ancestors of the better families now in Montgomeryshire were his servants and raised by him and he delighted so much in hospitality as having a very long table twice covered every meal with the best meats that could be gotten and a very great family. It was an ordinary saying at that time when they saw any fowl rise, 'Fly where thou wilt, thou wilt light at Black Hall,' a low building of great capacity my grandfather erected in his old age." In spite of this generous expenditure, however, he and his son were great buyers of land, and the author of the autobiography must have been a very rich man. Indeed, his own accounts of expenditure make this sufficiently evident. Edward, afterwards Lord Herbert, was born at Eyton, the home of his mother, who was a Newport, and was the eldest of ten. Various childish ailments, though accompanied by a phenomenal precocity, prevented his learning the alphabet till he was seven. At nine he was sent to a learned member of the old family of Thelwal in the vale of Clwyd, to study not only classics but Welsh, so that he might converse with his tenants and humbler neighbours in Montgomeryshire. A Tertian ague, however, prevented our hero from acquiring either Welsh or any other of the tongues in which his tutor seems to have been remarkably proficient. He made up for lost time afterwards, however, with Mr. Newton of Diddlebury, for at twelve he was ripe for Oxford and entered at University College, where he "disputed in logic as proved up to the standard of both Latin and Greek." His father now died, and succeeding to the estates and honours at the age of fifteen he was married by family arrangement to the wealthy heiress of another branch of the Herberts from near Caerleon, six years older than himself. Soon after this ceremony he went back into residence at Oxford, accompanied both by his wife and mother ; upon the whole I should imagine as singular an entourage for an undergraduate of fifteen as University records could show. This, together with a thirst for learning, and apparently a prodigious fund of common sense and foresight, made his academic career a profitable though a secluded one. Besides his classical course he taught himself French, Italian and Spanish. After spending the greater part of six years at Oxford he divided his time between Montgomery and London, and at twenty-one had three living children, two if not three having died. He was also an enthusiastic physician, and tried his hand on his own servants in Montgomeryshire and great ladies in London with equal success. Edward Herbert (as he then was) was anything but a mere student, for he cultivated his physical powers by every manly exercise at his Welsh home with the same ardour that he trained his mind, and became probably the most formidable person to pick a quarrel with, and certainly the most ready to pick one, of any notable man of his day, as well as a very daring and accomplished soldier. He gives us his views on all active pursuits and their relative value to a man of quality. Dancing, for which he had little time himself, he does not rate high in his comprehensive scheme of life. Hunting he regards as a necessary but minor art, concerning which a man of station should know enough to take a part in but not waste too much time over. Fencing, however, riding and training the " great horse " were vital and serious matters in his opinion, and he wrought hard at both of them.

Our author treats at length of the breaking of the war horse, on whose perfection a man's life may at any moment depend. He should be familiarized with martial sounds, by the beating of drums and the firing of pistols in the stable at feeding time, and with martial sights, by hanging suits of burnished armour on a post in a meadow against which the animal should be ridden at all paces. The correct seat, and methods of handling and guiding a horse by touch of rod on flank or neck, and in the battle or duel by movements of the thigh, knee and heel, are exhaustively dealt with. Racing, Lord Herbert would have none of, on account of the trickery inseparable from the sport. Archery, as useful in war, he wholly approves, and a little bowling is desirable " so that the company be good." It may seem strange to us that the French should have been at that time the highest exponents of equestrian art ; for Lord Herbert not only quotes them freely, but writes of his first long sojourn in France as a good opportunity for perfecting himself under the best examples.

In due course the young Herbert repaired to court, and when Elizabeth saw him " she swore her usual oath " and asked who he was, and being informed by Sir James Crofts of his various claims to recognition, the aged queen looked earnestly at him and swore again, saying it was a pity he had married so young, and gave him her hand to kiss. When James came to the throne Herbert was made a Knight of the Bath, and by his person and accomplishments found great favour at court but was proof against its temptations. He then returned to Montgomery as high sheriff and plunged once more into his "beloved studies." In a formal family interview quaintly described, in which the children are paraded, he reminds his wife that as he is very young and she not so very old, either might die and the survivor might marry again and have offspring. He asks her therefore to settle her fortune on their children and he will do the same : but the lady refused the suggestion point blank, saying that "she would not draw her cradle over her head,"

COTTAGE AT CHIRBURY.

so her young husband gave her a week to think better of it, upon which she left the room in a pet. Nor at the solemn conclave held that day week when the children were again present did she relent, whereupon his Lordship replied, that having married too young to enjoy the usual pre-nuptial rovings and liberties he proposed to make up for it now. But still, if she would yield the point at issue he would give up all and remain with her in Montgomeryshire. To this she retorted that she would be sorry to lose his company, but entirely refused to make the requested settlement.

So with a clear conscience the young Sir Edward repaired to France, first to Paris, where he was well received, and thence on a long visit to Montmorency, Constable of France, at his splendid estate of Merdun. Herbert had taken his oath of the Bath very seriously as a potential champion of dames. For at Merdun he picked the first of his many quarrels with a Frenchman, who had playfully plucked a ribbon from a little girl's hair. When the duke left Merdun he placed the whole establishment at Herbert's disposal, forests full of game, hounds, huntsmen, fifty "great horses" and tenants by the hundred to beat the woods, which they did, with drums and fire-

CETHY COED, FROM NEAR CHIRBURY.

arms, while he himself had many adventures with boar, wolf and stag, and has related them with much vigour. After eight months of this Herbert repaired to the Court of Henry IV, who embraced him like a son, while at the balls and routs which followed, the queen would have him always next her "to the envy of some and the wonder of others."

On returning to England with Sir Thomas Lucy their ship was driven upon Dover pier by a storm and shattered, and the two sea-sick gallants got ashore in boats with difficulty. Having kissed King James' hand and given him all the gossip of the French Court, Herbert repaired to his Welsh home, his studies in philosophy and other literature, and to the riding

of " great horses," of which his stable was full. War in the low
countries, however, tempted him anon from his rural retreat,
and he repaired to the siege of Juliers, where was the Prince of
Orange, Lord Chandos, with Sir Horace Vere, Sir Edward
Cecil and four thousand English, besides a French corps under
Marshall de Chartres. Here he had a characteristic adventure
with one Balagny, the most daring man of the French Court.
This cavalier hearing that Herbert was known as one of the
bravest men of his nation, challenged the Englishman to
follow him against the enemy's lines and " see who would go
furthest." He then leaped out of the trenches, sword in hand,
with Herbert after him. Having run the gauntlet of a heavy fire
directed on them, the Frenchman remarked it was getting
somewhat hot, but Herbert replied that if Balagny was willing
to proceed he would assuredly follow. So the latter ran
swiftly on in a crouching attitude while Herbert walked upright
with much deliberation behind him. By a miracle both got
safely back, and the Prince of Orange, one is not surprised to
hear, pronounced it an extremely foolish business.

Herbert next challenged Lord de Walden to a duel on horse-
back, which was prevented at the last moment by the authorities. He then challenged Ballagny to fight him for the beauty
of their mistresses. But Ballagny laughed and did not think the
fairness of their ladies was worth it. Soon after Sir Thomas
Somerset at the head of a dozen men said something uncivil
to our author, in passing between the camps, whereat he leaped
from his horse, drew his sword and charged the entire squadron.
He got off, however, with a few scratches, the *mêlée* being
fortunately stopped.

The town at length surrendered, when Herbert, after protracted visits to many capitals and courts, returned to England.

Now ensued the greatest personal encounter of his life, which
is interesting if only as an example of the desperate rough
and tumble fights which even persons of quality engaged
in at that time. The beauty of Herbert's person and his
chivalric disposition made copies of his portrait in some
request, and the wife of Sir John Ayres having fallen
in love with him had procured his miniature by stealth,
which her husband discovered hung round her neck,
and assuming the worst as it so happened quite
wrongly, swore dire vengeance. Herbert is perfectly candid
in the matter of his gallantries which, for his period
and peculiar circumstances, were less than moderate, but in

the Ayres matter he was entirely innocent. At this moment he was laid up with a serious fever, and Sir John Ayres vengeful and unbelieving designed to kill him in his bed. Herbert, hearing of this, sent his solemn word that Lady Ayres was innocent, but that he would meet Sir John as soon as he could "stand upon his legs." But Ayres' reply was ambiguous, and he evidently preferred some underhand method of revenge.

So soon as Herbert, though still weak, was out again, Sir John, hearing he was coming on a certain day to Whitehall with only two lackies, laid for him with his men in Scotland Yard. On Herbert's appearance Ayres rushed at him at once with sword

CORNDON BEACON FROM NEAR CHIRBURY.

and dagger, wounding his horse, while his armed retainers crowding round stabbed the animal severely, till lashing out in pain it cleared the arena for the moment and gave Herbert just time to draw. But on the first stroke he aimed at Ayres, his sword unfortunately snapped within a foot of the hilt on the other's guard. Then a passer-by who recognized Lord Herbert called out several times, " Ride away, ride away," but the Lord of Montgomery, " scorning a base flight upon what terms soever," proceeded to alight from his horse, and at the same moment Sir John, making a rush at the sorely wounded animal, caused it to upset Lord Herbert on the ground, where he lay with one foot caught in the stirrup. In this perilous plight all seemed over, but, just as Sir John was in the act of thrusting his sword into his prostrate foe, the latter by a frantic effort reached out and caught him by the leg and upset him flat on his back. "Then," says he, "one of my footmen a little Shropshire boy freed my foot of the stirrup, the other which was a great fellow having run away." This enabled Herbert to spring to his feet and put himself in the best posture he could with "that poor remnant of a weapon." "Sir John Ayres by this time likewise got up, standing betwixt me and some part of Whitehall with two men, his brother behind him and at least twenty or thirty persons, his friends." Herbert now ran at Sir John, who, only expecting a blow from a broken sword, held his own and his dagger on guard above his head, but his resourceful foe lunged him full in the chest so violently that he fell flat on the ground, his head striking it first. Four of Sir John's attendants now attacked Herbert. But Mr. Mansel from Glamorganshire and another gentleman from Scotland who were passing came to the support of their friend in the nick of time, leaving him only two immediate antagonists, "all I could well do to those two which remained was to ward their thrust. Sir John was now up a third time, when I, making towards him with the intention to close, put by a thrust of his with my left hand so coming within him received a stab with his dagger on my right side which ran down my ribs as far as my hip, which I feeling, did with my right elbow force his hand together with the hilt of his dagger so near the upper part of my right side that I made him leave hold. The dagger now sticking in me Sir Henry Cary, afterwards Lord of Portland and Lord deputy of Ireland, finding it thus in my body snatched it out." Lord Herbert now for the third time threw down Sir John, and bestriding him, "struck at him as hard as I could with my piece of a sword wounding him in four places and did almost cut off his left hand. His two men this while struck at me, but it pleased God even miraculously to defend me, for when I lifted up my sword to strike at Sir John I bore off their blows half a dozen times. His friends now finding Sir John in this danger took him by the head and shoulders and drew him from betwixt my legs and carried him along the stair at Whitehall. Sir Herbert Croft afterwards met him upon the water vomiting all the way. I remained master of the place and his weapons, having first wrested his dagger from him and afterwards struck his sword out of his hand."

Lord Herbert was cured of his wounds in ten days, during which time he had many " messages and visits from the best in the kingdom." He sent a message by Sir Robert Harley to Sir John, that though he could not have enough honour left to be worth taking, still he would like to meet him fairly in the field. The surly Sir John, however, only replied that he would shoot his adversary from a window on the first opportunity. But the verdict of society was dead against Ayres. Lord Herbert's innocence of this charge was beyond question, and the other's cowardly threats were resented by all. The case was submitted to the lords of the council, but the only result of this extraordinary fracas was the disowning and disinheriting of Ayres by his own father !

LYMORE.

In 1614, Herbert went again to the Low Countries to fight for the Prince of Orange. So little, however, was effected that late in autumn an unauthorized challenge was sent from the Spanish army, proposing that a champion from either side should engage for the honour of their respective mistresses. Herbert begged to represent the prince's army, but in the meantime a veto on the business had been sent by Spinola, the Spanish commander. Herbert, however, obtained leave to take another challenge to the enemy, but on presenting it Spinola would not hear of such a thing, though he entertained the challenger royally. Sir Edward now made a long tour

In the south, and at Lyons, where the governor proved officially impolite his would-be guest sent him a challenge, which was not accepted. Lord Herbert's re-crossing of the Channel to England is a significant illustration of seventeenth century travel. He made no less than three attempts to get over in as many weeks from Brill, under the encouragement of salvoes of artillery at each one of them from the courteous governor, who perhaps was afraid of being challenged, but he was beaten back upon every occasion, so gave up the attempt and returned to Brussels, proceeding to England later by Calais. At Brussels some Spanish officers at a tavern, not knowing Herbert, spoke slightingly of King James, upon which our hero revealed himself and offered to fight them all in turn, but handsome apologies were forthcoming. The impression may well have been gathered from these cursory anecdotes that this accomplished person was chiefly a swashbuckler; on the contrary he was now regarded as the fittest person to represent his country at the Court of France, where the honour of a monarch who had little of his own was most punctiliously upheld and his embassy most splendidly maintained. The ruling passion even here breaks out occasionally, and his Excellency gives a most amusing account of how he drove his coach past and took the road from the Spanish ambassador, whose funereal pace, part in fact of his dignity, had always hitherto been suffered by the diplomatic body. At Paris, Herbert became intimately concerned with European politics, and it is hard to say, remarks a biographer, whether his person, his courage, or his understanding were the most extraordinary. The fair, the learned and the brave held him in equal esteem, and Ben Jonson wrote of him :

> If men get name for some one virtue then ;
> What man art thou that art so many men,
> All virtuous Herbert ! on whose every part
> Truth might spend all her voice, fame all her art.

He held of course extremely free theological opinions, and is generally accounted a Deist. The last part of his life was spent in literary labours, and arguments against revealed religion, his *Life of Henry VIII* and his *de Veritate* being best known of his prose works, which are much better than his poetry. He was made a peer of England in 1636 with the title of Lord Herbert of Chirbury.

By the Civil War period his fighting spirit would seem

wholly to have given way to the literary habit. His neutral attitude in this great struggle however may be in part accounted for by his divided sympathies, though his sons fought for the king. He remained quietly in his castle at Montgomery, while the Royalist forces invested the town, and in response to an invitation from Prince Rupert to take a more prominent part, excused himself, writing that "though he would like to kiss His Highness' most valorous friendly hands he had just entered on a course of physic and must therefore decline." After the rout of the Royalists at Montgomery by Middleton's force in

THE SEVERN VALLEY ABOVE WELSHPOOL.

1644 it remained a Parliamentary stronghold and centre, Lord Herbert pursuing the even tenor of his way, though in greater sympathy so far as we know with the Puritan party. The castle was dismantled at the close of the war and the owner lived thenceforward at Lymore just below, of which a word or two presently. On his deathbed Lord Herbert sent for Archbishop Usher to administer the sacrament, but so shocked that prelate by accompanying his request with the remark that if the rite did him no good, it could at least do him no harm, that the eminent divine refused even to see him. So he turned his face to the wall and died peacefully, the philosopher that he had lived, eccentric to the last, though he tells us he had prayers read always twice a day by the chaplain of the castle and a sermon every Sunday. His brother was the saintly George Herbert, no less famous in a widely different sphere. Surely no stock in Britain counts so many outstanding members of its name as the Herberts!

The town of Montgomery was walled round in former days, and standing a mile beyond it to the southward beside its two large pools is, I think, the largest timbered mansion on the Marches.

Lymore is a plain gabled, black and white house of the Tudor period, but of great size and elevation, the property of Lord Powis and practically uninhabited for some generations. It is not accessible to the public, but the interior, apart from the panelling and picturesque detail inseparable from its date and consequence, has a further and quite peculiar interest. For though of deserted and in part dilapidated appearance, and though the living rooms are virtually stripped of furniture, most of the numerous square, low-pitched chambers upstairs contain the four-post bedsteads, hangings, wall-papers, and so forth that were in use early in the eighteenth century. That these are all much alike and of a quite plain description rather increases the interest of the situation than otherwise. They appeal to one in a different way from an interior kept up as a museum of old treasures, or again from one still occupied and animate with the trifles of daily life and the addition of modern accessories. But Lymore, as regards its upper storeys, except for the fact of being kept clean and aired, suggests a house suddenly abandoned and locked up in the time of George II and recently opened. At any rate these galleries of silent, half-furnished, long-forsaken rooms are extremely realistic, and as a matter of fact have not been inhabited since about 1750. Some very valuable tapestry work is a possession of the house, and when I was there experts from London were busy at work repairing the ravages that time had made on it, preparatory to its removal to Powis castle. The road approaching the house from Montgomery divides the two large pools already mentioned. Not long ago the armour and skeleton of a Cromwellian trooper were fished up in one of them and are preserved in the house. It is conjectured that their owner, either as pursuer or pursued in one of the skirmishes round Montgomery, and possibly in the night, got off the narrow roadway and thus met his fate.

Montgomery church warrants more attention than space admits of here. There is a good tower, a fine oak roof and a rood screen; while among the tombs are recumbent effigies of two knights, one of them with long hair thought to be Mortimers of late fourteenth century date. Also a wonderful canopied tomb on which Richard Herbert and his lady recline amid elaborate armorial panels, while eight of their children, Herbert of Chirbury among them, gaze dutifully down from niches above.

From the rock of Montgomery you may see much that I

THE BREIDDEN FROM NEAR WELSHPOOL.

should be tempted to dwell on, if only for old acquaintance sake, so perhaps it is well that space is denied for such plilanderings. Corndon is much the most luminous hill of the Stiperstone range as viewed from this Welsh side, and raises its sugar-loaf summit finely against the eastern sky. On the upper wild of Corndon are three curious groups of stones of no great height, but the seat of many ancient superstitions and of antiquarian speculation. One of these groups, numbering a dozen or so of mostly low stones, is known as Mitchell's

Fold, to which attaches a well-known legend. For here in the remote days of local famines, a sore dearth once fell upon these dwellers on the skirts of Corndon, and the only sustenance available was the milk of a mysterious white cow which presented itself nightly at this lonely spot for the benefit of the country side. Its supply proved inexhaustible so long as each milker took but a pailful, according to general agreement. But one day an old hag named Mitchell came along and milked the cow into a sieve till she had drained it dry, after which the benignant animal disappeared, leaving the people it had sustained to perish of want. But the wicked old witch was turned into a stone, and the other stones were placed in a circle round, to keep an eye on her, we may presume, and the circle has been known ever since as Mitchell's Fold.

On the hither side of Corndon is Marrington Hall, a good specimen of a sixteenth century black and white gabled manor house, perched on the brink of a deep wooded dingle of notorious beauty down which the Camlad tumbles and ripples for two miles beneath a maze of foliage. Its leafy recesses come readily back to me one by one at the call of memory, for many a by-day in the more important business of September we used to woo the somewhat indifferent " back end " trout with a red tag as a dropper for the casual grayling. The Camlad is, I believe, the only stream which rises in England and ends in Wales. This is to say that its source is in Shropshire near Bishop's Castle, and its mouth in the Severn near Montgomery. On the lawn at Marrington there used to stand, and doubtless still stands, an ancient sundial co-eval with the house, a square pillar with the crest of the builder, Richard Lloyd, and several other coats of arms engraved upon it as well as these lines :

> From day to day these shades do flee,
> And so this life passeth away.

Chirbury village is supposed to have been a royal Mercian outpost, and the church is a good one of the twelfth century foundation. I had set Montgomery as my northern limit so far as these pages are concerned, so it will not do to seriously travel the seven miles of road from Chirbury to Welshpool. I will only remark what a pleasant stage it is, and what fine views there are over the Severn vale as you top the high " bank " overlooking it. Following down the Severn, too, there are some striking peeps of the Breiddon Hills, which to the eastwards so effectually shut out this country

POWIS CASTLE

from England proper, part Shropshire though it be ; while the towers of Powys Castle—the Castell Goch or Red Castle of the ancients—rising amid its splendidly timbered and swelling park, makes a fine approach to Welshpool.

There is not much left of interest in this cheerful bustling market town, which is well, as there is the less temptation to exceed my bounds, which I have already filled to overflowing with much matter very far from relevant had I set up to be writing a guide book. Welshpool or " Pool," as universally called in the neighbourhood, was a gateway town like Hay in the Wye valley, half English and half Welsh. It was much damaged by Glyndwr, but remained true to the Charltons, its then lords, and had its charter so widely extended, out of gratitude for its loyalty, that its limits cover to-day some twenty thousand acres. But this will never do ! The story of Powys castle and its ancient borough goes back through the Civil War, where it played an important Royalist part, to the mists of antiquity, and should be dealt with respectfully or left alone. It will be enough to say here that the Welshpool end of Montgomeryshire, with the neighbouring fragment of Shropshire cut off by hills from its own county, is still part Welsh and part English. The latter mainly in the flat low lands, with a Welsh farmer as a settler here and there, but in the hill countries that do business in Welshpool or Montgomery, the native Welsh element still prevails, But now we have come within sight of uplands where men are not only Welsh, but still habitually speak and think in the ancient tongue. So I feel it is full time to cry a halt to these northward wanderings, and with the first month of autumn to retrace my steps and turn my face towards the Land of Morgan.

INDEX

INDEX

INDEX

INDEX

Robert of Ewyas, 48
Robin Hood, 145
Rodney family, 79

Salweys, The, 173
Scott, Sir Walter, 224
Scudamore, Barnabas, 16
—— Lord, 15, 54
—— Sir John, 166
Scudamores, The, 33
Shelley, 92
Sherwood Foresters, 124
Shobden, 209
Shon Tir, 164
Shrewsbury, 2, 3
Sidney, Sir Henry, 190, 193
Skenfrith, 41–44
Skerrid, The, 77, 95
Snodhill Castle, 59
Southey, 93
St. David, 86
Stanbury, Bishop, 9
Stephen, King, 9, 177
Stiperstones, 252
Stockley Hill, 59
Stokesay, 232
Sugar loaf, 95
Sutton Walls, 5, 149
Sweyn, 6

Tatteridge Hill, 211
Teme, R., 170, 211
Tomkyns family, 72, 145, 146
Tretower, 114, 115
Trewyn, 75, 78
Trollope, Sir Andrew, 186

Turnastone, 58
Usk, Vale of, 107–126

Vaughan, David, 164
—— Roland, 57
—— Silurist, 114
—— Sir Roger, 64
Vinnal, The, 200
Vowchurch, 58

Walcot, 256
Watling Street, 168, 235
Wellington, 149
Welshpool, 278
Wenlock Edge, 234, 246
Wentnor, 252
Weobley, 140–145
Whitcliffe, 200
White Castle, 43
White Cross, 128
Whittington, 150
Wigmore Castle, 13, 166, 202
William the Conqueror, 7
Windsor, Lord, 201, 202, 229
Woodhouse, Sir M., 214
Wordsworth, 116, 134, 135
Wormbridge, 30
Worm Brook, 26
Wrekin, 236, 246
Wright, Antiquarian, 176
—— Dr., 214
Wycherley, 221
Wycombe, William of, 89
Wye, R., 21, 22

Yarpole, 170
Yatton Court, 168